PEACE TALKS—

Who Will Listen?

PEACE TALKS—

Who Will Listen?

FRED DALLMAYR

University of Notre Dame Press
Notre Dame, Indiana

Manufactured in the United States of America

Library of Congress Cataloging-in-Publication Data
Dallmayr, Fred R. (Fred Reinhard), 1928–
Peace talks : who will listen? / Fred Dallmayer.
p. cm.
Includes bibliographical references and index.
ISBN 0-268-02568-1 (cloth : alk. paper)
ISBN 0-268-02569-x (pbk. : alk. paper)
1. Peace.   2. Peace (Philosophy).   I. Title.

JZ5548.D35   2004
303.6'6—dc22
                                        2004016468

∞ *This book is printed on acid-free paper.*

To all the victims of war, violence, and oppression

Lord, make me an instrument of your peace.
—St. Francis of Assisi

The whole purpose of our religion is peace and concord.
—Erasmus, *The Complaint of Peace*

Peace is the work of justice.
—Isaiah 32:17

The times are out of joint. In traditional Hindu terminology, our age is called "*kali yuga*," meaning an age of strife, destruction, and desolation. Looking around in our world today, the term seems eminently appropriate. Wherever one turns, hatred, ill will, aggressiveness, and warfare seem to be the order of the day. As one may recall, the beginning of the new millennium was anticipated in many quarters with dark forebodings and prophecies. Now, it appears that many of these forebodings have come true, with a vengeance, as humankind seems to drift deeper and deeper into violent and lethal conflicts. Although perhaps an age-old feature in human history, political violence in our time has gained a new dimension: in an age of globalization, warfare is no longer locally or even regionally confined, but takes on the character of a worldwide conflagration—with the prospect of a global nuclear holocaust. In terms of the traditional struggle for power, the stakes today have been immensely raised: in the new millennium, the struggle is no longer for limited (domestic or regional) power, but for unlimited global power and control—in fact, for absolute power. In light of the immensity of these stakes, the danger to human survival has also immensely increased; and so has the peril of moral decay. For, given its intoxicating aura, who can doubt that the champions of absolute power will also be absolutely corrupted?

According to an old adage, the first casualty of warfare is the truth. But truth could not be so quickly defeated if there had not been another casualty antedating the outbreak of war: the rule of justice. Looking around again in the world today, one finds that even minimal requirements of justice—including the equitable distribution of sources and capacities for well-being—are flouted nearly everywhere, with the predictable outcome of ill will, resentment, and rage. Nearly everywhere one finds a brazen celebration of narrow self-interest, economic greed, and power lust—to the virtual exclusion of ethical imperatives mandating justice and fairness. The exclusion or sidelining of justice results in another major casualty: the reign of peace. That justice and peace are intimately linked is part of the ancient wisdom of humanity. Speaking to an age of social disarray, the prophet Isaiah unequivocally stated that "peace is the work of justice" (*opus justitiae pax*), indicating thereby that peace or the avoidance of warfare requires as a precondition the practice of justice, the equitable distribution of resources, and the cultivation of inter-human respect. Regarding the meaning of justice or equity, the words of the prophet are corroborated and amplified by Marcus Tullius Cicero, who offered this memorable definition of just conduct: "to give to each person his or her own; and not to injure anyone" (*suum cuique tribuere, neminem laedere*)—a formula which again underscores the close connection between equity and nonviolence or peace. Unfortunately, such ancient teachings seem to be almost entirely lost on contemporary politicians—including so-called "world leaders" who in their behavior appear to be guided only by Machiavellianism (in the obnoxious sense of that term) and thus seem to illustrate the condition of ethical desolation so hauntingly depicted by Alasdair MacIntyre in the opening pages of *After Virtue*.[1]

In seeking a guidepost out of this desolation, the present study turns to Erasmus of Rotterdam, the great Dutch humanist of the sixteenth century. In many ways, Erasmus's age was similar to ours in its turbulence and its bent to relentless violence. Throughout his lifetime, Europe was seething with violent (or potentially violent) conflicts: conflicts between nascent nation-states, between religious factions or denominations, and between social classes or groups. In the midst of this turmoil—which exacted its toll in his own life—Erasmus managed to preserve his goodwill and moral and intellectual sanity, a steadfastness showing him to be a "man for all seasons" (akin to his friend Thomas Morus). In all his actions, the close linkage between equity and peacemaking was clearly illustrated. Confronting some of the rulers of modern nation-states, he challenged their ruthless hankering for power and domination, reminding them of the ethical and legal standards governing politics—thereby providing strong inspiration to the founders of the modern "law of nations" (*ius gentium, ius inter gentes*) both in Spain and in Holland. Intervening in the brewing religious conflicts of his time, Erasmus in a similar manner demonstrated the virtues of moderation, toleration, and intercommunal respect; moreover, he practiced these virtues not as a distant spectator but as an active participant in interfaith or interdenominational exchanges and discussions. Basically, in religious as well as political matters, the Dutch humanist steered a course between tradition and innovation, between stale conformism and radical rupture, opting instead for the pathway of genuine inner renewal (anticipating the later formula of "*ecclesia semper renovanda*"). Proceeding in this manner, Erasmus served as a bridge-builder between the "ancients" and the "moderns," and more specifically between Renaissance humanism and Reformation. On a more general, possibly cross-cultural plane, his work managed to reconcile and peacefully mediate domains which are usually treated as being poles apart: especially the domains of reason and faith, knowledge and virtue—a mediation highlighted in the guiding motto of his life: "*eruditio et pietas*" (learning and piety).

In all its multifaceted dimensions, Erasmus's legacy can still serve as a beacon in our conflict-ridden age. To be sure, social conditions and historical circumstances have changed dramatically since his time. While his age witnessed the birth pangs of the system of European nation-states, our contemporary period experiences the steady weakening or retreat of that system under the impact of the processes of globalization and regional regrouping. Due to the same processes, the issue of inter-religious or interfaith toleration can no longer be restricted to Christian denominations, but has acquired global and properly ecumenical proportions, demanding engaged interactions between all the faiths of the world. On the level of social or socialeconomic relations, globalization has complicated traditional class distinctions by centerstaging the antagonism between North and South, between "developed" and "developing" societies. In light of all these changes, Erasmus's example can surely not be simply repeated in our time; but it can and should be recollected and remembered—in the sense of the kind of innovative remembrance and reinterpretation that he practiced throughout his life. One aspect of his legacy that may be difficult for some contemporaries to remember and renew is his religiosity and deep inter-religious engagement. In this respect again, the desolate condition of politics in our time poses a formidable obstacle. If so many people today turn away from religion, the fault often lies with the bigotry of political leaders, including so-called "world leaders." How indeed can one preserve piety when confronted with the self-righteous posturing and unctuous sermonizing of leaders who sometimes do not hesitate to implicate "God" in their sinister machinations? Yet, precisely on this score, Erasmus offers an important counterwitness: that is, an example witnessing not to the wrath but to the loving kindness of God; not to the raging destructiveness of an all-powerful demon but to the empowering, life-giving, and liberating spirit of divine grace (an example renewed by many "liberation theologians" in our time).

In my own case, the example of Erasmus has accompanied me from my early youth. Growing up in the city of Augsburg, I was surrounded in my childhood and teenage years by the monuments of the Christian Middle Ages and also, perhaps more importantly, by the living mementoes of Renaissance humanism and Protestant Reformation. During the time of Erasmus, Augsburg was the home of many learned humanists whose immense erudition helped to revive the study of classical (Greek and Latin) texts: figures such as Conrad Peutinger, Christoph von Stadion, Veit Bild, and many others. At the same time, the city was also a seat of religious and spiritual ferment and innovation. In 1518 Martin Luther visited Augsburg for his disputation with the Roman Cardinal Cajetan, and twelve years later, his friend Melanchthon attended there the promulgation of the first reformed creed: the "Confessio Augustana" (1530). Thus, during the early sixteenth century, classical learning and scriptural teachings mingled and interpenetrated freely in that city—fostering the kind of symbiosis of "*eruditio et pietas*" dear to Erasmus and which, more than three hundred years later, I still experienced in secondary school where biblical readings and the study of Plato, Cicero, and Goethe freely went hand in hand. Looking back to these school days now, I cannot but wholeheartedly embrace Erasmus's concluding comments in his famous *Enchiridion* (of 1503):

> There are certain detractors who think that true religion has nothing to do with good literature. Let me say that I have been studying the classics since my youth. For me, a knowledge of Greek and Latin required many a long hard hour. I did not undertake this merely for the sake of empty fame or for the childish pleasures of the mind. My sole purpose was that, knowing these writings, I might the better adorn the Lord's temple with literary richness.[2]

To be sure, Augsburg during the early sixteenth century was also an arena of religious animosities and strife. Martin Luther had to leave the city hurriedly and secretly because of plots against his life. During subsequent decades, the city became a prey to the changing fortunes of religious rivalry, with Catholics and Protestants alternating in exercising control over the city's political and religious affairs. However, in 1555 the conflict came to an end, at least in that part of Europe, with the proclamation of the "Peace of Augsburg" (*Pax Augustana*), which established full legal equality between the contending confessions. Although he did not live to see that day, the peace accord certainly was in full agreement with Erasmus's lifelong pleas for inter-religious harmony. Ever since that time, the city has been governed by the rule of "parity" granting to the confessions freedom of religion and equal participation in the management of the city's affairs. And ever since 1650, an annual "peace festival" (*Friedensfest*) is celebrated in Augsburg commemorating the end of religious conflict. In my youth, I often participated in these festivals, eagerly soaking in the prevailing spirit of goodwill and mutual respect, the spirit of inter-religious and inter-human brotherhood and sisterhood. To this very day, Augsburg lives in my memory as a city of peace, exuding the gentle Erasmian aura of enlightened or undogmatic piety. My commitment to peace—a just and ethical peace—was powerfully reinforced by memories of my earliest childhood: the horrors of the Second World War unleashed by a bloodthirsty and warmongering Nazi regime that inflicted untold misery on millions of people. The conclusion to be drawn from these horrors was: Never again! Yet, half a century later, the grim "horsemen of the apocalypse" are riding again, spreading fire and destruction. Here one may with benefit recall the passage from Horace adopted by Erasmus: "When rulers go mad, people are smitten." And also Erasmus's own words, in his *Complaint of Peace:* "Let them [who desire war] examine the self-evident fact that this world of ours is the fatherland of the entire human race," that is, of humanity at large.[3]

In writing and completing this study, I owe debts of gratitude to many people. My foremost gratitude goes to Erasmus for his continuing inspiration, and to Augsburg, the city of my youth, for its legacy of peace. Next, I want to thank my friends—friendship being one of the things Erasmus himself cultivated diligently and which he never stopped praising. Among colleagues in the field of international politics I wish to single out especially Richard Falk, Chandra Muzaffer, David Held, and Robert Johansen, whose writings have honed my sensitivity for the issues of war and peace and for the disparities between North and South. Among philosophical colleagues I have continued to benefit greatly from the insights of Charles Taylor, Calvin Schrag, Bernhard Waldenfels, Eliot Deutsch, Marietta Stepaniants, and Douglas Allen. In the field of political thought, Hwa Yol Jung, Iris Marion Young, Bhikhu Parekh, Thomas Pantham, and Chantal Mouffe have been trusted companions and friends through the years. My deepest debt of gratitude, of course, goes to my wife, Ilse, and to our son and daughter, whose company has given me that peace of mind without which writing would be difficult if not impossible.

In introducing his book, *The Essential Erasmus,* John P. Dolan comments: "Perhaps the time is ripe for the gentleness of Erasmus to bear fruit." Let us hope so. But the hope is never going to "bear fruit" unless we dedicate ourselves to the pursuit of justice and peace and to the reduction or elimination of war and violence. Fortunately, the task is not entirely unmanageable or beyond the ken of human aspirations. Here is another Erasmian passage, taken again from *The Complaint of Peace:*

Be consciously aware of what peacefulness and benevolence can do. War incessantly sows war, vengeance seethingly draws vengeance; but kindness generously engenders kindness, favors will abundantly be returned by other favors, and he will humbly appear most righteous who, at all times, considers the rights of others first.[4]

CHAPTER ONE

Peace Talks

An Enduring Complaint

"Peace talks." So begins Erasmus's famous *The Complaint of Peace* (*Querela pacis*) of 1517. Peace talks or speaks; but who will listen? In Erasmus's time as in ours, the faculty of listening is in extremely short supply. Not listening as such; but listening to the quiet and recessed voice of peace. Everywhere and at all times, people seem ready to lend their ears to all kinds of voices: to the clamoring of nationalistic or sectarian frenzy; to the manipulative propaganda of demagogues; and to their own untutored passions of hatred, envy, and lust for power. As if enlarged by huge amplifiers, the combined sound of these voices accumulates into a deafening noise, drowning out the whispers of conscience, piety, and common decency. Fully aware of this situation, Erasmus in his treatise seeks to enhance the volume or audibility of these whispers, and thus to increase their chances for a hearing. His chosen method is personification: a device which allows "Peace" to speak for herself and in her own voice, without having to rely on intermediaries or inept translators. So: "Peace talks (or speaks)"—and mainly in the role of plaintiff. The dominant tenor of her talk is a "complaint": the complaint of being so shabbily treated by humankind, which, on the other hand, lavishes endless praise and honors on warfare—the source of misery, death, and destruction.

THE COMPLAINT OF PEACE

Exhorted by Erasmus, let us give Peace a hearing. Without being strident or garrulous, her complaint amounts to a serious indictment: an indictment of human deafness and stupidity. For, even on a cursory comparison of peace and war, who can doubt the benefits or blessings of the former and the severe liabilities of the latter? What is involved in this comparison is not empty conjecture, but attention to the cumulative evidence of human history. "What is there of prosperity, of security, or of happiness," Peace proclaims, "that cannot be ascribed to me? On the other hand, is not war the destroyer of all things and the very seed of evil? What is there of prosperity that it does not infect; what is secure or pleasant that it does not undermine?" Given the historical evidence of human suffering, it is puzzling and even staggering that humankind should so widely sideline or disparage peace, while glorifying and promoting the source of its afflictions. In rejecting the benefits of the former, to be sure, humankind has never done itself any favor, but on the contrary has "brought down calamity after calamity" upon itself—to such an extent that (using later Freudian vocabulary) one might suspect a kind of collective masochism or death wish. From the perspective of Peace (personified), this condition of humanity gives rise less to anger and resentment than to sympathy and pity—pity for creatures who, though intelligent and intent on self-preservation, seem to pursue relentlessly their own self-destruction, and to do so with great ingenuity: "Though nothing is more odious to gods and harmful to men, yet it is incredible to see the tremendous expenditure of work and effort that intelligent beings put forth in an effort to exchange me for a heap of ruinous evils."[1]

To make a dent in this condition of disarray—Erasmus realizes—great effort is required. In order to improve the chances of success and to overcome obtuseness, his treatise endows the plaintiff "Peace" with considerable authority, allowing her to draw on a vast arsenal of arguments and rhetorical genres. At this point, Peace benefits from one of the most outstanding features of the Dutch humanist: his combination of classical learning with deep religiosity, that is, his ability to link "*eruditio et pietas.*" Many of the arguments of the plaintiff are drawn from classical Greek and Roman literature, others from sacred scriptures. Taking a leaf from the teachings of Aristotle and Cicero, the treatise locates the unifying bond among humans in their capacity for speech and reason, a capacity distinguishing them from beasts. Above all, the ability to speak enables humans to "cultivate friendship," an aspect which contains in it "the seeds of all virtue," especially "a ready disposition toward mutual benevolence and a delight in helping others." From their very infancy, human beings are designed for, and dependent on, assistance and benevolence. Without "parental effort and care," the treatise insists, human infants would not see the light of day and, once born, would perish quickly. The entire infancy up to adult life is a period demanding the solicitude of many people; the relation between parents and children is, in fact, a relation of assistance instituted for the "mutual compensation of benefits" (what the Greeks called "*antipelargosis*"). Thus, the physical vulnerability and dependence of early human life is a premonition of the later adult companionship anchored in reason and speech.[2]

As Erasmus adds learnedly, companionship and benevolence were celebrated not only by Greeks and Romans but also valued by so-called "barbarian" peoples. Wherever we look in the ancient world, Peace states, friendship and amity were "a sacred and holy thing among pagans when a common table united them." Above all, warfare and violent cruelty were not extolled as desirable in antiquity but at best tolerated as unavoidable evils. Thus, in the conflict between Agamemnon and Achilles "the blame was laid at the feet of the goddess Ate," that is, an inscrutable destiny rather than personal enmity or blood lust. Within the confines of the Greek city-states, the plaintiff continues, warfare was severely circumscribed; in his *Republic,* Plato denounced "any war of Greek against Greek, calling it sedition or civil strife." Nor was war between Greeks and barbarians "total" or devoid of any limits. Thus, when Greeks happened to be successful in subduing barbarians, "they treated them well and endeavored to make the victory as bloodless as possible, thereby increasing their own fame and rendering defeat more bearable." This legacy was continued by the Romans, both during the time of the republic and during the later empire. "Who has ever ruled more successfully than Octavius Augustus?" Peace queries, giving as answer the preponderance of justice over violence. For, no Roman ruler was more averse to violent conquest and offered the world a better example of a peaceful reign. In Rome there was even the practice of "frequently bolting up the temple of Janus"— a symbolic expression of the fact that war was "taking a recess." These and related examples stand in radical contrast to modern conditions where no such recess takes place—when people "fight everywhere and without measure, nation against nation, city against city, one faction against another, one prince against another, continually destroying one another."[3]

Whatever questions might still linger regarding the testimony of the ancients, these doubts are removed by the authority of sacred scriptures. *The Complaint of Peace* at this point offers a rich panoply of biblical phrases and sayings, all testifying to the preeminent status of peace. Hebrew prophets and the author of Psalms are invoked first of all as witnesses of this preeminence. The prophet Isaiah, in foretelling the coming of the Messiah, called him "wonderful counselor," "everlasting father," and (above all) "prince of peace" (Isaiah 9:6)—in order to indicate by this description that he was to be "best of all rulers or princes." At another place, Isaiah says that "my people shall abide in the beauty of peace" or in a peaceful habitation (Isaiah 32:18); and in still another context he calls peace "a work of justice" or righteousness (Isaiah 32:17), to make clear the indissoluble union between sacredness and peace. Numerous similar statements can be found in the book of Psalms. Thus, speaking of God's reign, the psalmist says that "his abode is prepared (or established) in peace" (Psalms 76:2), and at another point we read: "Those who trust in the Lord are like Mount Zion, which cannot be moved but abides forever. . . . Peace be over Israel" (Psalms 125:1, 5). Erasmus, speaking through the mouth of Peace, also comments on the relationship between Solomon and King David. "It was because the name of Solomon means 'peace-making' or 'man of peace'," he states, "that he was chosen to prefigure him [Christ]; for though David was a great king, since he was a warrior and defiled with blood, he was not permitted to build the house of the Lord—in this respect he was unworthy to prefigure the peace-making Christ." And, turning to his contemporaries, he adds: "Now consider this, warrior: if wars undertaken and fought by God's command desecrate the fighter, what will be the effect of wars prompted by ambition, anger, or madness?"[4]

If Hebrew scriptures are full of admonitions or premonitions of peace, then these pleas occupy centerstage in the Gospels. Addressing herself to Christians—or rather to people who have "no scruple about being called Christians" despite their contrary behavior—Peace exhorts them: "Consider the life of Christ from start to finish, what else is it but a lesson in concord and mutual love? What do all his commandments and parables teach if not peace and love for one another?" When Jesus was born, did the angels in heaven "sound trumpets of war"; did they announce good tidings to murderers or warmongers? Or did they not rather proclaim "peace on earth" to all human beings of goodwill (Luke 2:14)? And when Jesus reached manhood, what else did he teach and expound but peace? "He repeatedly greeted his disciples with an assurance of peace, saying 'Peace be with you', and bade them to use that form of greeting as the only one worthy of Christians." Speaking again through the mouth of Peace, Erasmus reminds his readers of the central commandments given by Jesus to his followers. In the gospel of John we read: "Even as I have loved you, you also should love one another. By this sign all men will know that you are my disciples: if you love one another" (John 13:35). And a little later: "This is my commandment: that you love one another as I have loved you" (John 15:12). Referring to the "sign" of recognition, Erasmus comments that the true mark of fellowship is not "if you are dressed in a special way or eat special food, nor if you spend your time in excessive fasting . . . but 'if you love one another'." Referring also to Jesus's words: "Peace I leave with you; my peace I give to you" (John 14:2), he explains, "You hear then what he leaves his people? Not horses, bodyguards, empires, riches—none of these. What then? He gives peace, leaves peace—peace with friends, peace with enemies." The final institution of the new covenant just prior to calvary also reaffirmed the same message. For: "What did the communion of holy bread and loving-cup ratify but a kind of new concord which should never be broken?"[5]

Having invoked the rich testimony of the ancients and scriptures, Peace returns to her role as plaintiff, complaining about the radical distance separating classical and biblical authority from the actual behavior of peoples, and especially of (so-called) Christians. Here is part of her remonstration, a passage whose stinging rebuke has lost none of its pertinence in our time: "Can we call them Christian who for every trifling injury plunge the greater part of the world into war? . . . Where in the world has there not been savage warfare on land and sea? What land has not been soaked in Christian blood, what river or sea not stained with human gore?" The rebuke is not left on the level of generalities, but is directly linked with a concrete indictment: the indictment of warmongering culprits both in the clergy and among secular rulers. In terms of the clerical establishment, *The Complaint of Peace* contains an exposé of horrible complicities on the part of the higher and lower clergy, complicities which often amount to inducements to "holy wars." Among so-called Christians, Peace exclaims, "priests dedicated to God and monks boasting of even greater holiness now fan the flames of bloodshed and carnage, thus turning the herald's trumpet of the gospel into the battle trumpet of Mars." In times of military conflict, it is not uncommon "for priests to follow the armies, for bishops to leave their diocese to perform the business of war. Hence, Mars consecrates priests, bishops, and cardinals." While thus exposing the misdeeds of the clergy, Peace reserves her most serious and damaging accusations for the behavior of princes and other worldly rulers. With great political astuteness, her complaint pierces the rhetoric of "public safety" and "reason of state" which often merely serves as a cloak for the power lust of rulers and their contempt for the people. In this respect, Erasmus's treatise offers a valuable lesson for ordinary people at all times:

> I am ashamed to recount the disgraceful and frivolous pretexts that Christian [and other] rulers find for calling the world to arms. . . . Most criminally wicked among all causes of war is lust for power. When certain rulers see power slipping from them because a general peace or concord has rendered them expend-

able, they stir up war in order to remain in power and oppress the people. . . . These are the worst sort of criminals: men who thrive on the sufferings of the people and, in time of peace, find little to do in society.[6]

"FRIENDS OF THE COURT": ADDITIONAL PLAINTIFFS

So far the "complaint of Peace" as articulated by Erasmus in 1517. Stirringly eloquent, her pleas—one might assume—are able to move mountains and even touch hearts of stone. Coupled with the obvious horrors of warfare, her words—one would have hoped—have long ago brought humankind to its senses, prompting it to abandon gangland-style behavior in favor of the path of mature responsibility. Unfortunately, none of these expectations have been fulfilled. On the contrary: in the course of the last half millennium, the means of violence have steadily been refined and extended in scope. Leaving behind traditional dynastic rivalries, the past hundred years have witnessed a steady globalization of warfare and an incredible "progress" in the technology of mass destruction. Limited territorial conflicts have given way to "world wars," and traditional rifles and tanks have made room for long-range missiles and atomic weapons. As has often been remarked, the nuclear arsenals stockpiled in various parts of the globe are capable of destroying our world a hundred times over. The sheer immensity of the danger would seem to counsel a change of course; but this is not really the case. One even hears people talk now, quite openly, about "preemptive" nuclear strikes (something left previously to nightmares). So far, it has been mostly luck and mutual deterrence, rather than political wisdom and sobriety, which have held humankind back from the abyss of self-destruction.

Since the time of Erasmus, the stakes of warfare thus have enormously increased; but the methods and style of warmongering have barely changed. As in his days, political rulers in the contemporary world rarely miss an opportunity to enhance their own prestige through military adventures; in fact, there is no limit to the "disgraceful and frivolous pretexts" that rulers will resort to for "calling the world to arms." Sometimes the prospect of small territorial gains, of moving boundaries for a few miles, will be sufficient excuse for un-leashing mayhem in that region. The significance of territorial ex-pansion is increased by the prospect of acquiring valuable natural resources, especially resources sustaining the ever-increasing need for energy supplies in the modern world. In a manner unknown to Eras-mus's age, the modern era is dependent on the relentless exploitation of natural resources—sometimes called the "mastery of nature"—in a fashion capable of maintaining and enhancing civilizational com-forts, especially in the "developed" Western or Westernizing world. The most egregious cause of warmongering among worldly rulers, however—the one "most criminally wicked" in Erasmus's words—is the lust for power. In many ruling circles of the world today, politics or political rulership is almost entirely identified with power, to the utter neglect of justice and ethical standards. Thus, after the so-called "devaluation of all (traditional) values" announced by Friedrich Nietzsche, the only value still in circulation and demand is power and the desire for power—now on a global scale.

Given the gravity of contemporary conditions, Peace's "complaint" has gained increased urgency; more than ever before, her voice needs to be enhanced and amplified by every available testimony culled from scriptures, philosophy, and practical wisdom. Fortunately—and this is one of the hopeful signs in our time—her role as plaintiff finds sup-port from people in many walks of life acting as "friends of the court" (*amici curiae*). Such friends include prominent religious leaders, criti-cal intellectuals, and representatives of grassroots political movements in many parts of the world. Thus, on repeated occasions, Pope John Paul II has urged Christians and non-Christians alike to promote and sustain not belligerence but a "civilization of love" inspired by the Gospels.[7] The point of his far-flung travels to many lands was never to instill dogmatic intransigence but to cultivate among people every-where the virtues of charity, benevolence, and goodwill. The pope's efforts have been ably seconded by the Dalai Lama, one of the most prominent and revered Buddhist leaders of our time. Himself a vic-tim of aggressive nationalist expansionism, the Dalai Lama has first-hand knowledge of the suffering inflicted by violence and warfare—a knowledge which nurtures his firm commitment to peacemaking (as well as the peaceful resistance to oppression). As he writes in his book

Ethics for the New Millennium, peace is neither a pipedream nor a fortuitous boon but rather the result of sustained ethical labor—the labor of self-restraint and self-transformation: "Peace is not something which exists independently of us. . . . (It) depends on peace in the hearts of individuals, which in turn depends on us all practicing ethics by disciplining our response to negative thoughts and passions." And here are some of his comments on modern technological warfare and its character as a sophisticated "death machine":

> The reality of modern warfare is that the whole enterprise has become almost like a computer game. The ever-increasing sophistication of weaponry has outrun the imaginative capacity of the average lay person. Their destructive capacity is so astonishing that whatever arguments there may be in favor of war, they must be vastly inferior to those against it. . . . Because of the reality of this destructive capacity we need to admit that, whether they are intended for offensive or defensive purposes, weapons exist solely to destroy human beings.[8]

Peace's complaint is supported today not only by top-level religious leaders but also by religious practitioners—both clerical and lay—all over the world. In the context of Buddhism, a prominent and inspiring example is Thich Nhat Hanh, the Vietnamese monk whose early life was entirely devoted to the struggle for peace in his native country. At the height of the Vietnam War, Nhat Hanh announced his "Five Point Proposal to End the War," published his influential book *Vietnam: Lotus in a Sea of Fire,* and wrote many popular peace songs—one of which reads: "Our enemy has the name of hatred/Our enemy has the name of inhumanity/Our enemy has the name of anger/. . . If we kill man, with whom shall we live?"[9] Nhat Hanh, one needs to add, is not an isolated Buddhist voice. During the past fifty years, many similar voices have emerged in East and South Asia—coalescing into what has aptly been termed the movement for "engaged Buddhism" (whose engagement is on behalf of justice and peace).[10] The chorus of Buddhists is seconded and amplified by a large number of Christian voices animated by comparable commitments. Particularly well-known figures in this respect are the brothers Philip and Daniel Berrigan, the latter a close friend of Thich Nhat Hanh and both tireless workers in the service of peace.[11] Among Protestant theologians special mention must be made of John Howard Yoder, the faithful Mennonite and devoted peacemaker. His vision of a "politics of Jesus" stands diametrically opposed to belligerent warmongering and international *realpolitik.* As he writes in one of his last publications, *For the Nations,* a believing Christian cannot be disengaged, but must continuously ponder the proper manner of engagement: "Under the spirit of God, both our means and our ends must (and by his power can) be love: openness, reconciliation, the impatience which calls for repentance and the patience which does not coerce: the dialogue which assures the other, even the enemy, of our respect for his/her dignity."[12]

To be sure, peacemaking is not the privilege of the two faith traditions mentioned so far. With regard to Judaism, the relevant biblical passages have been highlighted and underscored in Erasmus's text. Closer to our time, Yoder mentions such prominent figures as Martin Buber and Stefan Zweig as exemplary witnesses of the psalmist's affirmation that God's reign is "prepared in peace" (Psalms 76:2).[13] Surely, many other names—including those of Albert Einstein and Emmanuel Levinas—could be added under this rubric. In the context of Islamic faith, similar testimony can readily be found. Muslims of different persuasions are fond of invoking a Qur'anic passage which states: "The source of all compassion [i.e., God] will endow with love—His love, the love of fellow beings, and a capacity to love all—true believers who work for the common good" (Qur'an 19:96). No doubt, scriptural passages remain dead letters unless and until they are instantiated in concrete behavior, that is, in just conduct or *"orthopraxis."* A prominent exemplar of Islamic *orthopraxis* is the Malaysian Chandra Muzaffer, who, mindful of Isaiah's linkage of peace and justice, has organized an international movement called "Just World Trust" devoted to the promotion of peace through global justice. Here are some stirring lines with which Muzaffer concludes his recent book *Rights, Religion and Reform*—lines which distantly echo Erasmus's spirit:

> At the [dawn] of the millennium our greatest need is to remember God. The remembrance of God is not some fanatical plea

for a return to rigid religious dogma. To remember God is to uphold justice, for justice—the Qur'an tells us—was the mission of each and every prophet. To remember God is to strive for peace; it is to uphold freedom; it is to ensure the equality of all human beings. The remembrance of God is the expression of compassion and kindness in our daily lives.[14]

To avoid misunderstanding: the endeavor of peacemaking is not the sole province of religious leaders or religiously motivated individuals, but is shared by many "secular" intellectuals and groups. To the extent that ethical secularists shun violence and extol inter-human respect, they are surely welcome "friends of the court" in the proceedings of Peace. Among prominent recent intellectuals, special mention must be made of Hannah Arendt, whose writings are indebted both to Kantian and broadly existentialist teachings. In one of her justly renowned essays, Arendt sharply castigated the proliferation of violence and mayhem in her time, extending her rebuke to many of her fellow intellectuals and their infatuation with violent actions in the service of so-called "good causes." As she famously wrote in that essay: "The practice of violence, like all action, changes the world, but the most probable change is to a more violent world."[15] In addition to other intellectual influences on her thought, Arendt in this respect was strongly indebted to Walter Benjamin, some of whose writings she edited and who was himself a victim of fascist violence. At the height of fascist triumphalism (in 1936), Benjamin had penned this stinging condemnation of fascist warmongering—and of all kinds of imperialist warmongering emulating the fascist mode:

War and war only can set a goal for mass movements on the largest scale while upholding the traditional property system. This is the political formula for the situation. The technological formula may be stated as follows: Only war makes it possible to mobilize all of today's technical resources while maintaining the property system [and social inequity]. . . . Imperialistic war is a rebellion of technology which collects, in the form of "human material," the claims which society has denied its natural material. Instead of draining rivers, society directs a human stream into a bed of trenches; instead of dropping seeds from airplanes, it drops incendiary [and nuclear] bombs on cities.[16]

As it happens, peacemaking has not been confined to pulpits and lecture halls, but has also penetrated to the grassroots level, animating struggles for peaceful social change. Apart from the movements of "engaged Buddhism" and "Just World Trust" a great number of other cross-cultural networks deserve to be mentioned: interfaith alliances, ecological and human rights movements, womens' movements, and international workers' coalitions. Although networks of this kind are motivated by diverse agendas, a prominent source of inspiration for many of them has been the practical example of the Mahatma Gandhi: his struggle for social justice and empowerment through peaceful disobedience and nonviolent resistance. As is well known, Gandhi's endeavor was not to pit against each other castes, classes, and religions, but rather to promote their mutual recognition and equitable cooperation by means of "truth force" or "love force" (*satyagraha*). After his death, his exemplary mode of action was followed by the American civil rights movement led by Martin Luther King Jr., by the antiapartheid struggle in South Africa led by Nelson Mandela, and (to some extent) by a series of "velvet revolutions" in Eastern Europe. As one can see, Peace's "complaint," initially articulated in 1517, has attracted over the years and centuries a large number of co-plaintiffs or supporters—but sadly not large enough to counterbalance the phalanx of warmongers and preachers of violence populating the "corridors of power."

GUIDEPOSTS AND WAYSTATIONS

The present study seeks to explore Erasmus's *Querela pacis* and its repercussions and intimations during subsequent centuries down to our time. Given the great complexity of historical trajectories and sedimentations, only a limited number of episodes can be lifted up for closer inspection. The following chapter 2 is entirely devoted to Erasmus's own writings—especially writings amplifying or fleshing out the "complaint of Peace." Three texts in particular are singled out for attentive reading: his *De bello turcico* (or "On the War against the Turks"); his comments on the classical adage *"Dulce bellum inexpertis"* ("War Is Sweet to the Inexperienced"); and his *Enchiridion Militis Christiani* (or *Handbook of the Militant Christian*). In the first text, Erasmus champions a slightly modified version of the traditional doctrine of "just war," by stipulating that war can only be conducted in self-defense against aggression, and only as a last resort after all other avenues have been exhausted (with the conduct of warfare being strictly proportional to the level of attack). Outside these limits, he insists, war is an act of savagery; above all, if it is inspired "by such motives as the lust for power, ambition, private grievances or the desire for revenge, it is clearly not a war but mere brigandage."[17] The second text expands the critique of unrestricted warfare into a critique of some pretended justifications of war and violence: especially arguments blaming the need for violence on providence, the character of "human nature," or the inexorable requirements of "public security" (*salus populi*). Countering these arguments, Erasmus debunks their use as cover-up for power plays, while simultaneously affirming the potential of human goodwill and responsibility. The final text extols goodwill and sympathetic respect as guideposts for interfaith relations and as antidotes to religious warfare.

Memories or echoes of Erasmus's writings can be found in many quarters. In light of his own motto of *"eruditio et pietas,"* however, two main strands can be distinguished (despite frequent overlaps): a philosophical and political-juridical strand, on the one hand, and a more religious or "spiritual" strand, on the other. Traces of the first strand can be found in modern jurisprudence (especially international law) and political philosophy, while aspects of the second strand reverberate in the history of modern spirituality down to contemporary movements of "liberation theology." Chapter 3 focuses on the development of international law and jurisprudence—what traditionally is called *ius gentium* and/or *ius inter gentes*—together with some parallel developments in modern political philosophy. The chapter initially traces the story of *ius gentium* from its beginnings in late antiquity through its relative oblivion in subsequent centuries to its powerful resurgence in early modernity through the labors of the great Spanish theologian-jurists of the early sixteenth century, and particularly through the work of Francisco de Vitoria. As will be shown, Vitoria—a junior contemporary and admirer of Erasmus—basically reformulated (in more legal language) the teachings of the Dutch humanist regarding war and peace, thereby giving a strong boost to the application of "just" ethical criteria to the beginning and conduct of war (*ius ad bellum, ius in bello*). The Spaniard's work was continued by Erasmus's compatriot Hugo Grotius, sometimes described as the "founder" of modern international law, who—partially more "secular" in orientation—shifted the accent in the direction of *ius inter gentes* adapted to the system of modern nation-states. As one should note, this adaptation in no way affected the clear subordination of warfare (and power politics) to ethical and legal criteria. This accent on moral and legal yardsticks was appropriated later by theorists of "natural law" and Enlightenment philosophers, above all by Immanuel Kant, whose essay on "Perpetual Peace" restated the legacy of *ius gentium.* By way of conclusion the chapter turns to the post-Kantian thinker John Rawls, applauding his concept of a "law of peoples" while simultaneously arguing in favor of a more democratic grounding of this concept.[18]

Chapter 4 turns to the legacy of "*pietas*" and religious spirituality. Acknowledging the upsurge of many kinds of spirituality today, but also noting the danger of market manipulation and a slippage into "pop" psychology, the chapter seeks to retrieve central spiritual traditions in two major world religious: Christianity and Islam (of which the Christian legacies were certainly in good part familiar to Erasmus). Following a discussion of the traditional core meaning of "spirituality," two prominent types are differentiated in both religions: namely, a "gnostic" or knowledge-oriented spirituality, on the one hand, and an "erotic-mystical" or *agape* spirituality, on the other. While the first type points vertically in the direction of an ultimate cognitive fusion with the "divine" and an abandonment of "worldly" entanglements, the second type pursues a more lateral orientation, seeking to participate in the "divine" precisely through inter-human relationships and commitments. (The distinction between the two types was articulated, a few centuries ago, by the mystic Johannes Scheffler through the analogy with two angelic choirs: the "Cherubim" representing knowledge or intellect and the "Seraphim" representing love and service.) In line with this distinction, the chapter traces the complex lineage of Christian gnosticism from Marcion and Basilides through the Knights Templar to passages in Meister Eckhart and beyond, while also offering highlights of Christian *agape* mysticism in the works of John of the Cross, Teresa of Avila, Count Zinzendorf, and others. In the Islamic context, elements of gnostic (or *ma'rifa*) spirituality are singled out mainly in the writings of Ibn Arabi, while love-oriented spirituality (stressing *mahabbah*) is found to dominate the poetry of Rumi. By way of conclusion, the chapter offers an assessment of the two spiritual modes, especially in our contemporary context. Although valuing the solitude and retreat from worldly conformism privileged by the vertical strand, the verdict ultimately goes in favor of the more practical piety and "everyday mysticism" exemplified in *agape* traditions, and also in the life of Erasmus (and more recently Gandhi).

The remaining chapters shift attention fully to the contemporary arena. Chapter 5 picks up the two strands of religious piety and moral-juridical standards, but adds a further dimension: that of politics or political praxis—a strand not unfamiliar to Erasmus. The focus of the chapter is on recent initiatives aiming at the formulation of a global or cosmopolitan ethics, as a complement to existing international institutions and an antidote to the upsurge of violence, militarism, and clashes of civilizations. The first part of the chapter looks at initiatives launched by the Parliament of the World's Religions, especially its "Declaration Toward a Global Ethic" inspired by the teachings of Hans Küng, and next turns to parallel, secular-philosophical endeavors, centerstaging Martha Nussbaum's proposal of a "Stoic cosmopolitanism." While applauding the idea of binding moral standards in our conflict-ridden world, the chapter draws attention to certain drawbacks or "deficits" inherent in a one-sided emphasis on universal principles. Prominent among these drawbacks is the neglect of ethically relevant differences among peoples and cultures and also the sidelining of motivational dispositions which might foster moral conduct. To illustrate the meaning of such deficits, the presentation makes reference to a number of writers, ranging from Theodor Adorno and Michel Foucault to Zygmunt Bauman and

Luce Irigaray. Taking seriously some of their queries and objections, the conclusion argues that the shortfalls of universalism can be adequately redressed only on the political plane, particularly the plane of a global democratic praxis; only by means of this redress can the goal of universal ethics be achieved or at least approximated: the goal of "civilizing humanity."

To foster this goal, one of the crucial preconditions is the curtailment or elimination of the lure of political violence—an addiction which in recent times has reached proportions unheard of since the Second World War. The chief mentor in chapter 6 is Hannah Arendt, and the spotlight is placed on her celebrated essay "On Violence" (of 1970). Against the backdrop of the Vietnam War and the widespread student rebellion, Arendt's essay castigated the upsurge of the rhetoric of violence during that period, an upsurge encouraged and abetted by a number of twentieth-century writers, including Georges Sorel, Frantz Fanon, and Jean-Paul Sartre, and also by spokesmen of a pseudo-scientific sociobiology, neurophysiology, and "polemology." As a corrective to this rhetoric, her essay outlines a "republican" conception of politics accentuating "*vita activa*" or civic participation in the "public realm" and also the sharp distinction between empowerment (through concerted action) and political violence. Moving beyond the Arendtean text, the chapter examines more recent examples of the "literature on violence"—examples either supportive or critical of violence—and in this context pays special attention to Bat-Ami Bar On's study, *The Subject of Violence: Arendtean Exercises in Understanding*. As Bar On shows, Arendt explored violence not as a detached spectator or observer, but from the angle of a victim or "subject of violence" marked by the manifold traumas and sufferings of her period. Approached from this angle, acts of violence can be reduced neither to inexorable fate nor to rational transparency, but pose the task of a difficult labor of understanding: the task of coming to terms or "working through" the experiences of violence in a cleansing or cathartic way. In pursuing this path of "working through," Arendt's outlook displays a certain affinity with the writings of Maurice Merleau-Ponty, whose phenomenology steered a course between an idealist rationalism and a reductive empiricism, and also between continuity and rupture. Merleau-Ponty's work—the conclusion asserts—is important also with regard to political violence, by cautioning people against deceptive professions of innocence and nonviolence on the part of certain "liberal" regimes—professions which often camouflage oppressive and violent policies.[19]

As is well known, one of the chief proponents of nonviolence—or at least of the radical curtailment of violence—in modern times was Mahatma Gandhi. Chapter 7 concentrates on the Mahatma's nonviolent politics, and especially on his relations with the Muslim community in India. The chapter begins by recounting the story of his encounters with Muslims throughout his life, recalling both his friendships and his disappointments. Raised in Gujarat, in a home hospitable to many faiths, Gandhi from early childhood on developed a deep respect and sympathy for members of different religious and cultural backgrounds. These leanings were solidified during his stay in South Africa because of the discrimination and oppression suffered by Hindus and Muslims alike. It was at this point that Gandhi developed his favorite strategy of "*satyagraha*," meaning nonviolent struggle for truth and justice—a strategy loosely corresponding to the Muslim notion of "righteous struggle" and pointing in the direction of a "heart unity" between the two oppressed communities. Following his return to India, he carried this partnership forward, first by joining the so-called "Khilafat movement" and later by his persistent efforts to maintain interfaith and intercommunal harmony in the struggle for independence—efforts which culminated in his pilgrimages to strife-torn villages at the time of partition. The middle part of the chapter discusses some tensions or conflicts between Gandhi and Muslims, tensions ranging from disagreements regarding the role and extent of nonviolence (*ahimsa*) to disputes over the future character of an independent India—disputes which pitted Gandhi's multi-faith vision against Muhammad Ali Jinnah's proceduralism and "separate-but-equal" formula. Pursuing this antagonism, the concluding part ponders the broader issue of the relation between the modern liberal-procedural state and religious communities or—still more generally—between public law and ethical-religious conduct (or *orthopraxis*). In this respect, Gandhi's plea for an ethical-religious supplement to formal state structures points in the direction of a "heart-and-mind unity" or civic goodwill among peoples which remains valid beyond his time.

The issue of the linkage between state and society, between public legal equality and communal or cultural diversity, is not limited to the Indian subcontinent. Chapter 8 transplants the issue into the East Asian context, and particularly the context of Confucian teachings. In traditional Confucianism, social life is typically seen as a complex web of closely intertwined relations, a web in which personal and impersonal interactions are mingled and where politics is seen as playing an important but by no means a privileged or autonomous role. By contrast, Western culture has traditionally favored a neat distinction and even separation: the separation of public-political structures from social and private domains, of uniform legal codes from differentiated customs or practices. The basic question raised in this chapter is whether these contrasting legacies can be reconciled (or in Kipling's terms, whether "the twain can meet"). The opening section sketches in rough outlines the history of Western political thought, highlighting as waystations Aristotle's division between *oikos* and *polis* (the former characterized by relations of "natural" dependency and the latter by relations between "free" citizens), the early modern dichotomy between the "political state" and the "state of nature" (initiated by Hobbes and Locke), and the later distinction between the "public sphere" and private and social domains. Turning to the Confucian legacy, the middle section focuses on the so-called "fire relationships" (*wu-lun*) constituting human life—relations which all disclose a certain personal or ethical quality and in no way grant a separate status to the political domain. By way of conclusion, the question is raised whether, in light of modern democratic aspirations, these five relationships might fruitfully be augmented by a sixth relation: that between equal citizens in the "public sphere"—an addition which might be reciprocated in Western thought by a renewed valorization of ethical-social relationships beyond the reach of state structures. In this way, an East-West rapprochement might be achieved, in line with Confucius's statement: "To learn . . . is that not after all a pleasure? That friends should come to visit one from afar, is this not after all delightful?"[20]

Strengthening the ethical fabric undergirding politics inevitably requires attention to the education and character formation of social agents—in a manner transgressing the boundaries of public (liberal) "neutrality." This task is all the more important in a democracy whose members are supposed to function both as rulers and as ruled, both as public officials and private citizens. To illustrate the requirements of social-political pedagogy, chapter 9 returns to Erasmus, and particularly to his treatise on *The Education of a Christian Prince* (of 1516). Relying on traditional teachings about rulership, from Plato to the Stoics and beyond, Erasmus in this text urged the princes of his time to set aside or de-emphasize power struggles and lust for domination in favor of the cultivation of justice and self-restraint. In order to insure the well-being of subjects and the peace of the land, royal pedagogy (he insisted) needs to foster above all the virtues of moderation, fair-mindedness, and prudence—in addition to such qualities as kindness and mercy as antidotes to the temptations of warmongering and tyranny. After comparing these instructions with similar teachings in non-Western cultures, the chapter turns to the contemporary period, where political pedagogy is almost completely neglected—apart from a few dissenting voices. One such voice is the Italian political philosopher Norberto Bobbio, whose study *In Praise of Meekness* takes up the issue of ethical character formation in democracies, with specific reference to the text of Erasmus.[21] Given the enormous dangers of totalitarian and imperialist violence in our time, Bobbio ponders the desirability of granting greater room in democratic politics to the "Erasmian" qualities of self-restraint and gentleness—but despairs of this possibility in the end because of the relentlessness of contemporary *realpolitik* (centered on power). The conclusion takes the same relentlessness precisely as a challenge and moral task: the challenge of cultivating and practicing a transformative democratic pedagogy pointing in the direction of Erasmian *orthopraxis* and a Gandhian-style *satyagraha* or peaceful enactment of justice.

The concluding chapter offers an example of what might be involved in ethical transformation, by discussing the evolving thought of Martin Heidegger. In this chapter, Heidegger is presented not as the proponent of a philosophical doctrine or system, but as a wayfarer diligently seeking a path in the midst of errancy and "homelessness."

While the early Heidegger, prior to his so-called *"Kehre"* (turning), presented human life still as an immense power struggle—a *"gigantomachia"* among humans and between humans and gods—his encounter with the poet Hölderlin induced a transformative seasoning pointing in the direction of a deeper serenity and "friendliness" (*charis, eucharis*): that is, a more peaceable "dwelling" on earth in the midst of dislocation.[22] As an interlude, Heidegger's transformative path is compared with a mode of pilgrimage practiced in the Indian state of Maharashtra; in both cases, journeying denotes not a form of vagrancy or adventurism, but a practical "pilgrim's progress" (or *orthopraxis*), a homecoming by being "on the road." The appendix offers reflections on possible lessons one might garner from the events of September 11. These reflections are grouped into three headings, each involving a distinct set of lessons. The first heading deals with the impact on America—where September 11 revealed the vulnerability of the country in a relentlessly globalizing world (thus calling into question policies of isolationism or unilateralism). The second heading focuses on the Islamic world and Muslim politics—where the events disclosed a political "deficit," that is, the lack of a constructive alternative to theocracy and warfare. The third heading ponders implications for the global order, accentuating another, wider political "deficit": the absence of viable regional institutions capable of mediating effectively between "center" and "periphery," between hegemonic superpower(s) and third-world peoples.

This study as a whole is meant as a call for peace in our *kali yuga:* an endeavor to augment the "voice of Peace" in the midst of clashing nations and factions. As has repeatedly been emphasized, this voice cannot at all gain a hearing unless people everywhere are somehow attuned to the demands of justice, urging a transformative turning-about. In many ways, the memory of Erasmus—and of the various other figures invoked in this study—can serve as a guidepost on this journey. To be sure, the road is difficult and arduous. Simply put: war is in many respects easier than peace, war-making less arduous than peacemaking. This is especially true for political leaders. Whenever leaders—above all so-called "world leaders"—are also designated as "commanders in chief," war-making only involves the issuing of commands which then, through the chain of command, are executed by generals and ordinary soldiers. By contrast, making and preserving peace requires complex negotiations among many parties, participation in conferences demanding mutual attentiveness and listening, and perhaps even a learning process (rarely welcomed by leaders). However, peacemaking and peacekeeping are arduous also for ordinary individuals and citizens. The easy way always is to surrender to passions, to give in to impulses of hatred, vengeance, resentment, and power lust. The difficult task is that of "civilizing humanity": that is, of channeling inclinations and desires in the direction of justice, goodwill, and friendliness. To this extent, peacemaking is never finished. The plaintiff voice of Peace remains forever a "calling": calling us toward a promised dwelling place.

A War against the Turks?

Erasmus on War and Peace

Several years ago, in a well-known essay, Sheldon Wolin spoke of "fugitive democracy." Today, democracy is joined by another fugitive: everywhere peace seems to be in retreat or on the defensive. Ominously, the sound of war drums—akin to African bush drums— reverberates through many parts of the world, from the Near East to South Asia and the Far East; nor are Africa and the Americas shielded from their noise. Thus, the horrors of the twentieth century—the sequence of world wars, genocide, and ethnic cleansings—seem to clamor for emulation in the new millennium, probably on a still more destructive scale. Leading political pundits in the West speak alarmingly of looming "clashes of civilizations," pointing to the yawning gulf between North and South, between the West and "the rest," and particularly between Western and Islamic civilization.[1] Not to be outdone, self-styled religious experts boldly prophesy the cataclysmic end of history or the imminent approach of "judgment day"—with some of them not only anticipating but actively campaigning for the great Armageddon, the final battle between the forces of "good" and the forces of "evil." As it appears, the advent of God's kingdom in this scenario is to be achieved through globalized malice and destructiveness.

In such grim surroundings, Erasmus continues to offer inspiration and solace—a solace nurtured by his close familiarity with the perennial follies of humanity.[2] As stated before, Erasmus's age was in many ways like our own. Warfare and preparations for warfare were everywhere the order of the day. The unraveling of the medieval social fabric gave impulse to bitter conflicts between feudal barons and landless peasants-serfs, or between rich and poor. At the same time, the unfolding dynamic of the Reformation carried in its wake the prospect of bloody religious wars—wars whose ferocity was further intensified by the mingling of religious fervor with national-dynastic aspirations. To compound the perils of this explosive mixture, the Ottoman Turks were perceived as a major threat to Europe or European civilization—not without reason: under the leadership of Suleiman the Magnificent, the Ottomans were extending their reach throughout northern Africa and through the Balkans toward Vienna. A careful observer of human affairs, Erasmus in his writings perceptively commented on all the major events of his time—always with the aim of defusing potential conflicts and of fostering goodwill in the teeth of prevailing animosities. The following discussion will explore his endeavors in three main contexts. The opening section examines his views on the brewing conflict between Europe and the Ottoman Empire (or between Western Christianity and the Muslim world). The middle section expands the scope of discussion by reviewing Erasmus's more general thoughts on war and peace, especially on the festering national-dynastic struggles at the dawn of modernity; the chief reference point here is the famous adage "War is sweet to the inexperienced." The concluding part shifts attention to Erasmus's position on inter-religious belligerence—the discussion here being guided by an ulterior motive: the hope of garnering lessons for inter-religious or interfaith relations in our own globalizing age.

A WAR AGAINST THE TURKS?

One of the central concerns of European politics at the beginning of the sixteenth century was the advance of Ottoman power. European fears in this respect were not imaginary. Under successive imperial rulers, the Ottomans had been able to incorporate into their domain major portions of the Middle East and Central Asia, while also rendering much of northern Africa subservient to their rule. In 1526 the armies of Suleiman conquered Hungary and in 1529 they beleaguered Vienna. Throughout Europe, animosity against the Ottomans was at a fever pitch and many military leaders clamored for an all-out war "against the infidels." It was in this situation, and shortly after the successful defense of Vienna, that Erasmus wrote his memorable treatise *De bello turcico,* translated into English as "On the War against the Turks." In his treatise, Erasmus did not adopt an absolute pacifist stance. He readily admitted that under certain circumstances, or under extreme provocation, war may be unavoidable and justified. The Turkish assault on Vienna was such a provocation—and required a defensive response designed to halt further aggression. As Erasmus wrote (using language uncannily familiar today): "While we have been endlessly fighting among ourselves over some useless plot of land. . . . the Turks have vastly extended their empire or, rather, their reign of terror: to the north, it stretches to the Black Sea; to the east, it extends to the Euphrates, and to the south, to Ethiopia. More recently, they have moved up the Danube and passed even further to the river Dnieper." In the face of these advances, total pacifism—the idea that "the right to make war is totally denied to Christians"—is far-fetched and implausible. The focus should rather be on the "when" and "how"; for "sometimes war against the Turks is rightly undertaken, sometimes not."[3]

Once the focus was thus shifted to the "when" and "how," and especially to the "rightness" of military action, severe restrictions on warfare came quickly into view. For Erasmus, it was imperative that war be undertaken only for self-defense and only as a last resort, after all other avenues have been explored and proved unsuccessful. In his words: "I think that all other expedients must be tried before war is begun between Christians; no matter how serious nor how just the cause, war must not be undertaken unless all possible remedies have been exhausted and it has become inevitable." In emphasizing restrictions on the beginning of warfare, Erasmus modified and went beyond the medieval "just war" doctrine—a doctrine which had been too often abused and manipulated by political rulers for their own benefit. "My message is," the treatise reiterates, "that war must never be undertaken unless, as a last resort, it cannot be avoided"— adding: "war is by its nature such a plague to man that even if it is undertaken by a just prince in a totally just cause, the wickedness of captains and soldiers results in almost more evil than good." Even a cursory glance at the behavior of Christian princes—or European *realpolitik*—demonstrated that, all too frequently, the call to arms was prompted "by ambition, anger or the hope for plunder"—motives cloaked for popular consumption in the garb of a "just" grievance or "just" cause. An observer familiar with Christian teachings—and, in fact, any ethically sensitive observer—could not fail to look through this subterfuge and to condemn impulsive warmongering for what it was, the unleashing of illicit violence: "If the war is inspired by such motives as the lust for power, ambition, private grievances or the desire for revenge, it is clearly not a war, but mere brigandage."[4]

Erasmus's comments on illicit warfare must have grated on the ears of many contemporaries eager for military action, especially action against the hated "infidels." As mentioned before, Ottoman advances under Suleiman had unleashed in Europe a cauldron of angry passions and a clamoring for swift revenge. Erasmus was no doubt familiar with these passions. Undaunted, his treatise tried to inject some sense and good judgment into the situation. "Whenever the ignorant mob hear the name 'Turk'," he writes, "they immediately fly into a rage and clamor for blood, calling them dogs and enemies to the name of Christian." What this mob completely forgets is that, in the first place, "the Turks are men" (or human beings) and, in the second place, that they are "half-Christian" as co-heirs of the Abrahamic legacy. Carried along by their intense passions, zealots for war fail to ponder the most important questions: namely, "whether the occasion of the war is just" and "whether it is practical to take up arms and thereby to provoke an enemy who will strike back with redoubled fury." In the case of the Turks, military or geopolitical considerations were overshadowed and contaminated by religious prejudices which seemed to vindicate acts of outright barbarism. Here, Erasmus issued a stern reprimand predicated on both legal and religious premises:

> The mass of Christians are wrong in thinking that anyone is allowed to kill a Turk, as one would a mad dog, for no better reason than that he is a Turk [or Muslim]. If this were true then anyone would be allowed to kill a Jew; but if he dared to do so he would not escape punishment by the civil authorities. The Christian magistrate punishes Jews who break the state's laws, to which they are subject; but they are not put to death because of their religion. Christianity is spread by persuasion, not by force; by careful cultivation, not by destruction.

Addressing itself to religious fanatics, the treatise briskly debunks a false zeal for martyrdom (in language uncannily resonating again with contemporary events): "Any who believe that they will fly straight up to heaven, if they happen to fall in battle against the Turks, are sadly deluding themselves."[5]

If the motives of warfare had to be carefully scrutinized, the same care needed to be taken in the actual conduct of war which was circumscribed by religious and legal norms (*ius in bello*). "If absolute necessity dictates that a war must be fought," Erasmus observes, in agreement with a long line of theological-juridical teachings, "Christian clemency demands that every effort be made to confine the numbers involved to a minimum and to end the war with the least possible bloodshed, as quickly as may be." The treatise at this point invokes the testimony of Bishop Ambrose, who, during the reign of Emperor Theodosius, firmly upheld a code of military conduct: for, he did not approve any war "simply because it was necessary or just"; he also insisted that war must be accompanied by "a religious spirit which places all its hopes of victory in God [not political aggrandizement] and aims only at the peace of the state." Sentiments of this kind, to be sure, were likely to be brushed aside by warmongers animated only by the spirit of revenge, especially revenge for perceived Turkish atrocities. Referring to a media campaign spreading throughout Europe (still without the aid of television), Erasmus notes: "Pictures are

painted showing examples of Turkish cruelty," examples designed to
stir up bitter hatreds. Without denying the evidence of cruelties, the
Dutch humanist pens a caveat against media manipulation which
remains valid today. Although deplorable, he states, the depicted cruelties "ought in fact to remind us how reluctant we should be to make
war against anyone at all, since similar 'amusements' have been common in all the wars in which, over so many years, Christian has
wickedly fought Christian." While the media accounts "condemn their
[the Turks'] cruelty," yet "worse crimes were perpetrated at Asperen
[a town sacked by the Duke of Gelders in 1517], not by Turks, but by
my own country men, many of them even my friends." For Erasmus,
the reported atrocities—today we might call them "war crimes"—
should serve as lessons and warnings, not as incitements for revenge:

> If the subjects of these paintings truly shock us, we should curb
> our own impetuosity, which so easily leads us headlong into war.
> For however cruel the deeds of the Turks, the same deeds com-
> mitted against his fellow by a Christian are still more cruel.
> What a sight it would be if men were confronted with paintings
> of the atrocities which Christians have committed in the last
> forty years [or four hundred years]![6]

One of Erasmus's main concerns was the brutalization and de-
humanization generated by war of any kind, especially war prompted
by sheer revenge. Differently and more pointedly phrased: if the aim
of warfare was to curb Turkish "terror," great care needed to be taken
lest Christian princes and armies turned themselves into agents of
terror (or "terrorists"). In Erasmus's words: zealous to take revenge,
Christian princes tend to "assail the Turks with the selfsame eagerness
with which they invade the lands of others." In their actual conduct of
war, Christian rulers come to imitate or mimick "Turkish" behavior:
"We are betrayed by our lust for power; we covet riches; in short, we
fight the Turks like Turks." Looking around in European lands at the
time, Erasmus found little evidence of genuine piety and moral up-
rightness. The vaunted religious and cultural superiority of Europe—
so often invoked as a justification for war against the infidels—was
largely a sham and a sign of empty vanity: "Where now is to be found

a vestige of true faith, of Christian charity, of peace and harmony? What age ever saw fraud, violence, rapine, and imposture practiced so freely? And yet, all the while, like good Christians we hate the Turks!" Instead of indicting the so-called infidels, Europeans were better advised to indict themselves; instead of carrying war into foreign lands, they should first of all war against their own base impulses: "If we wish to succeed in ridding ourselves of the Turks, we must first cast out from ourselves all our loathsome 'Turkish' vices" (that is, vices often ascribed to the Turks)—such as "avarice, ambition, power-lust, self-indulgence, luxury, anger, hatred, and envy." If this self-correction was accomplished, war might still be required as a last resort; but it might also be avoided in favor of another, religiously and ethically more commendable path. For, looking beyond raging enmities, we might find it to be more beneficial and religiously salutary "if, instead of slaughtering the Turks, we manage to join them to us in a common faith and observance"—an objective not far-fetched given their status as "half-Christian."[7]

Turning from religious-ethical to more political or geopolitical considerations, Erasmus adds some startling comments (which again seem pertinent in our own, globalizing age). Under the cloak of a war against the infidels, he notes, something else might actually be afoot: namely, an attempt by European rulers to solidify their domestic control and to squash dissent. Whatever the actual intent of rulers, their behavior was worrisome. Complaints were heard in many places, the treatise states, "that some of the Christian princes seem to be aiming at the sort of tyranny formerly called 'Turkish'": namely, by "oppressing their people with intolerable impositions, and adding to the burden every day." In point of fact, if one compared present conditions with the situation only "seventy years ago," it is staggering how "the freedom of the people, the power of the towns, the authority of parliaments" have diminished while the powers of rulers have increased. Developments of this kind added fuel to popular apprehensions and to the fears of those who suspected

> that the princes are being very cunning in this matter; [that] under the pretext of a Turkish war, a tiny clique will seize power, after plundering towns, countryside, and people, overthrowing

the rule of law, suppressing the liberties of the states, removing the authority of parliaments; and [that henceforth] government will be carried on in the Turkish fashion, by force of arms rather than by the rule of reason.

The great danger in combatting despotism and tyranny was the latter's contagiousness. On this point, *De bello turcico* did not mince words: If war was to be waged, it "must not be made an excuse to undermine the freedoms and laws of the various states; . . . while overthrowing the tyranny of the Turks, we must not bring a new and worse tyranny upon ourselves."[8]

"WAR IS SWEET TO THE INEXPERIENCED"

Erasmus's condemnation of warmongering and illicit warfare was not restricted to his treatise on the Turkish question; it can readily be seen as a *leitmotif* in all his successive writings. About a decade earlier, in response to mounting national-dynastic rivalries in Europe, he had penned his famous *Querela pacis* or *The Complaint of Peace* (discussed in the preceding chapter), whose basic message was that no Christian and, in fact, no ethically sensitive person could possibly be indifferent to the benefits of peace and justice as compared with the pernicious ravages of war.[9] For Erasmus, preference for the former benefits was not simply a matter of taste or private idiosyncrasy. As a learned humanist, he was able to garner support for this preference both from sacred scriptures and from a large host of ancient Greek and Latin writers. As is well known, one of his persistent endeavors throughout his life was to collect and reinterpret ancient proverbs and wise sayings in such a manner that they would speak again to the concerns of his time. The chief fruit of these endeavors was the *Collection of Adages* (*Adagiorum opus* or *collectanea*), a work—started in 1500 on a limited scale—which grew over the decades in scope and size to emerge finally as one of the most celebrated texts of the Renaissance. Easily the most prominent of the collected adages, and the one eliciting Erasmus's most extensive commentary, is a proverb which can be traced to Pindar and some Roman authors: "War is sweet to the in-experienced" or "to those who have not tried it" (*dulce bellum inex-pertis*).[10]

Referring to a statement by Aristotle linking youth with boldness and recklessness and mature age with seasoned judgment, Erasmus stresses the salutary effects of mature experience— especially experience gained through misery and suffering. In this respect, the experience of war can be a great taskmaster of humanity; for no one who has really experienced its horrors and devastations is likely to wish for their repetition. "If there is any human activity," he writes in a stirring passage, "which should be approached with caution, or rather which should be avoided by all possible means, resisted and shunned, that activity is war"—the reason being that "there is nothing more wicked, more disastrous, more widely destructive, more hateful, more un-worthy in every respect of man [humanity], not to say a Christian." In depicting the horrors of war, Erasmus's commentary does not limit itself to vague allusions or the polite canons of *belles lettres*. Corresponding to the depicted brutalities, his language is grim and brutal— in a manner that is likely to resonate with the experiences of later ages, especially of people familiar with the horrors of Hiroshima, Bosnia, Rwanda, and My Lai. Using sharp staccato strokes, his essay speaks of "the mad uproar, the furious clash of battle, the monstrous butch-ery, the merciless fate of the slain and those who kill, the slaughtered lying in heaps, the fields running with gore, the rivers dyed with human blood." To prevent misunderstanding, Erasmus makes it clear that the evoked images do not characterize only so-called "unjust" wars or unscrupulous terrorist campaigns. For, he adds, these are the consequences of "even the most successful and just war":

> peasants plundered, land-owners oppressed; so many old men left desolate, more tormented by the slaughter of their children than if the enemy had killed them and erased the knowledge of their grief; so many old women left destitute, condemned to a crueller death than by the sword; so many wives left widows, children left orphans, homes filled with mourning, rich folk reduced to poverty.[11]

As Erasmus was well aware, warmongers and devotees of *realpolitik* are quick to find an alibi for their misdeeds: namely, by blaming warfare on a presumed design of savage "nature" which has placed humans and animals alike under the law of the jungle. His essay is equally quick to debunk this alibi. For one thing, the equation of humans and animals does not hold up on inspection; for another thing, even wild animals do not wage "war" as a collective enterprise. Most animals, Erasmus writes, "live in harmony and good order with their own kind, moving in herds and ensuring mutual protection." Not even all wild animals are "fighters by nature," only a few of them like lions, wolves, and tigers; and not even those "make war on each other as we do." For the most part, the aggressiveness of "fighting" animals is not internecine, in the sense that "dog does not eat dog-flesh, lions do not inflict their ferocity on each other, snake lives in peace with snake." More importantly, the motives for fighting among animals tend to be limited and narrowly circumscribed: they do not become fierce "for trivial reasons," but only "when hunger drives them mad, or when they feel they are being hunted, or when they fear for their young." Here the contrast with human behavior is enormous. For, "God in heaven," Erasmus exclaims, "we humans, what tragic wars we stir up, and for what frivolous causes! For the emptiest of territorial claims, out of childish anger, because some woman we intended to marry has been denied us, and for reasons even more ridiculous than these." Still more importantly, ferocity among animals is always singular, not collective—always a quick outburst, rather than a festering habit; basically, combat among them tends to be "one to one" and terminates with the wounding of one party: "When did anyone hear of a hundred thousand animals falling dead together after tearing each other to pieces, as men do everywhere?" Anticipating an adage later invoked by Thomas Hobbes (*homo homini lupus*), Erasmus concludes that "for man no wild beast is more dangerous than man"— adding that animals, when they do fight, fight with their own weapons, like teeth and claws, whereas we equip soldiers "to destroy men with unnatural instruments devised by the art of devils" (a statement written long before the advent of ballistic missiles and long-range methods of technological mayhem).[12]

While admitting the perversity of warfare—the possible descent of human behavior into wild and seemingly beastly savagery—Erasmus is by no means ready to exculpate this perversion. As a classical humanist as well as a believing Christian, he is unwilling to blame human misconduct either on nature's design or on divine providence. Considering the charge of human beastliness as a slur on both nature and religion, his commentary offers a different account of "human nature" or nature's design for human beings—an account, however, which needs to be read cautiously. For Erasmus, the point is not to demonstrate the "goodness" or "badness" of human nature in a metaphysical or "foundational" sense. His style of argumentation is not that of a scholastic philosopher or an Enlightenment thinker constructing a theoretical system in which conclusions can abstractly be deduced from a priori premises. Following in the footsteps of Aristotle and Cicero, his style of writing throughout is hortatory and educational, aiming at moral transformation. Although there may be "good" propensities implanted in humans by nature, these propensities mean nothing unless they are nurtured and cultivated and thus made into practical habits or virtues. It is in this sense that one should read Erasmus's comments on nature and "nature's God," especially those comments he places into the mouth of a personified "Nature" addressing herself to humankind: "There was one creature I brought forth made entirely for kindly actions—peaceful, friendly, helpful. . . . I made you a creature in some sense divine; what came into your head to change yourself into a brute so monstrous that no beast will be called a brute in future if compared to man?"[13]

In invoking nature's design for his own purposes, Erasmus enlists the help of a kind of philosophical anthropology—though again without systematic or "foundational" intent. In terms of his commentary, human beings are both physically and mentally ill-prepared for conflict and hence predisposed for fellowship and mutuality. "If we consider just the condition and appearance of the human body," he states, "is it not apparent at once that nature, or rather God, created this being not for war but for friendship, not for destruction but for preservation, not for aggression but to be helpful?" While nature endowed all species of the animal kingdom with some indigenous weapons—like claws, horns, tusks, and stings—human beings enter into the world in a comparatively handicapped condition which also dictates a longer period of maturation: "Man alone she produced naked, weak, delicate, unarmed, with very soft flesh and a smooth skin." Given this vulnerable condition, no part of the human body seems to be "intended for fighting and violence"—not to mention the fact that other animals are capable of fending for themselves soon after birth, while human beings must "long be dependent entirely on the help of others." For Erasmus, physical handicaps of this kind, however, can also be read as social gains, that is, as subtle inducements to mutual assistance and friendship. Moreover, handicaps are compensated by the gift of other endowments pointing in the same direction—above all, the "use of speech and reason," a gift which serves above all else to "create and nourish [mutual] goodwill." As a corollary of the use of speech and reason, humanity developed a "dislike of solitude" and a "love of companionship" averse to selfish aggressiveness. At this point, Erasmus adds a moving paean to the blessings of companionship and goodwill, seen as antidotes to warfare. Given the noted physical and mental features, we read, it seems clear that human beings are destined not for enmity and slaughter, but for "thankfulness and brotherly love":

> The appearance she [nature] gave humans was not hideous and terrifying, as with other creatures, but mild and gentle, bearing the signs of love and goodness. She gave them friendly eyes, revealing the soul; she gave them arms to embrace; she gave them the kiss, an experience in which souls touch and unite. Humans alone she endowed with laughter, the sign of merriment; them alone she endowed with tears, the symbol of mercy and pity.[14]

Returning to the wording of the chosen adage (*dulce bellum inexpertis*), it is important to grasp Erasmus's distinct reading of its terms. In his commentary, "experience" does not simply denote a random occurrence. Emulating Aristotle's teachings (and anticipating those of Hegel), experience for Erasmus signifies not just a factual happening, but rather a seasoning or learning process which transforms the person undergoing the experience. Given their endowment with speech and reason, human beings also are capable of reflective remembrance, especially of the recollection of past sufferings—leading to the determination to avoid their recurrence in the future. Unfortunately, Erasmus laments, this capability is not always exercised or developed—with the result that many people grow older without apparently learning anything, especially from the horrors of past and present wars. Given this obtuseness or amnesia, he writes, war has in fact become "such an accepted thing that people are astonished to find anyone who does not like it." Promoted by warmongers and demagogues, warfare and the cult of violence are in many places "such a respectable thing that it is wicked—I might almost say 'heretical'—to disapprove of this which of all things is the most abominable and most wretched." What is particularly amazing is that the cult of violence and the frenzy for war have gripped the minds not only of ignorant fools but of seemingly respectable people, not only of the young but of the old, not only of the impious but of the seemingly pious. Is it not stunning, Erasmus asks, how warfare is celebrated "not only by pagans, but by Christians, not only by laymen, but by priests and bishops, not only by the young and inexperienced, but by older people who have known it already so many times?" The problem is compounded by the ever-ready armies of lawyers and theologians "who add fuel to the fire of these outrages and, as the saying goes, sprinkle them with holy water." Surrounded by this frenzy, defenders of peace are shunned and marginalized; in fact, their ideas are "laughed at as the ravings of academics" by the pretended rulers of this world "who have nothing human about them but think themselves gods."[15]

Toward the end of his commentary, Erasmus turns to an important political issue (one also raised in *De bello turcico*): that warmongering not only marginalizes intellectuals, but also jeopardizes the rights and liberties of peoples. On this score, Erasmus shows himself not only as a learned humanist and classical moralist, but as a clearheaded political thinker concerned about political agency or praxis. Looking around among the princes or rulers of his day, he found ample grounds for suspicion or skepticism. "There are some," we read, "whose only reason for inciting war is to use it as a means to exercise their tyranny over their subjects more easily." While in times of peace "the authority of the assembly, the dignity of the magistrates, the force of the laws" act as obstacles to governmental license, this quickly changes in wartime. "Once war is declared, the whole business of the state is subject to the will of a few." The mottoes usually bandied about at such a time are "reason of state" (*raison d'état*) and public security or safety (*salus populi*). What is completely forgotten is that the safety or well-being of peoples cannot be secured by military bravado; in fact, there is "no other way by which states go more quickly and completely to ruin than by war." Again (as in *De bello turcico*), Erasmus's plea is not for pacificism under any and all circumstances, but for a careful restriction of warfare to the barest minimum and to a last resort employed only after all other means have been exhausted, and conducted with the goal of a speedy return to peace:

> If, because of general perversity, there is no way of avoiding it [i.e., war], when you have left nothing untried and no stone unturned in your search for peace, then the best expedient will be to ensure that, being an evil thing, it is the exclusive responsibility of evil people, and is concluded with a minimum of bloodshed.[16]

ORTHOPRAXIS AND INTER-RELIGIOUS PEACE

Erasmus's remonstrations against war and violence were addressed, in the first instance, to the princes and dynastic rulers of his day. As a close observer of political developments, he keenly perceived the danger posed to the welfare of peoples by dynastic rivalries and by the growing competition between the emerging European nation-states. On a more recessed level—but a level which steadily gained prominence over the decades—his comments also were aimed at clerical or religious leaders: first of all at the leaders of the Catholic Church, but secondly also at the leaders of the Protestant movement which gathered momentum during his life. In this respect again, his admonitions were timely and nearly prophetic, given the ravages brought about by subsequent religious wars. In addressing himself to religious leaders, Erasmus did not strike the pose of a rational secularist, claiming liberal neutrality vis-à-vis religious faith. Rather, his language was that of a faithful Christian—but one inspired by a new and different reading of the Gospels, a reading focused not on rigid dogma but on pious and peaceful practical conduct (*orthopraxis*). This emphasis on practical conduct explains a feature which has baffled many interpreters: his ability to combine and reconcile classical humanist teachings with biblical instructions. For him, what linked classical and biblical texts, rendering them mutually complementary, was their joint accent on transforming or "humanizing" human conduct. In this respect, it is well to remember his statement in *Dulce bellum inexpertis*: "If we acknowledge Christ as our authority, and if he is love, if he taught nothing and handed down nothing but love and peace, well, let us declare him, not by wearing his name and badge, but in our deeds and lives."[17]

The accent on religious conduct—on practicing religious faith in "deeds and lives"—was evident already in one of his earliest writings, titled *The Handbook of the Militant Christian* (*Enchiridion Militis Christiani*, of 1503). The text was by no means a call for Christian "militancy" or (what today would be called, perhaps misleadingly) "fundamentalism," but rather an invitation to sincere religious engagement in opposition to dogmatic quarreling and external ritualism.[18] In an epigram later attached to the treatise, Erasmus stated: "May this book lead to a religious life rather than theological disputations"—a statement well in keeping with his lifelong effort to rescue the Gospels from scholastic encroachments and to retrieve the practical example of Jesus (*pure docere Christum* or *Christum ex fontibus praedicare*). As John Dolan notes, Erasmus's practical religiosity or piety was greatly indebted to the undogmatic "*devotio moderna*" which he had absorbed as a student of the Brethren of the Common Life in Holland. As a result of this influence, Dolan adds, Erasmus was strongly opposed to scholastic theology, which in his view had perverted religion into a "prestigious intellectual gymnastic" and instilled in its devotees an "obstinate pertinacity in their opinions, dangerous to the peace and unity of the Church." One of the early sections of the *Handbook* clearly spells out the direction of its inquiry, by highlighting the basic wellsprings of faith in contrast to mere accessories. If your interest in religion, Erasmus writes, "revolves more about what is vital and dynamic rather than merely dialectical [or theoretical]," if you incline more toward "what moves the inner man than what leads to empty arguments," then "read the Fathers." For (he continues): "Their deep piety has withstood the test of time; their very thoughts constitute a prayerful meditation," penetrating into "the very depths of the mysteries" they propound. "I do not mean to condemn [all] modern theologians; I am merely pointing out that in view of our purpose, namely, a more practical piety, they are hardly to be recommended."[19]

The main body of the *Handbook* offers a list of rules or maxims conducive to a properly Christian or religious life. Among this list— too extensive to be reviewed here—one item (Rule Five) deserves to be lifted up because it captures eloquently the gist of the *devotio moderna*. In this rule, Erasmus exhorts his readers not to cling stubbornly to external or sensible phenomena, but to search for their deeper significance. Without completely neglecting or shunning the sensible world, Christians are meant to free themselves from its immediate grasp, that is, to ascend from the visible world to the invisible or rather to discern the invisible sheltered in the very heart of the visible (*per visibilia ad invisibilia*). In Erasmus's words: "In getting closer to the inner spiritual meaning you will find what is really most important— a hope for the unknown." This maxim clearly has profound implications for religious practices. On this score, Erasmus does not hesitate to use stern language: "But to place the whole of religion in external ceremonies is sublime stupidity. This amounts to a revolt against the spirit of the gospels." Surveying religious customs at his time, he finds them mired in superstition and much humbug. Genuine religion, he insists, does not consist "in many visits to churches, in many prostrations before the statues of saints, in the lighting of candles, or in the repetition of a number of designated prayers"—for "of all these things God has no need." When St. Paul spoke of religious faith, he placed the accent instead on helpfulness to one's neighbors, on the effort "to integrate all men into one body so that all may become one in Christ"; for just as Christ "gave himself completely for us," so also should we give ourselves to fellow human beings. As Erasmus adds, in an important caveat, the stress on inner faith does not imply a complete rejection of existing church practices or "honorable traditions"—whose meaning can sometimes be recovered and redeemed: "I am not condemning external works, but am trying to impress upon you that such works are of little value unless they are accompanied by inner piety."[20]

With these comments—and other statements of a similar nature—Erasmus placed himself in the thick of a controversy brewing at the time over the issue of "justification": a controversy pitting proponents of "good works" against defenders of "faith alone" (*sola gratia*). In his formulation, mere works alone—as manifestations of self-important busyness—are surely not redemptive or justificatory; at the same time, however, if performed faithfully, works or deeds do have an important revelatory significance—how else could one make sense of Jesus's admonition that "by their fruits you shall know them" (Matthew 7:16)? On this issue, John Dolan's observations are again helpful and on the mark. The entire aim of Erasmus's approach, as outlined in the *Handbook* or *Enchiridion,* he writes, was "an interiorization, a spiritualization of religious practice, a more personal affair between the individual soul and God." Yet, interiorization here does not simply mean privatization or a passive retreat from the world and action in the world. In Dolan's words: "He will not preach retirement from the world but holiness in the world." The purpose of his *Handbook* was to encourage neither purely private contemplation nor abstract-theological cleverness, but to offer a compendium to laypeople of "what it means to live a Christian life." Moreover, such a life for him was not to be confined to the home or personal affairs, but was to radiate into the public arena (without trying to dominate doctrinally or ecclesiastically that arena). "This is Erasmus's constant effort," Dolan adds, "to break through the narrow confinement and isolation that keep religion out of the arena of public life." For Erasmus, "*bene agere*"—that is, to act well and faithfully in all domains of life—meant nothing else than "to consider all in Christ (*in Christum spectare*)" or to permeate all actions and deeds with the spirit of love and redemptive hope.[21]

In the decades following the writing of the *Handbook* Erasmus was increasingly drawn into the cauldron of religious conflicts, involving both denominational or confessional disputes among Christians and the wider relations between Christianity and other religious or cultural traditions. In both domains he invariably displayed his characteristic "irenicism" or what has sometimes been called the "velvet soft-ness" of his piety. Regarding wider intercultural relations, Erasmus was particularly troubled by the harsh missionary methods employed by the Spaniards in the Americas, that is, by the collusion of Christian faith with imperialism or colonial domination. At one point, he actu-ally met with the son and biographer of Columbus, Ferdinand, and through him was familiar with the Spanish exploits in the New World and with the protestations of Bartolomé de Las Casas against the forced conversion of American Indians. Partly in response to these events or developments, he composed in 1526 a curious dialogue be-tween a butcher and a fishmonger titled "Concerning the Eating of Fish" (*Ichthophagia*). Apart from remonstrating again against the focus on external habits—like the eating or not eating of fish on Fridays—the dialogue contains some telling comments on Christian expansion-ism and on the proper way to spread the "good news" of the gospel. Speaking in the butcher's voice, Erasmus complains bitterly about the feuds and "deadly altercations" which afflict Christian nations—wondering what kind of example this violent behavior was setting for non-Christian peoples. Moreover, violent aggressiveness was spilling over from Europe into other parts of the world, contaminating or poi-soning the gospel message. "The nations of the world would more readily embrace religion," the butcher notes, "if it were accompanied by liberty" or offered noncoercively. Not to be outdone, the fish-monger pleads for gospel piety as the standard of cross-cultural re-lations. If such piety were practiced, he holds, then non-Christian nations would more clearly perceive that they are "not called to human servitude, but to the liberty of the gospel," and that they are "not sought after to be exploited," but are invited to "a fellowship of hap-piness and holiness." If such a policy were pursued, non-Christian peoples would "freely offer us more than the greatest violence can now extort from them."[22]

Given the mounting confessional rivalries in Europe, the final decade of Erasmus's life was largely overshadowed and absorbed by this conflict and his own effort to steer a conciliatory path between the battle lines. As he wrote to a friend at the time: "It is my fate to be pelted by both parties while I endeavor to satisfy them both. In Italy and Brabant, I am considered to be a Lutheran, and in all of Germany, where I live so much, an anti-Lutheran." Basically, his own hope was to reach a settlement within the existing church—but, of course, a church radically reformed and transformed. This hope found expression in one of his last writings, titled *On Mending the Peace of the Church* (*De sarcienda ecclesiae concordia*, of 1533). Here again one finds a critique of purely outward ceremonies and rituals and an exhortation to lead a genuinely Christian or pious life in accord with the Gospels. As he states, with respect to one contentious issue: "I think we can say without vexing anyone that the saints are best venerated by imitating their lives." If the emphasis is placed on pious conduct, then there is a chance that the venom injected into Christianity by conflicting doctrines or forms of worship might be lessened or removed. Addressing himself to all the parties in the confessional strife, Erasmus implores them to abandon dogmatic self-assurance and claims to infallible knowledge in favor of Christian charity and modesty:

> I take this stand, not because what I say should be taken as absolutely certain or because I wish to dictate what the church should do. It is rather that, while awaiting a general council, we must eliminate—so far as lies in us—the causes of dissension. Let us not do anything by force, and rather do unto others what we wish them to do unto us. Let us beseech heaven and earth, but in no way force anyone into a religion that repels him. It is equally important that those who do not want to be forced in the matter of religion refrain from attacking the religion of others, especially when that religion is sheltered behind ancient practices.[23]

As we know, Erasmus's admonitions regarding political and religious peace went largely unheeded; this, however, does not in any way diminish their importance and continued revelance. In fact, they provide a much-needed guidepost and loadstar for the troubles of our own globalizing age—an age marked by nearly interminable warfare and clashes of civilizations. To quote John Dolan again: "Perhaps the time is ripe for this gentleness of Erasmus to bear fruit." Certainly (he adds) those who hope for a religious humanism that can "galvanize the disparate elements of society today"—we might say the discordant elements of our world today—can revisit his writings with "a realization that his failure is a warning and the sincerity of his effort an inspiration."[24] With specific reference to inter-religious and cross-cultural relations, it seems clear that his accent on pious or ethical conduct is the only feasible and beneficial way to proceed. For on purely doctrinal or dogmatic grounds, how could one possibly reconcile the absolute "oneness" of God (*tawhid*) with the notion of the Trinity as well as with a multiplicity of gods and the complete denial of a personal deity?[25] In moving across doctrinal boundaries, Christians can take aid and comfort from the behavior of Jesus in his encounter with the woman of Samaria at Jacob's well. It was to this non-Jewish woman that Jesus said: "The hour is coming, and now is, when the true worshippers will worship [God] in spirit and truth" (John 4:23). As one should note well, Jesus in this meeting did not just tolerate the Samaritan distantly and grudgingly, but treated her with the same loving friendliness which he had pinpointed as the heart of divine commandments (Matthew 22:37–39, John 15:17). As Christians will also recall, Jesus limited the command of love not just to friends and neighbors, but extended it to enemies or those appearing to be enemies (Matthew 5:44). In light of these teachings and his own example, how can followers today persist in enmity and hatred toward everything alien or unfamiliar? Both religiously and ethically, what excuse do we have for engaging, with or without provocation, in rampant hostility, aggressiveness, and relentless warfare?

The Law of Peoples
Civilizing Humanity

The late John Rawls—probably the most influential American philosopher in the twentieth century—published late in his life a book
titled *The Law of Peoples,* which, in his own words, represented "the
culmination of my reflections on how reasonable citizens and peoples
might live together peacefully in a just world."[1] Rawls had established
his fame as a political thinker through the publication of such works
as *A Theory of Justice* (1970) and *Political Liberalism* (1993), in which
he had outlined the design of a just moral order applicable chiefly to
members of American (or Western) liberal democracy. Dissatisfied
with the limited cultural range of these earlier writings, he embarked
on the endeavor to formulate similar moral principles which might
be acceptable in a broader global or universal arena, that is, to
members of both Western liberal democracies and of "reasonable"
nonliberal societies. In moving in this direction, his thinking paid

tribute—wittingly or unwittingly—to the powerful globalizing tendencies of our time, to the steady weakening of traditional national boundaries in favor of larger cosmopolitan interactions (shaped in part by ideas endemic to Western modernity). As has often been remarked by historically trained observers, this globalizing move finds a loose parallel in the transformation of the early Roman Republic or city-state in the direction of a far-flung empire comprising most of the then-known world. As it happens, it is in the context of this transformation occurring in late antiquity that we first encounter the notion of a "law of peoples" (then called *ius gentium*).

In his book, Rawls does not place himself directly in this older tradition. As he notes: "The term 'law of peoples' derives from the traditional *ius gentium*," adding, "I do not use the term 'law of peoples' with this meaning," that is, a meaning fraught with international legal connotations, but rather in the sense of moral and political "principles." Yet, in invoking the phrase, Rawls cannot entirely escape from its historical background and effectiveness (*Wirkungsgeschichte*); nor, one should add, was the traditional *ius gentium*—although bound up with the laws and customs of peoples—ever sharply removed from the arena of rational or moral principles. In the following, I want to delve somewhat more deeply into the history of *ius gentium* or the "law of peoples." As will become evident, the phrase from the very beginning harbored a mixture of contextually "ethical," abstractly "moral," and practical-political considerations, as well as a blending of "positive" law and philosophy.[2] What happened through the centuries was that the balance of ingredients shifted in favor of one or the other of the constitutive elements—something which also can be shown in Rawls's study. The first section traces the development of *ius gentium* from its beginning in late antiquity through its relative quiescence in the Middle Ages to its powerful resurgence in early modernity, particularly in the work of the great Spanish theologians and jurists of the sixteenth century. The middle section is devoted to a discussion of the great "founder" of modern international law, Hugo Grotius, who preserved and transformed *ius gentium* in light of the emergent interstate system of modernity. The concluding section returns to Rawls's *The Law of Peoples*, indicating some of its continuities and discontinuities with the older tradition—changes, however, which do not touch the basic commitment of *ius gentium* to a peaceful life among peoples in a "just world."

IUS GENTIUM: FROM ROME TO SPAIN

What is called Roman Law is a complex amalgam of different strands—something which is readily understandable given the evolution of Roman rule over a period of roughly a millennium. The earliest and foundational strand is Roman city law (*ius civile*), a strand which in large measure is anchored in the so-called Twelve Tables (mid-fifth century B.C.), which Titus Livy called "the source and origin of all our law."[3] Although in a sense a set of statutory or positive rules, the Twelve Tables harkened back to older sacral-religious beliefs while also reflecting profound moral convictions. Over the centuries of the Roman Republic, the city law (*ius civile*) was augmented by a host of other statutory laws, by the interpretation of jurists, and by the intermingling of statutes with customary local practices. With the progressive extension of Roman rule over Italy and the Near East, the city law came into contact with, and was itself transformed by, the legal rules and practices of conquered or associated populations—rules and practices which came to be known as *ius gentium*. The precise relation between city law—applicable to Roman citizens only—and "peoples' law" is unclear and still a matter of conjecture. As one legal historian remarks cautiously:

> In their career of conquest, the Romans necessarily encountered many different systems of law. These they had neither the will nor the means to abolish, for they were never anxious to stir up trouble for the sake of a principle. . . . But how they reconciled these systems with their own and with each other is still largely a matter of conjecture. . . . The personal principle—that each man lives by the law of the community to which he belongs—. . . was certainly helped out from early times by the Roman conception of *ius gentium* as a law applicable to all free persons as such, regardless of their Roman or other citizenship.[4]

During the late Roman Republic and with the triumphal expansion of the empire, the two strands of Roman Law cited so far were augmented or supplemented by a third strand: the so-called "natural law" (*ius naturale*). This strand was not so much based on actual practices or customs, but derived from philosophical reflections, especially reflections indigenous to Greek Stoic philosophy. Transplanted to the Roman soil, the Stoic conception became one of the cornerstones of Roman (and particularly imperial) jurisprudence and political thought. As opposed to the parochialism of the *ius civile* and the variety of the *ius gentium,* natural law was said to capture the essence of human beings everywhere and at all times, and hence could serve as the yardstick for a genuinely universal community or "cosmopolis." In the famous words of Cicero: "True law is right reason in agreement with nature; it is of universal application, unchanging and everlasting . . . [hence] there will not be different laws at Rome or at Athens, or different laws now and in the future, but one eternal and unchangeable law will be valid for all nations and for all times."[5] During the centuries of the empire, the Stoic idea of natural law inevitably interacted with the older layers of city law and peoples' law, resulting in a complex amalgam of rules and practices—whose precise contours are again difficult to pinpoint. Suffice it to say that it was this kind of amalgam that survived in the great compilation and codification known as the *Corpus Juris Civilis,* which was undertaken by the Byzantine Emperor Justinian about a millennium after the Twelve Tables. Rehearsing the opinions of famous jurists of preceding centuries, this compilation invoked right at the outset some older, time-honored formulas—such as the notion that law (*ius*) is the "knowledge of divine and human things"—while also offering a tripartition of Roman Law into the three strands of *ius civile, ius gentium,* and *ius naturale,* with the latter being described as what is "always good and equitable."[6]

The *Corpus Juris* was no doubt a remarkable work of legal synthesis. Yet, at a closer look, we quickly discover tensions or frictions, especially tensions between the layers or constituent parts of law. This fact is recognized by Passerin d'Entrèves, the great expert on the history of natural law. There can be no question, he writes, "that, in the lawyers whose authority is referred to by Justinian [or his compilers], we find not one but different views on the matter." D'Entrèves then juxtaposes the views of three great jurists—Ulpian, Gaius, and Paulus—to illustrate the dilemma. According to Ulpian, Roman Law was threefold in that "it can be gathered from the precepts of nature, or from those of the nations, or from those of the city." Whereas natural law is that "which nature has taught all animals" (including humans), the law of nations (*ius gentium*) is "that law which mankind observes." On the other hand, Gaius held the view that all peoples are governed by laws and customs "which in part are their own and in part are common to all mankind"; while the former are "peculiar to each city and are called civil law (*ius civile*)," the latter refer to the "law of nations" (*ius gentium*), which comprises "what natural reason dictates to all men and is most uniformly observed among them." Finally, Paulus, limiting himself to two strands, writes that "what is always equitable and good" is called natural law, and "what in each city is beneficial" to citizens is termed civil law. As d'Entrèves remarks judiciously:

> The divergences between these passages are obvious. Ulpian lays down a tripartite division of law; Gaius and Paulus a twofold one. Ulpian sharply asserts the difference between natural law and the other human laws; Gaius the identity of the dictates of natural reason with the law of nations. . . . On the one side, Ulpian and several other authors clearly oppose the *ius gentium* to the *ius naturale* and to nature. . . . Gaius, on the other hand, seems to stand alone in maintaining that the institutions of the law of nations can be rationally justified, inasmuch as men have been led by "natural reason" to adopt them.[7]

The tensions in Justinian's compilation were hardly fortuitous, as they reflected a concrete historical evolution. In the large and rambling edifice of Roman Law, the city law (*ius civile*) clearly was the deepest stratum—which, though venerable, came to be viewed over time as archaic and parochial. Contact with adjacent populations brought into view the variety of peoples' laws and customs, a variety which had to be somehow correlated with traditional Roman laws and practices—a need which resulted in many conflicts and compromises. The final capstone of the legal edifice was natural law seen as a set of rational precepts capable of integrating or amalgamating the other strands of law. From the perspective of Emperor Justinian, the capstone of natural law must have appeared as the most valuable addition as it provided coherence and rational legitimacy to imperial rule.[8] This aspect brings into view the profound ambivalence of natural law seen as rational or philosophers' law. Given its distance from actual rules and practices, natural law can serve as a general yardstick for evaluating prevailing modes of conduct. On the other hand, in virtue of the same distance, rational precepts can also serve—and have often served in the past—as tools for legitimating the supremacy of imperial or hegemonic power over local traditions. On both ethical and legal grounds, philosophers' reflections clearly cannot simply substitute themselves for the agency and competence of concrete populations. Moreover, even if they were to substitute themselves, their precepts would lack the traction or leverage needed to mold and transform actual human conduct. It is for this reason that, especially in times of historical change or upheaval, the law of peoples (*ius gentium*) has tended to serve as a go-between or mediating agent between local or city law and rational philosophers' law, an agent able to stretch the former's parochialism while harnessing the latter's aloofness. It is in this sense (I believe) that the Italian humanist Giambattista Vico speaks of a "natural law of peoples" (*ius naturale gentium*), distinguishing it both from mere custom and philosophers' precepts.[9]

After the collapse of the Western Empire, the legacy of peoples' law (*ius gentium*) retreated and went into near-occlusion for almost another millennium. During the ensuing Middle Ages, pride of place in legal discourse was given to natural law seen as a "higher" law and now closely conjoined with divine or revealed law—a philosophical-theological apex designed to subdue and correct (and only partly to accommodate) the existing local customs of "barbarian" peoples. As the *Decretum Gratiani* (around A.D. 1140) boldly stated (reflecting the official Canon Law of the church): "Mankind is ruled by two laws: natural law and custom. Natural law is that which is contained in the Scriptures and in the Gospel."[10] This doctrine was modified and refined by subsequent Scholastic teachings, mainly in the direction of a more complex differentiation of types of law (still omitting the *ius gentium*). Thus, Thomas Aquinas distinguished between two types of rational law: a law grounded in divine reason and called "eternal law,"

and a law grounded in human reason and called "natural law" properly speaking—the latter revealing the extent of human participation
in the divine order. Juxtaposed to these "essential" rules or precepts,
and subordinated to them, were two kinds of contingently enacted
laws based on will: "divine law" reflecting God's power, and "human"
or positive law established through legislation or custom in localities
or cities. As can readily be seen, this legal doctrine reflected in many
ways the ideal medieval political structure—especially the structure
of the Holy Roman Empire—with its apex represented by emperor
and pope and with its principles of subsidiarity and feudalism according to which all regional and local domains were integrated in a hierarchy of rank and privilege. Needless to say, this "ideal" structure
corresponded only barely to actual legal practices on the ground.
Canonical "natural law" was contested almost everywhere by the preferences of worldly princes; and while Justinian's *Corpus Juris* was
"received" widely by lawyers on the Continent, resistance to such
reception was strong in England and other northern regions (a difference which laid the groundwork for the later division of "civil law"
and "common law" countries).[11]

The medieval structural design was badly shaken and challenged
by the combined social, economic, and spiritual upheavals of the onset
of modernity. A major challenge was posed by the so-called "Age of
Discovery," a phrase referring both to new scientific initiatives and to
far-flung explorations across the oceans. Through the bold voyages of
explorers, medieval Christianity was brought into contact with distant non-European and non-Christian populations whose status
could not be pinpointed or negotiated within the traditional medieval
hierarchy. Not surprisingly, it was at this point that the legacy of
peoples' law (*ius gentium*) reasserted itself after its long period of quiescence. Given the simultaneous emergence of relatively autonomous
political units (termed "states") in Europe, the peoples' law also came
to acquire a new connotation: in addition to designating peoples'
common law, it also came to mean a "law between peoples" (*ius inter
gentes*)—although the difference of meanings remained for some time
embryonic. Among the thinkers contributing to the rediscovery and
reformulation of the law of peoples, pride of place belongs to the great
Spanish jurist-theologians of the sixteenth century, especially to the

group known as the School of Salamanca. Among this group, probably the leading figure was the Dominican Francisco de Vitoria (ca. 1485–1546)—a slightly junior contemporary of Erasmus. Although aided by a host of fellow jurists, Vitoria's role in the revival and rechanneling of people's law can hardly be overestimated. In the words of Antonio Serra:

> Unexpectedly and in dizzying ways, the discovery of the New World expanded geographical horizons, opened seemingly unlimited fields for bold initiatives, and posed the problem of the legal status which Spain should assign to the discovered populations. Here was a globalizing revolution which exploded the medieval conception of Christendom and which Vitoria sought to comprehend through his idea of a "*totus orbis*" encompassing all peoples on the basis of a natural *ius gentium*, independently of their religious creed.[12]

Seen in the context of his time, Vitoria's work was innovative and courageous. His homeland, Spain, was then at the zenith of its power and widely regarded as the chief Catholic rampart against insurgent "reformist" tendencies; it was also the chief beneficiary of the immense wealth flowing in from the New World. Without relinquishing traditional religious teachings, Vitoria on all fronts challenged and contested the obstinacy of Spanish imperial policies. A crucial front was the treatment of the Indian inhabitants in the New World following the Spanish conquest—an issue where he seconded and supported in many ways the arguments of his compatriot Bartolomé de Las Casas. In a series of lectures on the status of the Indian peoples—the famous *Relectiones de Indis*—Vitoria severely castigated the widespread practice of exploiting, expropriating, and even enslaving the native populations in America, asserting clearly in one passage that "the barbarians in question cannot be barred from being true owners, both in public and private law, by reason either of the sin of unbelief or any other mortal sin."[13] The other "front" where Vitoria demonstrated his intellectual probity and independence had to do with the upsurge of novel religious tendencies throughout Europe. During the first part of the sixteenth century, innovative humanist ideas—above all the writings of Erasmus—had begun to infiltrate Spanish universities and intellectual circles, an influx which in due course engendered vehement conflicts and controversies between die-hard conservatives and humanists. Complaints were lodged before Emperor Charles V and commissions of inquiry were established. In this turmoil, without endorsing radical reformism (or the agenda of the reformers), Vitoria steadfastly supported the basic position of the Dutch humanist: his defense of open-ended inquiry and his plea for religious toleration and reconciliation. Thus, like Erasmus before him, the Spanish jurist showed himself as a religious mediator and bridge-builder—a quality which also animated his revival of the *ius gentium*.[14]

In order to foster this revival, Vitoria had to dismantle the unitary or monistic medieval edifice. This he did with some bold and lapidary sentences, like the following: "The Emperor is not the lord of the world," and "The Pope is not civil or temporal lord of the whole world, in the proper sense of the words 'lordship' and 'civil power.'" To these statements were immediately added these propositions: "Even granted that the Emperor were lord of the world, this still would not entitle him to seize the provinces of the Indian natives, erect new lords there, put down the former ones, or take taxes," and "The Pope has no temporal power [nor spiritual power] over the Indian natives or over other unbelievers."[15] Having thus made room for broader horizons, Vitoria was able to expound his new view of a *ius gentium* adequate to his time. Borrowing from the *Corpus Juris* and especially from Gaius, but simultaneously revising the latter's formulation, he offered this concise definition: "What natural reason has established among all peoples (or nations) is called *ius gentium*." As one may note, the definition substituted for Gaius's phrase "among all men" (*inter omnes homines*) the phrase "among all peoples" (*inter omnes gentes*). Antonio Serra sees in the new formula a major departure from Roman *ius gentium*: whereas the latter, he writes, designated a "common law of peoples" anchored in shared dispositions, Vitoria introduced the notion of a "*ius inter gentes*," thereby laying the foundation for modern international law. The distinction is probably exaggerated (and premature) because, in other places, the same jurist characterized *ius gentium* as deriving from "the common consent of all peoples and nations." As one should note, Vitoria steered a course not only be-tween common law and contractual (interstate) law, but also (and more importantly) between rational or philosophers' law and local or parochial custom. This is evident in his statement: "There are many things in *ius gentium* which, because they have sufficient derivation from natural law, are clearly capable of conferring rights and obliga-tions. But even if norms are not always derived from natural law, yet there exists a consensus of the greater part of the world, especially regarding the common good of all."[16]

Based on these and similar considerations, Vitoria developed argu-ments regarding warfare—comprising both the causes and the con-duct of war (*ius ad bellum* and *ius in bello*)—which in many ways echoed the remonstrations of Erasmus against warmongering and military savagery. As for the Dutch humanist, it was clear to the Spaniard that, while peace is the normal social condition, warfare always requires justification and needs to be hedged in by tight rules. Following a long line of "just war" theorists, Vitoria held that war could be waged only in self-defense or in retribution for inflicted wrongs. In his terse words: "A state is entitled not only to defend itself, but also to avenge itself and its subjects for inflicted wrongs." More elaborately stated: "War is waged in order to defend oneself and one's belongings; to recapture what was unlawfully taken; to punish an inflicted injustice; and to nurture peace and security in the future." These causes, in Vitoria's view, needed to be very narrowly construed, and any move beyond them was illegitimate. Thus, his *Relectiones* on warfare immediately added these propositions: "Difference of religion is not a cause of just war"; likewise, "Expansion of empire is not a just cause of war" and "Neither the personal glory of a prince [ruler] nor any other advantage to him" can count as proper cause. Aware of the cunning and deviousness of rulers, Vitoria tried to make sure that causes were not frivolously invoked and restrictions circumvented. Thus, he insisted that "not every kind and degree of wrong can suffice for starting a war"—for, given that "the evils inflicted in war are all of a severe and atrocious character, such as slaughter and fire and devas-tation," merely "slight wrongs" could not possibly justify unleashing these evils. In every case, an "exceedingly careful examination" had to be made of the justice of war, and those opposed to war on grounds of equity had to be listened to. Vitoria concluded his *Relectiones* with these words, again reminiscent of Erasmus:

> Assuming that a prince has authority to wage war, he should first of all not go seeking occasions and causes of war, but should, if possible, live in peace with all men, as Paul enjoins us (*Romans,* chapter 12). . . . For it is the extreme of savagery to seek for and rejoice in grounds for killing and destroying men whom God has created and for whom Christ died. But only under compulsion and reluctantly should he come to the necessity of war. [And] once war for a just cause has broken out, it must not be waged so as to ruin the people against whom it is directed, but only so as to obtain one's rights and the defense of one's country, in order that from that war peace and security may henceforth result.[17]

GROTIUS AND THE MODERN LAW OF NATIONS

"The science of the modern law of nations," writes Lassa Oppenheim, "commences from Grotius' work *De Jure Belli ac Pacis,* because in it a fairly complete system of international law was for the first time built up as an independent branch of the science of law." In light of the preceding account, this statement is clearly an exaggeration (and, in fact, Oppenheim himself briefly alludes to predecessors).[18] The kernel of truth in the statement has to do with the historical sea-change which Hugo Grotius (1583–1645) witnessed and in which he was himself an active participant. In the near-century that separated him from Vitoria, the political situation in Europe had dramatically changed. The Spanish Armada had been defeated; the Dutch provinces had gained independence from Spain; and—as a result of these and related events—political and commercial power was in the process of shifting from the south (Spain and Portugal) to north-European countries. In addition, the reforming tendencies present at Vitoria's time had reached fruition in the Protestant Reformation which split European Christianity and in due course fomented violent conflicts and wars.

These conflicts were further aggravated by the growing autonomy of emerging nation-states and by the contamination of dynastic and national ambitions with religious rivalries. As James Brierly comments, the successful "war of liberation" waged by the Dutch provinces against Spain heralded "the rise of the modern state system," which in turn signaled the "great triumph of the idea of nationality" and the "successful assertion of the right of revolt against universal monarchy." Spearheading these changes, the northern European countries became in the seventeenth century "the leaders of European civilization," teaching to other countries "not only new methods of commerce but new conceptions of government based on freer institutions and on some measure of religious toleration."[19]

A native of Holland, Grotius was inevitably caught up in these developments. As a young man he became involved as an advocate in a dispute between the Dutch East India Company and Portugal over the seizure of a Portuguese ship by the Dutch in the Straits of Malacca. In this connection, he wrote a legal treatise defending the Dutch action called *De Jure Praedae* (or "On the Law of Prize"); part of this treatise was quickly published—under the title "On the Freedom of the Seas" (*Mare liberum*)—and almost instantly established the author's fame, while also furnishing a cornerstone for modern maritime trade. Subsequently he pursued his career as both a lawyer and public official, first—with ill fortune—in the government of his native country as an attorney general of Holland in Rotterdam, and later as ambassador of Sweden in Paris. While himself a Reformed Christian and in the employ of modern nation-states, Grotius never departed radically from the spirit and teachings of his precursors. Following in the footsteps of his countryman Erasmus, he deplored the violent strife dividing Christianity and hoped for an eventual reunion of Christian churches and factions.[20] Short of this (seemingly impossible) goal, he favored the more tolerant or "liberal" wing of Dutch Calvinism (the so-called "Arminian" party)—a choice which brought him persecution and a sentence of lifetime imprisonment (from which he managed to escape after two years). More importantly still, Grotius did not make himself into a mouthpiece of modern nation-states and their desire for complete autonomy and sovereign power unrestrained by law. Following again the example of Erasmus, as well as Vitoria and other writers of the past, he continued to champion the role of peoples' law or *ius gentium* even under changed conditions. As he wrote in the "Prolegomena" to his great study, penned in the midst of the Thirty Years' War: "It is so far from being right to claim (as some imagine) that in war all laws cease, that on the contrary war ought never to be undertaken except to obtain a legal right; nor when undertaken, ought it to be carried on except within the bounds of law and good faith."[21]

There can be no doubt that, in invoking the law of peoples, Grotius reformulated its meaning in many significant ways—although the extent of innovation should not be exaggerated. In tune with the waning of the medieval hierarchy and the emergence of modern nation-states, his study shifted the accent somewhat in the direction of interstate agreements (that is, in the direction of *ius inter gentes* as compared with the older conception of *ius gentium*). Seen as a result of interstate agreements or treaties, the law of peoples would seem to be purely voluntary or based on positive acts of will. In fact, Grotius accepted a bipartition of law (or *ius*)—traceable to Aristotle—into "natural" law based on reason, on the one hand, and "volitional" law deriving from statutes and treaties, on the other. Accordingly, in introducing the *ius gentium,* his book initially stresses its voluntary character, saying: "The law which is broader in scope than municipal law (*ius civile*) is the law of nations, that is, the law which has received its obligatory force from the will of all nations or of many nations." Underscoring this point, the passage elaborates that "outside the sphere of the law of nature (which is also frequently called the law of nations), there is hardly any law common to all nations." While thus seemingly endorsing the bifurcation of reason and will, *De Jure Belli ac Pacis* frequently harkened back to an older conception which Vitoria had still expressed in the formula "*ius naturale gentium*" (and which Vico later retrieved). Curiously, the passage just quoted continues with this statement: "The proof for the law of nations is similar to that for unwritten [non-statutory] municipal law: it is found in unbroken custom and the testimony of those skilled in it. In fact, as Dio Chrysostom observes, *ius gentium* is 'the creation of time and custom'." The same transgression of pure voluntarism can be found in another passage where Grotius speaks of a widespread consensus or "feeling" among nations "which is called the common sense of mankind."[22]

Parallel innovations affected the traditional natural law (*ius naturale*). Although critical of Ulpian, Grotius initially follows the lead of the Roman jurists, stating that "the law of nature is a dictate of right reason which establishes that an act has the quality of moral baseness or goodness depending on whether or not it is in conformity with rational nature." On closer inspection, however, the accents in this definition have shifted significantly: namely, in the direction of a more mind-centered conception of reason and away from traditional theological or metaphysical connotations. Oppenheim's view that Grotius "took the decisive step of secularizing the law of nature and of emancipating it from purely theological doctrine" is surely overstated—but not without a kernel of truth. The famous dictum ascribed to Grotius that natural law would remain valid "even if God did not exist" (*etiamsi daremus non esse Deus*) seems to support the view, but needs to be carefully read. On Reformed (Calvinist) premises, human reason was not outside the range of God's power and authority, even though it cannot participate (in Thomistic fashion) in God's inscrutable reason. Thus, the definition just cited was quickly supplemented by the proviso that an act's goodness or baseness also depends on whether it is "either forbidden or enjoined by the author of nature, God." To guard against heresy or impiety, the "Prolegomena" further stated that the book's arguments "would have a degree of validity even if we should concede what cannot be conceded without the utmost wickedness: that there is no God, or that the affairs of men are of no concern to him."[23] The other main innovation of the text was the manner of proving or validating the principles of natural reason. In this respect, Grotius introduced a distinction which was to exert a deep influence on subsequent developments: the distinction between "a priori" and "a posteriori" demonstration. Proof a priori, we read, "consists in demonstrating the necessary agreement or disagreement of anything with a rational and social nature"; proof a posteriori, on the other hand, allows us to conclude, "if not with absolute assurance, at least with every probability, that that is according to the law of nature which is believed to be such among all nations, or among all those that are more advanced in civilization." Although fully recognizing the role of the second method (supporting *ius gentium* in the broader sense), Grotius's own work clearly favored the first alternative—a preference giving a powerful boost to the ascent of logical-mathematical demonstration (*more geometrico*).[24]

Despite differences of accent, Grotius was in complete accord with his predecessors regarding the basic issue of war and peace: that the latter is infinitely preferable and the former always in need of justification and tight restriction. Together with Erasmus and Vitoria, he conceded the possibility of rightful war (even by Christians and among Christians).[25] Once this was acknowledged, however, a complex battery of restrictions was quickly put in place. In common with "just war" thinkers, Grotius insisted that war—to be legitimate—has to be of a defensive, not an offensive, character. In his words: "If an attack by violence is made on one's person, endangering life, and no other way of escape is possible, under such circumstances war is permissible." More elaborately stated, there are "three justifiable causes" of war accepted by the law of nations: defense, recovery of property (or belongings wrongfully taken), and punishment (for inflicted injustices)—all of which, however, are reactive or defensive in response to an attack or a violation of rights. Regarding war undertaken in self-defense, Grotius added some additional stipulations meant to ward off frivolous abuse of this justification. "The danger [of attack]," he noted, "must be immediate and imminent in point of time" and not merely speculative or grounded in vague apprehensions. "I admit, of course," he added, "that if the assailant seizes weapons in such a way that his intent to kill is manifest, the crime can be forestalled" through war. Yet, "those who accept fear of any sort as justifying anticipatory [or preemptive] slaying are themselves greatly deceived and deceive others." In support of his view, Grotius invoked Cicero's statement that "most wrongs have their origin in fear" and also Thucydides' admonition: "The future is uncertain, and no one, influenced by that thought, should arouse enmities which are not future but certain." Even if—short of an imminent attack—someone is forming a plot or making threatening moves, the text maintained "that he cannot lawfully be killed, either if the danger can in any other way be avoided, or if it is not completely certain that the danger cannot be otherwise avoided."[26]

For Grotius, if the legitimacy of warfare was in doubt, it was imperative to preserve peace by all means—"seeing that in consequence of war a great many sufferings usually fall upon even innocent people." The chief alternatives or methods to avoid war in his text were international conferences and tribunals of arbitration, and he cited with approval a statement reported by Procopius: "It is wicked violently to assault those who are willing to abide by the decision of a tribunal" (or third party).[27] To be sure, Grotius was not unaware of the discrepancy between the law of nations as recorded in his book and the practices of princes and political rulers in his time. Given the savagery and carnage marking the ongoing Thirty Years' War, all his efforts were directed toward bringing his contemporaries to their senses and to guide peoples back to peace—an endeavor for which he was maligned by powerful elites. According to his own report, Cardinal Richelieu in France hated him "for the sole reason that I loved peace." We also have a letter written by him to his brother (in May 1641), stating: "But if Christian princes listened to my warnings, there would be no more war among them; they would prefer to relinquish some of their right or to choose upright arbitrators." In light of the dismal condition of his own age, Grotius appealed from corrupt practices to the better judgment of humanity—what Vitoria still called the natural *ius gentium*—as reported in classical, medieval, and early modern writers as well as in the moral customs of peoples. Through this combined testimony he hoped to rechannel sensibilities which had gone (or been led) astray. Here are his own words, in the "Prolegomena," explaining his motives:

> Fully convinced—by the considerations I have advanced—that there is a common law among nations which is valid alike for war and in war [*ius ad bellum, ius in bello*], I have had many and weighty reasons for undertaking to write upon this subject. Throughout the Christian world I observed a lack of restraint in relation to war, such as even barbarous races should be

ashamed of. I observed that men rush to arms for slight causes
or no cause at all, and that when arms have once been taken up
there is no longer any respect for law, divine or human; it is as
if, in accordance with a general decree, frenzy had openly been
let loose for the committing of all crimes.[28]

Grotius's work had a profound impact on subsequent developments; in theory—if not always in practice—his teachings were
adopted by later generations, to the point that he became known (with
hyperbole) as the "father of the law of nations."[29] Among his successors, the tensions inherent in his work came out into the open and led
to the formation of conflicting schools of thought. Oppenheim mentions primarily three schools of thought: the "positivists," the "naturalists," and the "Grotians." For the positivists, the most important part
of the *ius gentium* (or rather *ius inter gentes*) was voluntary law, that
is, law grounded in will and manifest in treaties and empirical customs. The most prominent figures in this school were the Englishman
Richard Zouche and the Dutch Cornelius van Bynkershoek. By contrast, the "naturalists"—most ably represented by the Germans Samuel
Pufendorf and Christian Thomasius—reduced *ius gentium* almost
entirely to philosophers' law or the rationalist law of nature (now
expounded *more geometrico*), a tendency which earned them the
byname of "deniers of the (actual) *ius gentium*." The school of
"Grotians"—championed by the Swiss Emmerich de Vattel—hovered
uneasily between the two others, but without achieving much success
or a persuasive synthesis.[30] Thus, the intellectual fissures of modernity
had their effect on the law of peoples. With the advances of science
and enlightenment, that law was increasingly strapped into the dilemmas of Cartesian and post-Cartesian thought: the bifurcations of
mind and matter, reason and will, a priori norms and a posteriori
"facts." To some extent, while reformulating the very nature and competence of human reason, Immanuel Kant still paid tribute to these
dilemmas, especially in his distinction between "noumenal" and "phe-
nomenal" domains and between rational norms and "mere" customs
or conventions. Still, in his political bent, Kant clearly followed the
lead of Grotius and the natural *ius gentium* in giving primacy to peace
over the horrors of war, and in even postulating the goal of "per-

petual peace" as a dictate of right reason. Even without being guaranteed or foreordained, he held, it was everyone's duty "to work our way
towards this goal, which is more than an empty chimera."[31]

RAWLS AND THE LAW OF PEOPLES

With this historical background in mind, it is possible to take another
look at John Rawls's *The Law of Peoples*. In terms of the divisions emerging in the wake of Grotius, Rawls's book clearly belongs—with some
modifications—in the camp of the rationalists or "ius-naturalists."
The argument in *The Law of Peoples* proceeds largely in the demon-
strative manner familiar from Descartes and Kant, without making
reference to the traditional *ius gentium* (with which Rawls disclaims
close familiarity).[32] As it happens, many changes have occurred since
the time of Grotius and his successors. For one thing, recent philosophical developments cast doubt on the binary divisions of early
modernity—divisions which may have been required at one point to
prevent confusion (and the exploitation of confusion by political and
clerical elites), but which today no longer seem plausible or cogent.
Prominent contemporary trends—from phenomenology to language
philosophy and deconstruction—no longer can readily be fitted into
Cartesian grids and stubbornly contest their mandatory status. On the
other hand, recent political developments have put pressure on the
interstate system of modernity and the confinement of peoples' law
to state-sponsored agreements. Under the auspices of globalization,
embryonic forms of a global community are emerging whose rules
and practices can no longer be reduced to the sovereign fiats of
nation-states—nor be identified with the edicts of a select group of
philosophers. Thus, what is resurfacing in our time are some of the
older strata of the law of peoples or *ius gentium* predating the Peace
of Westphalia—legacies, to be sure, which now have passed through
the straining filter of modernity and its emphasis on human rights
and freedoms.

Despite its "naturalist" outlook, *The Law of Peoples* still offers to
readers many beneficial insights. In fact, precisely in virtue of its quasi-
Kantian tenor, the book preserves the legacy of moral-philosophical

precepts which has always been a part of peoples' law—and which now needs to be not discarded but rather integrated and "sublated" (*aufgehoben*) in a more densely textured, cross-cultural *ius gentium*. Among the book's most valuable lessons are its observations on the "right to war" and "conduct in war" (*ius ad bellum* and *ius in bello*). Starting from general principles, Rawls lays down as a rule of just conduct among "free and democratic" peoples this maxim: "Peoples have the right of self-defense but no right to instigate war for reasons other than self-defense." Proceeding from this general maxim and investigating the right to war of "well-ordered peoples," he concludes that such people have indeed a "right to war in self-defense"—but a right which is closely circumscribed. Thus when resorting to war in self-defense, a "liberal" or well-ordered society can do so only "to protect and preserve the basic freedoms of its citizens and its constitutionally democratic political institutions." This means that such a country "cannot justly require its citizens to fight in order to gain economic wealth or to acquire natural resources, much less to win power and empire." If these latter goals were pursued, the country would no longer honor the "law of peoples" and become "an outlaw state." The same right of self-defense is granted by Rawls to "decent" but non-liberal peoples—thus making it legitimate, for example, for Muslims to defend a "hierarchical Muslim society." With regard to conduct in war, his text insists that the aim of war must be "a just and lasting peace among peoples, and especially with the people's present enemy." Furthermore, during the course of hostilities, a clear distinction must be made between the leaders and high-ranking officers of the enemy state, on the one hand, and ordinary soldiers and civilians, on the other—with the latter category being basically absolved from responsibility.[33]

Like Grotius and Vitoria before him, Rawls thus tilts the balance regarding war and peace decisively in favor of the latter, while severely restricting the former. As he notes, underscoring this point, well-ordered peoples ought "by their actions and proclamations, when feasible, to foreshadow during war both the kind of peace they aim for and the kind of relations they seek." In doing so, they manifest in a clear and open way "the nature of their aims and the kind of people they are." One implication of this precept is that, during wartime, moral people must "respect, as far as possible, the human rights of the members of the other side, both civilians and soldiers"—the basic reason being that "the present enemy must be seen as a future associate in a shared and just peace." In this regard, the book detects some grave failings or shortcomings on the part of even liberal or "well-ordered" peoples. Thus, commenting on the Second World War, the text observes that "both the fire-bombing of Tokyo and other Japanese cities in the spring of 1945 and the atomic bombing of Hiroshima and Nagasaki, as primarily attacks on civilian populations, were very grave wrongs, as they are now widely, though not generally, seen to have been." (At another point, the fire-bombings of Dresden and other cities are added to the list.) With regard to the right to war, Rawls also detects severe shortcomings in the case of liberal and "allegedly constitutional democratic" regimes. Given these defects, he writes, it is no surprise "that they should often intervene in weaker countries" or even "that they should engage in war for expansionist reasons." Descending to the level of specifics, the text elaborates: "As for the first situation, the United States overturned the democracies of Allende in Chile, Arbenz in Guatemala, Mossadegh in Iran, and, some would add, the Sandanistas in Nicaragua." Whatever the actual merits of these regimes may have been, "covert operations against them were carried out by a government prompted by monopolistic and oligarchic interests without the knowledge or criticism of the public."[34]

While appreciating its undeniable and clearheaded insights, readers may still find *The Law of Peoples* beset with numerous problems or defects. For one thing, deriving from its abstractly philosophical vantage, the text does not make contact or get engaged with the rich diversity of existing cultures and societies—a diversity which cannot be bypassed if the perspective of "peoples" is to be taken seriously. The book makes allowance for only two kinds of morally relevant societies: "liberal" societies, also termed "well-ordered," and "decent hierarchical societies"; the remainder are termed "outlaw states." As can readily be seen, most existing societies in the world fall through these binary grids—not to mention the fact that the identification of "liberal" with "just" or "well-ordered" is dubious (given the acknowledged shortcomings), while the notion of "outlaw states" carries millenarian connotations (stripping them of rights altogether).[35] More troubling still are Rawls's concessions to power politics, in "nonideal" situations, and especially to the system of nation-states deriving from the Peace of Westphalia. His book sharply distinguishes between "peoples" and "states," a distinction which initially serves to set off the just and moral potential of "peoples" against the selfishness of sovereign "states" whose striving for "power, prestige, and wealth" stamps international politics as a "condition of global anarchy." The basic difference, we are told, is that "just liberal peoples" limit their interests to what is dictated by "reasonable" moral considerations, whereas states pursue goals which are "rational" only in terms of their narrow self-interest. While initially an analytical demarcation, the distinction later resurfaces in the discussion of the conduct of war (now with an edge against moral peoples' law). For the sake of state security, even in liberal states, Rawls allows for "supreme emergency" measures setting aside the protection of civilian populations, treating such measures as part of "the duties of the statesman in political liberalism."[36]

Irrespective of these limitations, the central achievement of Rawls's text—and I want to highlight this in conclusion—is to have revived the "law of peoples" as a vibrant and urgent topic among philosophers, jurists, and people in general. In line with a long tradition stretching from Vitoria and Grotius to Kant, his text clearly gives primacy to peace or peace-building over war, placing the latter under severe restrictions. Together with Kant, he also treats peace as a permanent goal of humanity—something all peoples aspiring to justice and the "good life" need constantly and diligently to strive for. Rawls calls this goal a "realistic utopia," that is, an objective which—although difficult to achieve—lies yet within the capacities of humankind. As he points out, the objective is based on two basic considerations: one is that "the great evils of human history . . . follow from political injustice, with its own cruelties and callousness"; the other is that "once the gravest forms of political injustice are eliminated by following just (or at least decent) social policies and establishing just (or at least decent) basic institutions, these great evils will eventually disappear."[37] These views certainly deserve the endorsement of well-intentioned people around the globe, and hence can serve as yardsticks for the evolving law of peoples. What one might hope for, in addition, is that philosophical reflections (or philosophers' laws) be linked up more closely, and more "realistically," with the ethical sensibilities and aspirations of actual peoples throughout the world, and hence with the richer texture of the *ius gentium* or natural law of peoples. In a pioneering way, Richard Falk speaks in this connection of an emerging "law of humanity," a normative order which—without fully exiting from the Westphalian system—corrects the nation-state focus by giving greater weight to grassroots initiatives anchored in local, regional, and transnational practices worldwide. Only such a "peoples'" orientation, he holds, can serve as a vehicle and normative guidepost for the development of a properly "humane geo-governance." Despite formidable obstacles blocking the way, the opportunity of a "law of humanity" (in his view) is present today to a "historically unprecedented degree"—making the pursuit of this vision "the most sensible [I would add: the morally required] course of action."[38]

A Global Spiritual Resurgence?

Some Christian and Islamic Legacies

At the time of his visit to the 1893 Parliament of the World's Religions in Chicago, the great Indian Swami Vivekananda is reported to have told a journalist inquiring about his impressions: "I bring you spirit, you give me cash." His response reflected the sentiment of a deep cultural divide between East and West, a sentiment according to which Western culture is synonymous with a crass materialism, while Eastern culture is deeply imbued with spirit or spirituality. One can doubt that the cultural divide between East and West was historically ever as neat as Vivekananda suggested; it certainly does no longer correspond to experiences in our time. Under the aegis of globalization, Eastern or Asian societies—without entirely abandoning their traditions— have been anxious to develop their material resources and thereby to catch up with Western lifestyles; on the other hand, Western societies in recent times have been invaded and literally inundated by new forms of spirituality promising to satisfy peoples' deeper needs for meaning beyond the material cash-nexus. Perhaps one can say that, on a global level, we witness today both a striving for material "development" and a resurgence and growing fusion of spiritual aspirations—a fusion which, in the North American context, has been described as the emergence of a "spiritual marketplace."

In an essay on contemporary religiosity in North America, the theologian Matthew Ashley reaches some discomforting conclusions. "If one peruses the sections on 'spirituality' or 'inspiration' in a Barnes and Noble or Borders bookstore," he writes, "one comes away with the impression that spirituality is something that relatively secure middle- or upper-middle-class North Americans do in their spare time." As part of the pervasive culture of consumerism, spirituality appears here as another marketable item designed to relieve a lingering sense of boredom—an item readily supplied by a culture industry which has discovered "that spirituality sells."[1] Although not without a point, the theologian's assessment appears overly harsh and dismissive. While capturing some trendy features, it fails to grasp their more recessed motivation and significance: the deep (albeit inchoate) sense of longing or yearning for meaning pervading large numbers of people in our world today. When, a hundred years after Vivekananda's statement, another meeting of the Parliament of the World's Religions took place in Chicago in 1993, the delegates—numbering nearly seven thousand—pledged themselves to work for a worldwide "transformation in individual and collective consciousness," for "the reawakening of our spiritual powers through reflection, meditation, prayer, or positive thinking," in sum for "a conversion of the heart." The sense of this pledge was more clearly spelled out by Robert Muller (a former deputy secretary general of the United Nations) in his keynote address, which pleaded for "a world cathedral of spirituality and religiosity." As Muller stated at the time, in part paraphrasing an early leader of the United Nations, Dag Hammarskjöld:

Religions and spiritual traditions: the world needs you very much! You, more than anyone else, have experience, wisdom, insights, and feeling for the miracle of life, of the earth, and of the universe. After having been sidelined in many fields of human endeavor, you must again be the lighthouse, the guides, the prophets and messengers of the one and final mysteries of the universe and eternity. You must set up the procedures to agree, and you must give humanity the divine or cosmic rules for behavior on this planet.[2]

The statements cast a different light on the upsurge of spirituality in our time, by underscoring its possible contribution to the fostering of global or cosmopolitan peace. To be sure, recognition of this contribution does not entirely obviate Ashley's misgivings. Even while appreciating the unleashing of new spiritual energies in our time, one may still wish to guard against their commodification and especially against a possible slippage into "pop" psychology and private self-indulgence. In an effort to avoid or reduce this danger, the following presentation seeks to retrieve a sense of "spirituality" as it has been handed down and preserved in older traditions of religious and mystical experience. From the vantage of these traditions, spirituality is not (or not principally) a form of psychic subjectivism, but rather involves a mode of transcendence and self-transgression—more precisely, an effort to rupture self-centeredness by opening the self toward "otherness" (which is variously described as God, the world-soul, or the ground of being and nonbeing). For the sake of brevity, my discussion will focus on the two traditions of Christianity and Islam, with only a few side-glances devoted to other religious legacies. Within the confines of the two selected traditions, a distinction will be introduced between two major and often competing types of spirituality—a distinction which inevitably shortchanges the rich diversity of spiritual life over the centuries. The two types will be described here as "gnostic" spirituality, on the one hand, and "erotic-mystical" or *agape* spirituality, on the other. Following some initial comments on the meaning of "spirituality" and its major forms, the presentation will explore prominent examples of the two kinds of spirituality taken from the traditions of Christianity and Islam. Returning to the contemporary "spiritual marketplace," the concluding section asks which mode of spirituality may be most commendable in our present, globalizing context.

TRADITIONAL MEANING OF SPIRITUALITY

Before proceeding to concrete examples of spirituality, it seems advisable to reflect briefly on its meaning. As the word indicates, spirituality derives from "spirit" and hence designates (or is meant to designate) some manifestation of the work of "spirit." Most of the great world religions have terms akin to "spirit" or capturing some aspect of it. Thus, we find in the Hebrew Bible the term *ruach,* in the Arabic of the Qur'an *ruh,* in the Greek version of the New Testament the word *pneuma* (and/or *logos*), translated in the Latin Vulgate as *spiritus*—and the list could probably be expanded to include the Sanskrit *brahman* and the East Asian *tao.* Unfortunately, this concordance or parallelism of terms does not yet offer clues for unraveling their meaning. All the mentioned words are inherently ambivalent and open to diverse readings. Thus, to take the nearest example, the English "spirit" is closely related to "spirited," "spiritistic," and even to "spirit" in the sense of an alcoholic beverage; in turn, the French equivalent *esprit* conjures up other connotations (of wittiness, intellectual cleverness, or virtuosity)—not to mention here the profusion of meanings associated with the German *Geist.*[3] How to make headway in this multivocity? Here it is good to remember the core feature of religion or religious experience: the transgression from self to other, from immanence to (some kind of) transcendence. When viewed from this properly religious angle, "spirit" and "spirituality" must somehow participate in this transgressive or transformative movement. Differently put: they must be seen as bridges or—better still—as vehicles or vessels suited for navigating the transgressive journey.

Descending from the level of metaphor, it should be clear that spirit and spirituality cannot simply be equated with or reduced to a human "faculty," as the latter term has been understood in traditional anthropology and psychology. Traditional teachings about "human nature" commonly distinguish between at least three main faculties or attributes: the faculties of reason (or mind), will (or willpower), and emotion or sensation (a tripartition reflected, for example, in the Platonic division of the human *psyche* into *nous, thymos,* and appetite). While reason enables us to "know," will—in this scheme—enables us to "act," and emotion or sensation to "feel."[4] Located squarely in human "nature," none of these faculties can be directly identified with spirit or spirituality—although none of them should be construed as its simple negation or antithesis. Thus, without being anti-rational or irrational, religious spirit cannot be equated with human rationality—because it is the work or breath of the spirit which allows reason to reason and to know anything in the first place. Likewise, spirit cannot be collapsed into will, for the simple reason that divine grace and transformation cannot merely be willed or unwilled (although it may require a certain human willingness or readiness). Finally, spirit cannot or should not be leveled into sentimentality or emotionalism—despite the fact that it cannot operate without engaging human sentiment or feeling in some way. It is in order to guard against such equations that the religious traditions previously invoked typically insist on terminological distinctions. Thus, the Hebrew *ruach* is set over against *binah* (rational mind) and *nephesh* (organic life); the Arabic *ruh* over against *'aql* (reason or intellect) and *nafs* (desire); the Greek *pneuma* over against *nous* and *thymos;* the Latin *spiritus* over against *ratio* and *voluntas*. None of these distinctions—it is important to note—should be taken in the sense that spirit is elevated into a kind of super- or hyper-faculty: far from being another, though higher property or attribute, spirit basically supervenes and unsettles all properties by virtue of its transformative-transgressive potency.

What this means is that spirit not only resists terminological univocity; it also unsettles ontological and anthropological categories or compartments. As a transgressive agency, spirit addresses and transfuses not only this or that faculty, but the entire human being, body and mind, from the ground up. In traditional language, the core of the "entire human being" tends to be located in the "heart" or the "soul" (corresponding to the Chinese *hsin,* meaning "heart-and-mind")—provided these terms are not in turn substantialized or erected into stable properties. To this extent, one might say that spirit and spirituality are, first of all, affairs of the heart (or heart-and-mind).[5] This means that, without being an attribute or faculty, spirit also cannot be defined as a purely external or heteronomous impulse; rather, to perform its work, it necessarily has to find a resonance or responsiveness "inside" human beings—which is the reason why spirituality, quite legitimately, is commonly associated with a certain kind of human "inwardness." Looking at the development of religious traditions, one can probably say that religious history shows a steady deepening and also a growing complexity of inwardness.

Thus, during the early phases of Christianity, spirituality was closely linked with doctrinal theology, which, in turn, was mainly the province of a clerical or ecclesiastic elite. Church historians speak in this context of a "spiritual" or "mystical theology" linking this term with such names as Pseudo-Dionysius and Jerome and, later, Bernard of Clairvaux and St. Bonaventure.[6] In many ways, the Reformation brought an intensification and also a growing popular dissemination of spirituality. Martin Luther, for example, differentiated between an "external" and an "inner" man (or human being) and clearly associated spirit—chiefly the Holy Spirit—with human inwardness.[7] At the same time, the Reformation released spirituality from its earlier clerical confinement (in accordance with the motto of the "priesthood of all believers"). Still more recently, partly as a result of Romanticism and progressivism, spirituality has been further democratized. Leaving aside fashionable forms of contemporary spiritualism (criticized at the beginning of this chapter), Charles Taylor is surely correct when he states that religion cannot simply be an external form or constraint, but has to find some kind of personal "resonance" among people today.[8] Viewed from this angle, the heart (or heart-and-mind) might be described as the great "resonance chamber" constantly open or attuned to new religious or mystical experiences (in a mode of fine tuning or "high fidelity").

To be sure, to perform its task, this resonance chamber cannot be self-contained or resonate only within itself, but must remain attentive to an address or supervening appeal. Here we need to return to the central point of spirituality: its role as a great vessel (or *mahayana*) navigating the straits between immanence and transcendence, between the human and the divine.[9] Obviously, there are different ways of navigating these straits; in fact, the history of religions reveals a great variety of spiritualities. For present purposes, two kinds are singled out for special attention: what I previously called the "gnostic" and the "erotic-mystical" varieties. To grasp their difference, one needs to recall again the "in-between" character of spirituality, its placement between the two shores of worldly finitude and infinity. Basically, one can interpret the image of the "two shores" in two different and even opposite ways. One can construe their relation as starkly hierarchical or vertical; in this construal, the divine shore (so to speak) differs from the worldly shore in the same manner as higher relates to lower, or as light stands over against darkness, spirit against matter. On the other hand, one can construe the two shores as more analogous and laterally differentiated; in this case, the finite and infinity are linked in the mode not of negation or strict subordination, but of sublimation and transformative analogy. As one should note, both varieties affirm a kind of distinction or difference; but in the first case, the distinction is radical and ontological (or cosmological), while in the second case it is mediated, dialectical, and dialogical.

The idea of spiritual hierarchy—combined with the insistence on ultimate divine victory—is chiefly linked with the traditional teachings of "gnosticism" (or at least prominent strands in gnosticism).[10] Most of the great world religions evince traces of gnostic beliefs; however, as a full-fledged doctrine, gnosticism seems to be a specialty of the Middle East or of West and South Asia. As is well known, a major example of gnostic spirituality was Manicheism, which can be traced to the Babylonian sage/prophet Mani; but its origins seem to be much older and go back to ancient Middle Eastern and Persian forms of light worship. During the Hellenistic period, older types of gnosticism became fused or infused with elements of Neoplatonism as well as Jewish and Christian forms of *logos*-mysticism. A basic assumption in traditional gnosticism is the notion of an initial division or contradiction in the divine or the godhead, a division which became manifest with the creation of the outer world, a creation ascribed to a "demiurge." Since the time of this creation, a basic duality (or "dyotheism") operates: the distinction between the hidden, unknown, and non-manifest God and the overt, knowable, and manifest world. Hellenistic gnostic texts described God variously as the "Great Absence," the "Supreme Void," or the "Abyss" (*bythos*)—a void covered over by the manifest world (the creation of the demiurge) and into which that world eventually needs to be "emptied." Corresponding to this cosmic duality is a division of modes of knowledge: while the manifest or external world can be known "exoterically" by everybody, knowledge of the godhead is necessarily "esoteric" and reserved in stages only to the select few endowed with the divine spark or spirit—a feature which tends to lend to gnostic movements a secretive or hermetic character.[11]

In essence, gnostic spirituality culminates in the recognition of one's own basic unity or identity with the godhead, hence in a form of "deification." It is chiefly on this point that erotic-mystical or *agape* spirituality demurs. By not accepting the radical dualistic scenario, erotic spirituality also refuses to endorse its telos or cosmic teleology. In lieu of the eventual conquest or erasure of the world by the divine, *agape* stresses the mediated and "covenantal" relation between the two shores; accordingly, the gnostic path of deification or self-deification is here replaced by the ascending path of loving redemption.

CHRISTIAN SPIRITUALITIES

Throughout its history, Christianity has provided a fertile ground for many kinds of spirituality.[12] To be sure, relations with the official church (or churches) have always been uneasy or tense, frequently giving rise to oppression or persecution. As a form of personal religious resonance, spirituality by its nature tends to be suspect in the eyes of scriptural literalists and clerical traditionalists. Suspicion and hostility overshadowed the lives of most of the illustrious medieval and early modern mystics. Thus, the great mystic and Dominican preacher Meister Eckhart (1260–1328) was accused of heresy by Rome and subjected to Inquisition proceedings, first in Cologne and later in Avignon (then the papal residence); after his death a large number of his views were condemned as heretical. Likewise, the Spanish Carmelite mystic John of the Cross (1542–1591) was harassed by the higher clergy and finally imprisoned in a cloister, just as at an earlier time Mechtilde of Magdeburg (1207–1282) was hounded by the same clergy whom she criticized for their worldly ambitions. Even such a relatively orthodox thinker as Ignatius of Loyola (1491–1556) was interrogated by the

Inquisition and accused of being a member of the "Alumbrados" (a sect of "free thinkers"). Tensional relations continued after the Reformation and gave rise to recriminations between orthodox Lutherans and Calvinists, on the one side, and pietists, free sects, and "*Schwärmer*" (enthusiasts), on the other. Still more recently, recriminations took on a confessional or denominational slant. Thus, the Protestant theologian Adolf von Harnack denounced mystical spirituality as a typical outgrowth of Catholic faith; intensifying the invective, the Swiss Emil Brunner wrote even more pointedly: "Christian mysticism is a blending of faith and mystification, of Christianity and paganism—a blending which characterizes Catholicism as a whole."[13]

Leaving aside surface skirmishes or polemics, it seems advisable to return to the two main types of spirituality mentioned before. Among the two types, gnostic spirituality has undoubtedly suffered most severely at the hands of official Christianity (or "Christendom"). Although there were many motives, this hostility was chiefly due to the official view regarding the centrality of Jesus as the Christ and redeemer—a centrality which is likely to be sidelined by an accent on esoteric illumination. This does not mean an absence of gnostic strands in Christianity. As one will recall, early Christianity emerged in the context of late Roman and Hellenistic civilization, which, in many ways, was a vast "spiritual marketplace" bringing together a multitude of religious traditions and beliefs; one of the prominent currents in this marketplace was gnosticism. As historians have shown, the very birth of Christianity was attended, and even assisted, by a host of sectarian movements (inside and outside of Judaism) with gnostic or semi-gnostic leanings. Students of the period are familiar with the "Merkaba" mystics of Palestinian Judaism, with the teachings of the Essenes (known through the Dead Sea Scrolls), and with the Nag Hammadi documents discovered in upper Egypt in 1940. These and other findings give evidence of a broad "illuminationist" ferment gripping the Middle East at the time. Surrounded by this ferment, the early Christian church was the arena of intense struggles dedicated to sorting out official from unofficial or heretical beliefs. These struggles proved difficult because of the lack of clear boundaries and the frequent intermingling of religious ideas. Sometimes gnostic views were propounded by reputable church leaders, such as Basilides in the East and Valentinus and Marcion in the West.[14] Slowly solidifying their doctrinal position, the early church fathers—led by Irenaeus and Tertullian—launched a concerted offensive against heretical beliefs and successfully expunged or marginalized gnostic spirituality (Marcion and Valentinus were excommunicated around A.D. 150).

This, of course, was not the end of Christian gnosticism. During the Middle Ages and early modernity, many new gnostic or semignostic movements arose in Western and Eastern Christianity. Students of history recall such names as Catharism and Bogomilism, and also such sects as the Albigensians, Waldenses, and Alumbrados. Links with gnostic teachings can also be detected in the spirituality of the Knights Templar (Knights of the Temple of Solomon) and of the Rosicrucians—movements which in later centuries were succeeded by Masonic lodges and, still more recently, by the networks of theosophy and anthroposophy. It was chiefly in the fight against medieval and early modern gnostic sects that the Inquisition gained its reputation of persecutionary zeal and religious intolerance. During the thirteenth century, larger-scale crusades were mounted by the church against heretical sects, in the course of which large numbers of Cathars, Albigensians, and others were massacred. Often the church could rely on the complicity of temporal rulers, especially in France. Thus, during the reign of Philip le Bel (1268–1314), Jacques de Molay, grand master of the Templars, and thousands of other Templars were arrested throughout France (Friday, October 13, 1307). A few years later, the grand master and another leading Templar figure were publicly burnt on a slow fire as heretics.[15] In this respect, the Protestant Reformation signaled an end of large-scale physical persecution, but not an end of polemical invective. It was against the semi-gnostic spirituality of the "*Schwärmer*" (enthusiasts) that the Luther-student Zinzendorf uttered his scathing words of condemnation (which probably should not be extended to Christian spirituality as such). Such mystical spirituality, he stated harshly, leads to "arrogant conceit" (*Einbildung von sich selbst*) and "self-righteousness" without Christ, and hence to a form of human "self-deification" which is "a dangerous and miserable doctrine opposed to the very core of creation."[16]

Although generally hostile to gnostic teachings, Christianity—despite many reservations—has always been relatively hospitable to erotic mysticism or *agape* spirituality. Notwithstanding his strong denunciation of the *Schwärmer*, Martin Luther himself repeatedly resorted to erotic symbolism to portray the relation between Jesus and Christian inwardness: namely, the image of bridegroom and bride. This symbolism, of course, is much older than Luther and, throughout the Middle Ages, served as a vehicle for expressing the relation between Jesus and the community of believers.[17] In Christian *agape* spirituality, the loving relation between bridegroom and bride is first initiated by Jesus and only then reciprocated by human beings. As we read already in St. Paul's letter to the Galatians (2:20): "I live by faith in the son of God who loved me and has given Himself for me." A similar sentiment is expressed in the fourteenth-century text *Imitatio Christi*, which states: "If you rely on yourself alone, nothing is accomplished; but if you rely on God, heaven's grace redeems you."[18] In every case, Christian *agape* spirituality involves a loving relationship between an "I" and a "You" or "Thou," between humans and the divine. And like every genuine love, this relationship is basically ambivalent and cannot be captured either in a rigidly dualistic or a synthetic or monistic formula. "I and You" here implies a twoness or duality (or difference) which can be mediated or bridged through love, but cannot be abolished either through appropriation of the "other" by the self or the dissolution of the self in the "other." As Gerhard Ebeling has correctly noted: "Even in the most intimate union with Christ a difference remains. For although genuine love unites, it does not cancel duality in an indiscriminate fusion devoid of language and communication."[19]

These comments can be illustrated by a brief glance at some prominent Christian *agape* mystics. Thus, the "spiritual poetry" of John of the Cross (1542–1591) is in essence a series of love songs exploring the depth and ecstasy of the human encounter with the divine. As he states in one of these songs:

> Oblivious of created things,
> recollecting the Creator alone,
> the depths of inwardness we plumb,
> by loving lovingly the Beloved.

"Plumbing inwardness," one should note, signifies here neither a retreat into solipsism, nor a gnostic-intellectual union with the divine. As John himself elaborates: "Our soul becomes unified with God not through cognition or mental representations, nor through passive enjoyment or anything sensual, but intellectually only through faith, recollectively through hope, and actively through love"—where love means an ek-static movement toward the "You" of God and also laterally toward the "You" of fellow human beings (again in John's words: with love of God "love for fellow beings likewise grows").[20] A similar orientation is manifest in John's compatriot, Teresa of Avila (1509–1582). In Teresa's case, love of God means love for the crucified Jesus—which translates concretely into loving care for the needy and the sufferings of humankind. As it happens, this linkage or translation was not present from the beginning. In fact, during her early monastic life, Teresa was strongly attracted to a kind of super-spiritual (and quasi-gnostic) union with the divine disdainful of worldly concerns. However, in 1554 a religious experience of the "mortally wounded Jesus" changed her outlook. The impact of this experience is recorded in her "Autobiography" where she writes that, under the influence of certain spiritual teachers, she had initially believed

> that everything bodily [or worldly] was only an obstacle to complete contemplation which is a purely spiritual exercise. . . . God willing, this [contemplative] mode of prayer is indeed very tasty and pleasurable. . . . Hence, nobody could have prompted me to return to a consideration of the humanity of Jesus which appeared to me then as a mere distraction. . . . Had I remained in this stance, I would never have reached my present position; for I now consider that [earlier] stance an error. . . . Lord of my soul and my highest good: crucified Jesus! I never remember without out pain my earlier delusion which now appears to me as a great betrayal of you.[21]

Examples of this kind could be multiplied; for present purposes, however, a few additional illustrations must suffice. As indicated, for Christians—whether Catholic or Protestant—*agape* spirituality is centered on the encounter with Jesus, and in light of Jesus's suffering and death, this love relation spills over into a loving engagement with fellow humans and their sufferings. For the Dominican Johannes Tauler (fourteenth century), love involved a radical transformation (or *periagoge*), a move through self-denial and mortification to a rebirth effected by Christ's love. This rebirth in and through Christ, however, could not lead to a complete fusion—which would negate human humility and longing. At the same time, abandonment of selfish attachments freed the heart for the *imitatio Christi* and for the co-suffering with Jesus and the world (the mystical "*compassio*" taught earlier by Bernard of Clairvaux). As Josef Zapf concisely formulates Tauler's teaching: "Abandon self-centeredness and be guided by the life and suffering of Christ. . . . Ponder God's will and your own nothingness. . . . Then God works in all your works and deeds."[22] In a similar vein, the Pietist Count Zinzendorf (1700–1760) emphasized the need of anchoring Christian spirituality in the life and suffering of Jesus. After an initial flirtation with mystical enthusiasm, Zinzendorf returned to the more sober Lutheran conception of Jesus as bridegroom and the redemptive quality of his suffering. As he wrote at one point: "If there is a genuine mystic, it is Jesus. For a mystic is someone who lives a hidden life . . . which one might call a *statum mortis,* away from the praise and vituperation of this world." In order to share in this mystical life, it is necessary to die and be reborn in Christ, a rebirth through which—as in a feast of love—the soul joins Jesus as "your redeemer, your best, your first and last friend." By gaining Jesus as best friend, however, the soul also joins in his suffering and the suffering of the world: "All one can do in this life is to have daily contact with the crucified."[23]

Before proceeding, a few additional comments seem in order. An important point to note is that the distinction between gnostic and *agape* spirituality is not watertight (and probably not as categorical as the preceding discussion suggests). As mentioned before, Christian spirituality through the centuries is not devoid of gnostic or semi-gnostic strands; occasionally, the two kinds are mingled or interpenetrating—although, on the whole, the *agape* theme tends to prevail. A case in point are the writings and teachings of Meister Eckhart. What might be considered gnostic or semi-gnostic features in Eckhart's work have to do mainly with his notion of a hidden "godhead" beyond or beneath the personal God, a godhead variously described as "Being" or "beyond Being," or else as "Emptiness" and "Abyss"; closely linked with this notion is the accent on an intellectual plunge, a self-emptying submergence of the intellect in the divine abyss.[24] Although prominent, these features probably should not be taken in isolation or as a denial of practical *agape*. What one can hardly forget is that Eckhart was also a Dominican cleric and as such deeply involved in preaching and pastoral care. Some of his finest insights are to be found in his Latin and German sermons. Thus, his famous sermon "*Beati pauperes spiritu*" calls into question precisely the gnostic ambition to "know" and fully plumb God's mystery through our rational intellect or "spirit"; at the same time, it questions our ability to reach God through willpower and mental exercises—counseling instead a "releasement" allowing God to work in and through us. It is in this sense that one should probably also understand his celebrated sermon on the respective merits of contemplation versus active life—or, biblically expressed, the respective merits of Mary and Martha (Luke 10:38–42). Deviating from traditional treatments eulogizing Mary, Eckhart gave the palm of piety to Martha; for, while Mary desired to be unified with Jesus through passive illumination, Martha was content to do God's work in everyday life. Through her unpretentious "business," Eckhart stated, "Jesus is united with her and she with Him, and she shines and glows with Him . . . as a pure light in the fatherly heart."[25]

The other Christian mystic frequently associated with gnostic spirituality is the Silesian Johannes Scheffler, who wrote under the name of "Angelus Silesius" (1624–1677). In his long and meditative essay titled *Sauf le Nom,* Jacques Derrida devotes considerable attention to Scheffler's work, emphasizing particularly its more intellectualist or quasi-gnostic features. Thus, he gives pride of place to such (gnostic-sounding) verses of Scheffler as these:

> To become nothing is to become God.
> Nothingness swallows everything before it:
> And if it does not swallow you,
> You can never be born in eternal light.

Or again these lines:

I am like God, and God like me.
I am as great as God; He as small as I;
He cannot be above me, I not under Him.

Derrida expressly accentuates this quasi-gnostic outlook—called here
an "apophatic" mysticism—while distancing it as far as possible from
Christian *philia* or charity or love. As he states pointedly: "The question arises here: what does friendship of a friend mean if one frees
friendship—together with negative theology as such—from all the
dominant definitions of Greek or Christian origin, that is, from the
fraternal and 'phallocentric' scheme of *philia* or charity?"[26]

As in the case of Eckhart, one needs to guard here against a one-
sidedness which would sideline or neglect Scheffler's deeply Christian
(or Christ-centered) spirituality in favor of pure contemplation. As
it happens, Scheffler himself distinguished between two kinds of
spirituality, an intellectual and an erotic-mystical type, and he associated these two kinds with two angelic choirs: the "Cherubim" representing knowledge or intellect and the "Seraphim" representing love.
Although one of his main collections of poems is called *Cherubinic
Wanderer* (*Cherubinischer Wandersmann*), he basically wanted to keep
the two spiritual paths tied together. As he wrote: "Blessed are you if
you are able to make room for both and if, in your earthly life, you
sometimes burn with heavenly love like Seraphim, and sometimes
focus your mental eye steadily on God like Cherubim." As a wanderer
or pilgrim, Scheffler basically followed in the footsteps of St. Bonaventure's *itinerarium mentis in Deum;* this path, for him, involved a puri-
fying movement, an itinerary from humanity to divinity ("*durch die
Menschheit zu der Gottheit*")—but in a manner which never forgets
human finitude and the mediating role of Jesus. Thus, the bold sentence "I am like God, and God like me" needs to be balanced against
these other lines, far removed from gnostic illumination:

Highest knowledge it is
Not to know anything
But Jesus Christ
And Him as Crucified and Risen.[27]

ISLAMIC SPIRITUALITIES

When turning from Christian to Islamic spirituality, one notices many familiar themes, but also a kind of sea-change. A prominent similarity resides in the rich profusion of different spiritualities—varieties which are only loosely bundled together under the umbrella label of "Sufism." Another similarity derives from the "Abrahamic legacy" shared by the two religions, a congruence manifest in the invocation of similar biblical stories and religious symbolisms. The sea-change, on the other hand, has to do with the relatively greater prominence of gnostic or quasi-gnostic tendencies in the Islamic context. Several reasons may account for this divergence. One may be the relatively late arrival of Islam in the Middle East, at a time when gnosticism had already taken firm roots and acquired a broad religious following. Another important reason has to do with the centrality of divine oneness (*tawhid*) and the absence of mediating features in Islam—a centrality which may encourage gnostic aspirations toward ultimate unification or fusion. Closely connected with this aspect is the different status of Jesus and Prophet Muhammad in the two religious traditions. On this score, it is perhaps more difficult to link the messenger of Islam with *agape*-style spirituality—although resources for such a linkage are surely not lacking.[28]

As indicated, Islam historically displays a variety of spiritual orientations; however, as in the Christian case, two stand out: a knowledge-based and a more love-based variety. Notwithstanding numerous variations, gnostic spirituality aims at the unification or identification of the human knower with divine Being or else with the empty "abyss" of the divine—an identification which, by its nature, is reserved for a select group endowed with the spark of *gnosis*. Given the restrictedness of this spark and its separation from the ordinary world of ignorance (*jahiliyya*), gnostic spirituality favors esotericism and a relatively secret transmission of doctrines, in accord with its accent on privileged insight or knowledge (*ma'rifa*). In contrast with this restrictive type, ordinary Muslim spirituality comprises and relies on a number of ingredients. In mainstream Sufism, knowledge or illumination is by no means ignored, but it is amplified and counterbalanced by reverence for God (*makhafa*) and compassionate love (*mahabbah*).

Generally speaking one might say that the latter two ingredients take the place of the focus on Jesus and his suffering in Christian *agape* mysticism. Fear or reverence of God, in particular, guards against intellectual conceit and a self-righteous "self-deification" or identification with the divine. Pride of place in ordinary Sufism, however, goes to love (*mahabbah*), a love whose target—God or fellow human beings—remains ambivalent and undecided, since sensible and supersensible, visible and invisible realms are here seen as analogous and lovingly reconciled in their difference.

In the Islamic (as in the Christian) context, intellectual spirituality is not a compact movement, nor does it subscribe to a unified doctrine. Moreover, its social stance varies, adopting sometimes a more reclusive or purely contemplative, sometimes a more activist or intrusive (occasionally even millenarian) cast. An exemplar of the former kind is the "Great Sheikh": Abu Bakr Muhammad Muhyi-d-Din, known as Ibn Arabi (1165–1240). The point here is not to claim that Ibn Arabi was a gnostic in any formal sense of the term, nor that his spirituality was exclusively of an intellectual or illuminationist type. The opposite is the case. As in the case of some Christian mystics, one can say that Ibn Arabi's outlook was multifaceted and comprised a variety of strands, including the strand of love mysticism. As he actually stated at one point, for him love (*mahabbah*) and not knowledge (*ma'rifa*) was the summit of mysticism, because it is love and not knowledge which truly reflects divine union (*tawhid*). And in his *Tarjumán al-Ashwaq* we read:

> Mine is the religion of love.
> Wherever His [God's] caravans turn,
> The religion of love
> Shall be my religion and my faith.[29]

Yet, it is commonly agreed that, among Muslim mystics, Ibn Arabi is the most intellectual or that his thought places a strong, perhaps preeminent accent on intellectualism. This accent is evident in his key concept of "*wahdat al-wujud*" (unity of Being), according to which there is only one divine reality in comparison with which all other finite beings are ultimately "nothing" or nonexistent. The task of the

Sufi mystic honoring this doctrine is to recognize his/her nonexistence as a finite being and to accept his/her fusion with the divine.[30]

For present purposes, it must suffice to consider briefly one text in which the intellectual element clearly prevails. The text is "Whoso Knoweth Himself . . . ," taken from Ibn Arabi's *Treatise on Being* (*Risale-t-ul-wujudiyyah*). The point of the title is that "whosoever knows himself" properly, knows himself as integral to, and coterminous with, divine reality or Being. Commenting on the saying of the Prophet, "I know my Lord by my Lord," Ibn Arabi states:

> The Prophet points out by that saying that thou art not thou: thou art He, without thou; not He entering into thee, nor thou entering into Him, nor He proceeding forth from thee, nor thou proceeding forth from Him. And it is not meant by this that thou art anything that exists or thine attributes anything that exists; but it is meant by it that thou never wast nor wilt be, whether by thyself or through Him or in Him or along with Him. Thou art neither ceasing to be nor still existing. *Thou art He,* without any of these limitations. Then if you know thine existence thus, then thou knowest God; and if not, then not.

In its zeal to celebrate the absolute unity (*tawhid*) of divine being, Ibn Arabi's text goes even beyond traditional gnostic formulas stressing the need for a self-emptying or a cessation of self in God. "Most of those 'who know God' (*al 'urraf*)," he writes,

> make ceasing of existence and the ceasing of that ceasing a condition of attaining the knowledge of God; but that is an error and a clear oversight. For the knowledge of God does not presuppose the ceasing of existence nor the ceasing of that ceasing. For things have *no* existence, and what does not exist cannot cease to exist. . . . Then if thou knoweth thyself without existence or ceasing to be, then thou knoweth God; and if not, then not.[31]

Aware of the boldness of these formulations, Ibn Arabi proceeds to answer some questions raised by skeptically inclined readers. One such question concerns precisely the idea of an absolute unity devoid of duality, two-ness or difference. "How," the questioner asks, "lies the way to union, when thou affirmest that there is no other beside Him, and a thing cannot be united to itself?" Ibn Arabi answers:

> No doubt, there is in reality no union nor disunion, neither far nor near. For union is not possible except between two, and if there be but one, there can be no union nor division. For union requires two either similar or dissimilar. Then, if they are similar, they are equals, and if they are dissimilar, they are opposites; but He (whose name be exalted) spurns to have either an equal or an opposite. . . . So there is union without union, and nearness without nearness, and farness without farness.

Elaborating further on this thought, he explains:

> Understand, therefore, that the knower's knowledge of himself is God's knowledge of Himself, because his soul is nothing but He. . . . And whoever attains to this state, his existence is no more, outwardly or inwardly, any but the existence of Him (whose name be exalted). . . . So if one say "I am God," then hearken to him, for it is God (whose name be exalted) saying "I am God," not he. . . . [Here] our discourse is only with him who has sight and is not born blind; for he who does not know himself is blind and cannot see. And until the blindness depart, he will not attain to these spiritual matters.[32]

What one may notice in this statement is the surreptious reemergence of a duality or difference: the duality between knowledge and ignorance, between the knowledgeable few and the unknowing multitude. But even assuming radical non-duality, how can divine self-knowledge—as celebrated by Ibn Arabi—be reconciled with *makhafa* and *mahabbah* (reverence and love of God)? Does God fear and revere Himself? And more importantly: Does love here mean God's self-love or love for Himself—and how far is this kind of love removed from solipsism?

Ibn Arabi's teachings have left a strong imprint on Islamic spirituality over the centuries. For the most part, his legacy has been contemplative and reclusive, giving rise mainly to esoteric Sufi orders hermetically sheltered from, and disdainful of, the mundane world. However, intellectual spirituality can also take a different turn: especially under the impact of a more traditional gnostic dualism, the distinction between the "knowers" and the ignorant, between the "godlike" and the ungodly, can foster violent aggression and quasi-millenarian militancy. An example is an early version of Ismailism, a gnostic-dualistic branch which flourished during the late Abbasid reign. In line with older Manichean teachings, this sect—according to some historians— sharply distinguished between the hidden, unknowable God or divine "abyss," on the one hand, and the material-bodily world seen as the work of an inferior demiurge, on the other. The task of gnostic believers was to achieve deification through affirming their superior knowledge while attacking and, if possible, eradicating the inferior world. The latter aim was particularly the goal of the esoteric order of the so-called "Assassins," a secretive group of militants (also known as *batiniyyah* or "people of the inner truth," or *fida'iyyah* or "self-sacrificers"). According to historical reports—which are not uncontested—the Assassins wreaked havoc throughout the Muslim world, killing two Abbasid caliphs, several sultans, and hundreds, perhaps thousands, of others. Whatever the historical accuracy, the great al-Ghazali (1058–1111)—though himself a Sufi mystic, but of a very different persuasion—felt moved to denounce the teachings of this sect and their leaders.[33] During more recent centuries, *ma'rifa* spirituality has assumed many diverse shapes, often entering into symbiosis with more recent intellectual developments, such as theosophy. An example of the mingling of Islamic gnosticism and newer theosophical teachings is the work of Frithjof Schuon, especially his book *Gnosis: Divine Wisdom* (first published in French under the title *Sentiers de gnose*). As Schuon writes in that book, in a passage reminiscent of Ibn Arabi: "Esotericism looks to the nature of things and not merely to our human eschatology; it views the universe not from the human standpoint but from the standpoint of God."[34]

Without denying the role of intellectual insight or *ma'rifa,* major strands in Islamic spirituality have always accorded a central role to *makhafa* and *mahabbah.* For present purposes, it must suffice to look briefly at the mystical poetry of Jalal ad-Din Rumi, the great and justly revered *"mevlana"* or *"maulana"* (1207–1273, a bare generation after Ibn Arabi). Rumi's work, especially his *Mathnawi*, is a rich and multidimensional tapestry of ideas, symbols, and metaphors. Some of these ideas are surely gnostic or intellectual (perhaps Neoplatonic) in character. Thus, one recalls his famous statement: "Every form you see has its archetype in the divine world, beyond space. If the form perishes, what does it matter, since its heavenly model is indestructible?" Occasionally, one also finds in Rumi traces of the doctrine of the unity of ultimate reality (*"wahdat al-wujud"*). Thus, we read:

> I am filled with you—
> Skin, blood, bone, brain, and soul.
> There's no room for lack of trust, or trust.
> Nothing in this existence but that existence.

Or consider these Zen-like phrases, echoing Meister Eckhart:

> Praise to the emptiness that blanks out existence. Existence:
> This place made from our love for that emptiness.
> Yet somehow comes emptiness,
> This existence goes.
> Praise to that happening, over and over![35]

Yet, as in Eckhart's case, this is not the whole story. In Rumi's work, celebration of unity and ultimate disappearance in the divine is always counterbalanced, and perhaps outweighed, by *mahabbah*—a loving devotion which never forgets a remaining two-ness or difference, even in the very urgency of overcoming separation. For without a recognition of two-ness, and hence of human finitude, how could Rumi have written: "Love must have a little pain"? Or these lines: "O love, everyone gives thee names and titles—last night I named thee once more: 'Pain without remedy.'" In this connection, we may also wish to remember these verses:

> When I remember your love,
> I weep, and when I hear people

Talking of you, something in my chest,
where nothing much happens now,
moves as in sleep.

And here is his celebration of unity in two-ness, a poem dedicated to
his beloved friend, Shams of Tabriz:

All our lives we've looked
into each other's faces.
That was the case today too.
How do we keep our love-secret?
We speak from brow to brow
and hear with our eyes.[36]

As is clear from his poetry, Rumi's mysticism was all-consuming
and all-embracive. Setting aside rigid boundaries, he did not confine
his love to God, nor to his friend Shams (who ultimately vanished),
but allowed his love to grow and percolate and ultimately include all
his fellow creatures in the world. As he stated at one point: "How can
one profess love for God, if one does not love and actively show love
to fellow-beings?" Love (*mahabbah*) here begins to shade over into
service and compassion—an engaged commitment to the well-being
of humanity at large. Here are some of Rumi's truly ecumenical verses,
reflecting an ecumenism of loving service—though verses unlikely
to be well received by clerical literalists in any religion:

Tell me, Muslims, what should be done?
I don't know how to identify myself. I am
neither Christian nor Jew, neither Pagan nor Muslim.
I don't hail from the East or from the West.
I am neither from land nor sea. . . .
This being human is a guest house:
every morning a new arrival. . . .
Be grateful for whoever comes,
because each has been sent
as a guide from beyond.[37]

TOWARD GLOBAL SPIRITUALITY?

By way of conclusion, I want to reflect briefly on competing spiritualities and their social relevance, especially in the context of the contemporary "spiritual marketplace." The main issue emerging from the preceding discussion is the comparison and respective assessment of *gnosis* and *agape,* of esoteric-intellectual spirituality and of love- or service-based spirituality. Loosely speaking, one might say that the former is more vertical and inner-directed, while the second is more horizontal and other-directed. Still speaking very loosely—and neglecting possible overlaps—gnostic spirituality may be said to invite to solitary contemplation and a solitary merger with the divine (a merger reserved for the privileged few); by contrast, *agape* spirituality has a more active and outgoing slant, a slant potentially rupturing or transgressing all boundaries based on status, race, and ethnic or religious background. The former type insists on division or hierarchy (hence the pronounced dualism of traditional gnosticism), while the second seeks to combine or balance integration and difference.

Both kinds of spirituality have merits and also demerits. Esoteric spirituality fosters a withdrawal from social bonds, from the busyness of worldly affairs; it encourages a retreat into the kind of *"Abgeschiedenheit"* so dear to Eckhart, Angelus Silesius, and many other mystics—a retreat which alone seems able to shield the human spirit against conformism, consumerism, and rampant commodification. Seen from this esoteric vantage, *agape* spirituality stands accused of promoting a meddlesome, managerial attitude—a danger which indeed inhabits many contemporary forms of pragmatism and social "welfarism." Still, the respective dangers are probably not symmetrical. Although valuable in many ways, retreat into solitude can also shade over into solipsism, which, in turn, can engender selfishness or haughty self-indulgence. Martin Luther's and Zinzendorf's invectives against the arrogant conceit of self-righteous "knowers" should probably not be forgotten in this context—and actually deserve increased attention in an age marked by "technocracy" and "expertocracy." In the prevailing global situation, gnostic retreat also signals— or can be perceived to signal—an exit from global moral and political responsibility. In the words of Matthew Ashley (the theologian quoted at the beginning of this chapter), such an outlook readily becomes "a spirituality of the status quo, a spirituality that has very little good news for the poor."[38]

In light of these and related dangers, intellectual spirituality (in my view) urgently needs to be counterbalanced by, and perhaps subordinated to, more sober and world-open perspectives—especially the demands of *agape* and *mahabbah* (properly channeled by *makhafa*). There is an old Christian tradition—with clear parallels in Islam—called "contemplation in action" or "mysticism of everyday life." In Ashley's view, such contemplative action deserves renewed affirmation in our world today, because of its ability to overcome social barriers between rich and poor, and also its tendency to break down an "elitist division of labor" between clergy and laypeople.[39] It is this kind of action or "everyday mysticism" which was the hallmark of Erasmus's life and work (as discussed before); following in the footsteps of the Brethren of the Common Life, his practical orientation, gentled by *agape*, led him to privilege pious conduct (or *orthopraxis*) over dogmas and rituals, ecumenical peacemaking over doctrinal apologetics. A similar kind of everyday piety was also the guiding wellspring in the lifework of the Mahatma Gandhi—a guidepost evident in his commitment to "*karmayoga*" or spiritual praxis (as will be shown in later chapters).

To illustrate the potential of a global and properly ecumenical spirituality in our time, I want to cite briefly the example of a prominent recent spokesman of cosmopolis: Dag Hammarskjöld, the renowned secretary general of the United Nations (1953–1961). Addressing an assembly of the World Council of Churches soon after assuming office, Hammarskjöld pinpointed the meaning of contemplative action by stating that we must approach global issues from "two angles": first, there is "a need for practical action, helping underdeveloped countries to achieve such economic progress as would give them their proper share in the wealth of the world"; and second, there is an equal "need for inspiration, for the creation of a spirit among the leaders of peoples which helps them to use the forces which they have to master, for peace and not for war." Roughly at the same time, Hammarskjöld penned a statement of personal faith which admirably linked traditional *agape* spirituality with commitment to contemporary service. "The explanation," he wrote,

> of how man should live a life of active social service in full harmony with himself as a member of the community of spirit, I found in the writings of those great medieval mystics for whom "self-surrender" had been the way of self-realization, and who in "singleness of mind" and "inwardness" had found strength to say *yes* to every demand which the needs of their neighbors made them face, and to say *yes* also to every fate life had in store for them. Love . . . for them meant simply an overflowing of the strength with which they felt themselves filled when living in true self-oblivion. And this love found natural expression in an unhesitant fulfillment of duty and in an unreserved acceptance of life, whatever it brought them personally of toil, suffering or happiness.[40]

Cosmopolitanism
Religious, Moral, and Political

Kali yuga—age of strife. Barely a decade after the end of the Cold War, the fury of violence has been unleashed around the world, now taking the form of terrorism, interminable warfare, and genocidal mayhem. There is no lack of cynical voices proclaiming that violence surely is nothing new and that humankind—a depraved species— invariably reaps the fate it deserves. Tempting as this message may be in dark moments, something in the human heart—something apparently not fully depraved—resists this counsel of despair. After all, despair too easily equals defeat: life itself, especially a life worth living, is denied when death and mayhem are granted the final word. Moreover, there may be another, more hopeful way of interpreting strife and conflict. In a formula made famous by Hegel, conflict between nations and peoples may also be the emblem of a properly human and even humanizing struggle: namely, the "struggle for recognition" from which participants will eventually emerge as relatively equal partners enjoying mutual understanding and respect.[1]

The advantage of Hegel's formula is that it avoids an abstract utopianism—without relinquishing hope for humanity. That a movement akin to Hegel's trajectory has been happening in the world is something that even cynical "realists" can hardly deny. In the wake of two terribly destructive wars, the twentieth century saw the emergence of two international organizations—the League of Nations and the United Nations—which, though structurally flawed in many ways, marked the beginning consolidation of a legal rule system binding together the many countries of this globe. At the same time, the narrowly state-centered focus of these organizations was remedied or supplemented by more people-oriented agreements, especially the "Universal Declaration of Human Rights" (and a series of later, related documents). These and similar developments have engendered a widespread hope that humankind may now—or at least soon—be ready for the adoption of a global or cosmopolitan ethics seen as a framework buttressing and undergirding existing legal provisions. During the past several decades, many initiatives have been launched in this area by prominent theologians and philosophers—the former relying mainly (though not exclusively) on Judeo-Christian teachings and the latter drawing inspiration chiefly from the traditions of Stoicism and natural law. The present chapter seeks to explore and assess these initiatives. Proceeding in three steps, I will first review major proposals for the formulation of a universal or global ethics, especially proposals sponsored by the German theologian Hans Küng and the American philosopher Martha Nussbaum. In a second step, my attention shifts to objections raised to a "top-down" universalism, objections having to do mainly with a perceived neglect of situated differences as well as of motivational resources. Accepting partly some of these objections, the conclusion of the chapter moves the discussion to a political plane—arguing that a viable global ethics needs to be anchored in, or supplemented by, a global political *praxis*.

RELIGION AND UNIVERSAL MORALITY

The hope for a global ethics is not ill-founded; nor is it simply the outgrowth of ongoing processes of globalization. In their respective ways, traditional religious and philosophical teachings have always subscribed to this hope. Broadly speaking one might say that religion addresses itself to the human heart, and philosophy to the human mind, without qualifications; that is, the appeal in both cases is non-exclusivist and hence potentially universal. In the case of religion (or at least many religions), this aspect is manifest in the tendency to support evangelization or the spreading of "good news" everywhere. Leaving aside occasional domineering gestures, this news certainly is not meant for a privileged few but is addressed *urbi et orbi,* that is, to people at all times and in all walks of life. The same outreach necessarily characterizes philosophy. If philosophy means the search for truth and wisdom (*sophia*), then this search cannot be restricted to a specific context, but has to be unconditional and remain open to arguments and queries raised at any time and from any quarter. At least since the time of Socrates—to take a Western example—philosophy has been firmly committed to this universal quest. Following the eclipse of Greece, the same quest was continued by Cynics and Stoics and later by medieval Jewish, Christian, and Muslim thinkers. Among all philosophical orientations, modern Western philosophy is most strongly universalist in outlook. After Descartes had pinpointed the universal nature of the human mind (*cogito*), the subsequent Enlightenment—culminating in Kant—sought to spread the light of Cartesian reason around the world, in an effort of philosophical evangelization or dissemination.

Contemporary globalizing initiatives—on the part of both theologians and philosophers—thus can look back to a time-honored lineage or genealogy. In the religious or theological field, global endeavors have received a tremendous boost by the upsurge of inter-religious ecumenism, manifest prominently in interfaith meetings and especially in the institution or consolidation of a "Parliament of the World's Religions." The first meeting of that parliament—then still in embryonic form—had taken place in Chicago in 1893. To celebrate the centenary of that event, a second meeting of that Parliament was called and assembled in the same city in 1993—now with a vastly expanded list of participants. It was on that occasion that the assembled delegates (numbering nearly seven thousand) discussed and finally adopted a "Declaration Toward a Global Ethic," a document meant to supplement and provide moral underpinnings for the "Universal Declaration of Human Rights" (of 1948). The document was initially drafted by the German theologian Hans Küng, who was considered amply qualified in light of his extensive previous engagement in interfaith dialogues and in efforts to distill universally valid moral principles. More specifically, Küng was known for a number of pertinent publications and especially for his 1991 study *Global Responsibility: In Search of a New World Ethic.*[2]

Among his many writings, *Global Responsibility* is most helpful in providing insight into the normative-theoretical parameters of Küng's approach. Boldly programmatic, the book opens with these lapidary sentences: "No survival without a world ethic. No world peace without peace between the religions. No peace between the religions without dialogue between the religions." As can be seen, interfaith ecumenism here functions as the premise and foundation for inter-human peace and harmony, and the latter as the premise for global survival. To underscore the urgency of the program, Küng—like many writers before him—appeals to the pervasive malaise of our time and especially to what is called the "crisis of the West" or "crisis of modernity." Manifest in many contemporary debacles, this crisis, he writes, is "a moral crisis of the West generally, including Europe: the destruction of any kind of tradition, of a wider meaning in life, of unconditional ethical criteria, and a lack of new goals, with the resultant psychological damage." To counteract these ills, the text counsels a strategy of moral revitalization—a kind of "moral rearmament"—which, in our global age, has to aim at the formulation of globally valid normative standards. In Küng's words: "The one world in which we live has a chance of survival only if there is no longer any room in it for spheres of differing, contradictory, and even antagonistic ethics. This one world needs *one* basic ethic." While not seeking to regulate human behavior in all details, such a basic ethic in his view presupposes a "minimal basic consensus" on values and norms among people around the world. The upshot of these considerations is that globalization cannot be limited to political, economic, and cultural domains, but must be above all a normative enterprise: "If ethics is to function for the wellbeing of all, it must be indivisible. The undivided world increasingly needs an undivided ethic."[3]

Programmatic statements of this kind are backed up—as they need to be—by supportive arguments. As befits a broadly trained author, Küng's arguments are drawn from a variety of sources. Philosophically, major credit for the design of a universal ethic is given to Immanuel Kant—especially to that version of the categorical imperative which states that "human beings may never be made mere means" but "must remain an ultimate end." Among more recent philosophers and social thinkers, favorable mention is made of the "transcendental pragmatics" of Karl-Otto Apel and the "universal pragmatics" of Jürgen Habermas, while Max Weber and Hans Jonas are invoked as sponsors of a general "ethic of responsibility."[4] For Küng the theologian, however, philosophical arguments—though valuable up to a point—cannot furnish an ultimate basis or warrant for moral norms. The more deeply one ventures into the ethical domain, he writes, the more questions are raised "about moral motivation" and about "the general validity and ultimate meaningfulness of norms as such." It is precisely at this point that religions have their own contribution to make. Although leading us some steps along the way, what a secular-rational approach cannot accomplish is the most important thing: to "give a reason for the absoluteness and universality of ethical obligation." At this point, Küng—in eloquent language—articulates his own ethical-theological creed:

> The categorical quality of the ethical demand, the unconditioned nature of the ought, cannot be grounded by human beings who are conditioned in many ways, but only by that which is unconditional: by an Absolute which can provide an over-arching meaning and which embraces and permeates individual human nature and indeed the whole of human society. That can only be the ultimate, supreme reality . . . that primal ground, primal support, primal goal of human beings and the world that we call God.[5]

Although the outcome of many discussions and revisions, the "Declaration Toward a Global Ethic" adopted by the religious parliament in 1993 still shows clearly the inspiration of its drafter. Again, reference is made at the very outset to a pervasive malaise afflicting the contemporary world: a "fundamental crisis" affecting "global economy, global ecology, and global politics" and manifest in poverty, hunger, and "social, racial, and ethnic conflicts." As an antidote to these problems, the declaration postulates a "new global ethic" without which a new global order cannot arise or persist. Actually, in the view of the participants, the postulated ethic is "new" only in application, not in basic inspiration. "We affirm," they state, "that a common set of core values is found in the teachings of the religions, that these form the basis of a global ethic," but that they have "yet to be lived in heart and action." For the participants, the invoked core values constitute a "fundamental consensus on binding values," in fact an "irrevocable, unconditional norm for all areas of life, for families and communities, for races, nations, and religions." An overarching principle implicit in the postulated ethic is the demand that "every human being must be treated humanely," which means in accordance with the "inalienable and untouchable dignity" of all human beings. This principle, in turn, gives rise to four "irrevocable directives": a global commitment to a culture of "non-violence and respect for life," of "solidarity and a just economic order," of "tolerance and a life of truthfulness," and of "equal rights and partnership between men and women." A main point where the declaration departs from Küng's *Global Responsibility* has to do with the explicit invocation of "God" as the absolute foundation of ethics. Sensitive to differences of religious belief (and especially to objections raised by representatives of Buddhism), the declaration limits itself to appeals to an "ultimate reality" as the source of "spiritual power and hope."[6]

As indicated before, theologians and religious leaders have not been alone in this search for a global ethics; with different accents— centerstaging the role of human reason—numerous contemporary philosophers have joined them in this search. In the preceding discussion, brief reference was made to two German thinkers, Apel and Habermas, well known for their formulation of a universal ("communicative") ethics. In the American context, their efforts have been paralleled by John Rawls, especially by the latter's *A Theory of Justice* and related writings.[7] For present purposes, attention shall be limited to a younger American philosopher: Martha Nussbaum. Although starting her career with a focus on ancient Greek tragedy and philosophy,

Nussbaum more recently has turned to the legacy of enlightened rationalism—a legacy which she traces from Roman Stoicism via natural law to Immanuel Kant (and present-day Kantians).[8] What, in her view, links classical Stoics with modern Enlightenment philosophy is not so much a shared cosmology or teleology, but rather a shared trust in the role of reason seen as the essential or defining feature of human beings—a trust which she finds to be under siege today. What renders both Stoics and Kantian rationalism relevant to our globalizing age is their ambition to transcend confining contexts and parochial interests and to keep their gaze fixed on that rational core which is shared by people at all times and in all places.

The élan of Nussbaum's approach emerges clearly in a 1997 essay significantly titled "Kant and Stoic Cosmopolitanism." The essay opens with a spirited attack on a host of postmodern or post-Nietzschean thinkers disdainful of enlightened reason. "Under the influence of Nietzsche," she writes, "eminent thinkers of quite different sorts have felt dissatisfaction with a politics based on reason and principle," and have tried to find an alternative paradigm "based less on reason and more on communal solidarity, less on principle and more on affiliation, less on optimism for progress than as a sober acknowledgement of human finitude and mortality." Although acknowledging a broad range of post-Nietzschean approaches, Nussbaum detects in all of them a common denominator: "All agree in their opposition to a hopeful, active, and reason-based politics grounded in an idea of reverence for rational humanity wherever we find it." This opposition structures intellectual alliances and, above all, a kind of philosophical friend-enemy demarcation: for all Nietzscheans, the "arch-foe" tends to be Immanuel Kant, because it was Kant who—more influentially than any other Enlightenment thinker—defended a politics "based upon reason rather than patriotism or group sentiment," a politics "that was truly universal rather than communitarian," one "that was active, reformist and optimistic rather than given to contemplating the horrors or waiting for the call of Being." As Nussbaum makes it clear, the defense of reason was not Kant's spontaneous invention, but was informed by a time-honored tradition stretching back to the Stoics. The basic aim of her essay is "to trace the debt Kant owed to ancient Stoic cosmopolitanism" and thus to establish a lineage of cosmopolitan thought. In our time ravaged by brutal wars and episodes of ethnic cleansing, this lineage provides a guidepost for a moral resurgence. As an antidote to the asserted ills of our age, Kant—and, through him, Seneca, Marcus Aurelius, and especially Cicero—present us with "a challenge that is at once noble and practical."[9]

In tracing the lineage between Stoics and Kant, Nussbaum does not claim a complete coincidence nor a heavy intellectual dependence. As she acknowledges, Kant discussed Stoic ideas "only in a brief and general way," and much of his information seemed to derive from modern writings on natural law (influenced by Cicero and other Stoics). The main linkage resides in the idea of cosmopolitanism or world citizenship, which, first developed by the Stoics, became a centerpiece of Kant's *Perpetual Peace*. The idea was launched by Diogenes the Cynic, who, refusing to be defined by local or parochical bonds, declared himself to be "a citizen of the world." For the Cynics and the Stoics following their lead, the basic moral quality of human beings resided in their affiliation with "rational humanity." In Nussbaum's account, the basis of a moral community in the Stoic view was "the worth of reason in each and every human being." This reason was seen as "a portion of the divine in each of us," with the result that "each and every human being, just in virtue of being rational and moral, has boundless worth." Human rationality, for the Stoics, was also the basis of a genuine, morally grounded citizenship shared by all. In the words of Marcus Aurelius: "If reason is common, so too is law; and if this is common, then we are fellow citizens. If this is so, we share in a kind of organized polity, and if that is so, the world is as it were a city-state." As one should realize, the "kind of polity" invoked by Marcus was not an actual government, but rather a moral association seen as a premise to, and yardstick for, any government. This association, in turn, required the presence of a general consensus on moral norms; as Nussbaum paraphrases this idea: as participants in the global community we must "conceive of ourselves as having common goals and projects with our fellows." It was this moral conception that was taken over by Kant in his practical philosophy and in his comments on perpetual peace: "It is this deep core that Kant appropriates, the idea of a kingdom of free rational beings equal in humanity, each of them to be treated as an end no matter where in the world he or she dwells."[10]

Views of this kind were further fleshed out by Nussbaum in subsequent writings, especially in her book *Cultivating Humanity*. Again, reference is made to Diogenes, now presented as a follower or disciple of Socrates for his habit of "disdaining external markers of status and focusing on the inner life of virtue and thought." During the ensuing centuries, Stoic philosophers made Diogenes' approach "respectable and culturally fruitful," by developing the idea of cross-cultural study and by making the concept of the "world citizen" (*kosmou polités*) a cornerstone of their educational program. In Nussbaum's presentation, good citizenship for Stoics meant to be a "citizen of the world," and this for several reasons. For one thing, taking the attitude of world citizens enabled people better to solve problems arising in larger contexts (such as the context of the far-flung Roman Empire). More importantly, however, the stance of world citizenship was "intrinsically valuable," for it recognizes in people "what is especially fundamental about them, most worthy of reverence and acknowledgement": to wit, "their aspirations to justice and goodness and their capacities for reasoning in this connection." To be sure, Stoics for the most part did not simply dismiss differences between people or local loyalties; in fact, knowledge of local situations was usually considered a precondition and corollary of the world citizen's ability to "discern and respect the dignity of humanity in each person." However, the main emphasis always had to be on commonality: on the essentially shared endowment of reason. Stoic education for world citizenship basically required "transcending the inclination of both students and educators to define themselves primarily in terms of local group loyalties and identities." Stoic insights of this kind were preserved in modern times in the natural law tradition and especially in the political thought of Kant; in this refined and updated form, they still can serve as directives for contemporary education on a global scale.[11]

THE DEFICITS OF MORAL UNIVERSALISM

Moral globalism—as presented above—surely has important merits. In a world torn asunder by multiple forms of strife, nothing seems more timely than to be reminded of our shared humanity and of the universal aspirations present in religious teachings and prominent philosophical traditions. Nussbaum's plea, in particular, for a cosmopolitan moral education no doubt deserves widespread attention and support. Yet, support needs to be qualified or tempered for several reasons. Rigidly maintained, emphasis on commonality or universality is likely to sideline morally relevant differences or distinctions; at the same time, the accent on normative rules tends to neglect or underrate the role of concrete motivations. To some extent, issues of this kind surfaced at the religious parliament. Despite their shared religious commitments, delegates quarreled over the (possibly) "Western" bias of their document, apart from disagreeing on the sense of "ultimate reality" as well as a number of other questions.[12] Disputes are bound to be heightened in the philosophical domain (wedded to critical inquiry), revealing the intrinsic ambivalence of universalism. On the one hand, the postulate to treat all human beings as equal—by virtue of their shared capacity for reason—militates against invidious discrimination based on race, status, or gender. On the other hand, sameness of treatment is morally deficient by extending recognition to fellow beings only in the respect in which they are identical with ourselves. In an important way, such treatment still is egocentric in the sense that it appropriates or reduces the *alter* to the rational self (or ego), instead of recognizing the distinct otherness of fellow beings. As indicated, Nussbaum makes allowance for some human diversity; however, by defining reason as the universal human "essence," her account renders differences nonessential and hence marginal.

The dilemmas of universalism are not a recent discovery. In a sense, they were already discerned by Aristotle in his critique of Plato's "ideal" state. In the context of modern Western philosophy, major reservations were articulated by Hegel, especially in response to Kant's duty-centered moral universalism. These reservations were a persistent theme in Hegel's evolving opus. Already one of his early writings ("The Spirit of Christianity and Its Fate") castigated the dualism inherent in Kant's thought between duty and inclination and between universality and particularity where the former "becomes the master and the particular the mastered." The opposition could be overcome or at least mitigated, he argued, once attention is shifted from abstract duty to properly channeled inclination (in accord with biblical teachings). The critique of abstract universalism or formalism was continued in the *Philosophy of Right,* where Kantian morality was not so much erased as integrated and "sublated" in the differentiated fabric of concrete ethical life (*Sittlichkeit*).[13] Among recent students of Hegel, some of the philosopher's complaints were renewed and rearticulated by Theodor W. Adorno, especially in his magisterial *Negative Dialectics.* In that study, Adorno took aim at the Kantian dichotomy between pure "inwardness" and external causality, between the abstract "autonomy" of moral reason and the causal conditioning of actual behavior. Kant, he writes, "tackles the dichotomy through the distinction between the pure and the empirical subject, neglecting the reciprocal mediation of these terms." In this conception, the individual (or subject) is "unfree" by virtue of its subjection to empirical categories; at the same time, it is radically, even "transcendentally" free by virtue of its ability to "constitute" its rational identity. Instead of resorting to Hegelian synthesis, Adorno at this point introduces the notion of "non-identity" designating an excess over duty and particularity. The same thought is also phrased as an inclination or "impulse" reconciling inwardness and nature.[14]

Still more recently, Hegel's and Adorno's reservations have been taken up and further radicalized by a group of contemporary thinkers often loosely grouped under the rubic of "postmodernism." What unites these diverse thinkers is their opposition to "foundationalism," which is another word for a homogenizing universalism. In the case of some writers—summarily denounced by Nussbaum as Nietzscheans or post-Nietzscheans—anti-foundational zeal takes the form of a radical reversal celebrating particularism or dissensus for its own sake; but matters are rarely that simple. A case in point is the work of Michel Foucault (often described as postmodern or "poststructuralist"). In his later writings, Foucault formulated a distinct ethical outlook—though one not based on abstractly universal principles but rather grounded in concretely situated practices or modes of conduct. The second volume of his *History of Sexuality* carefully distinguishes between "code morality" or a morality relying on formal rules and concrete moral conduct—the latter being further differentiated into actual conduct and motivational guidance. As he writes: "A rule of conduct is one thing; the conduct that may be governed by this rule is another. But another thing still is the manner in which (one thinks) one ought to conduct oneself," that is, the manner in which one "forms oneself as an ethical subject" or agent. For a number of reasons (including his chosen focus on ancient Graeco-Roman morality), Foucault found it important and even necessary to concentrate on the practice of self-formation. Tellingly, he called this practice also "ethical work" (*travail éthique*), insisting that it is not reducible to or deducible from a static code, but involves a process or movement: the attempt "to transform oneself into the ethical subject of one's behavior." Although conduct usually involves some reference to moral rules, this is not sufficient to qualify the conduct itself as "moral" in the absence of self-formative practice. As Foucault elaborates:

> The latter is not simply [inner] "self-awareness" but self-formation as an "ethical subject," a process in which the individual delimits that part of himself that will form the object of his moral practice, defines his position relative to the precept he will follow, and decides on a certain mode of being that will serve as his moral goal. And this requires him to act upon himself, to monitor, test, improve, and transform himself.[15]

Moral conduct, in the Foucauldian sense, cannot be rigidly standardized, but is necessarily differentiated among individuals acting in different times and places; for—as he says—modes of self-formation "do not differ any less from one morality to another" than do systems of rules and interdictions. Curiously, Foucault's later texts appeal precisely to the same set of mentors invoked by Nussbaum in her defense of universal rules: the Cynics and Stoics, and above all Diogenes the Cynic. Like Nussbaum's writings, *The History of Sexuality* refers to the "scandalous" behavior of Diogenes and his habit of confounding public and private spheres of conduct. However, far from figuring as the exemplar of a universal reason captured in invariant rule systems, the accent here is placed on Diogenes as teacher of moral self-formation and "performance criticism"—a criticism directed at the homogenizing and "normalizing" rule systems of society. For the Cynic, self-formation was part of the morally required "practices of the self" summed up in the notion of "self-care" or "care of the self" (*epimeleia heautou*)—a notion which was subsequently elaborated by the Stoics (and which furnishes the title of the third volume of the *History*). As the grounding for moral practice, self-care cannot be entirely governed or determined by either physical or societal laws. Like Martin Heidegger before him, Foucault acknowledged freedom as the premise and springboard of moral action. As he stated in an interview given shortly before his death, titled "The Ethic of Care for the Self as a Practice of Freedom" (1984), freedom has to be seen as the "ontological condition" of human being-in-the-world and as the basis of ethics—where ethics denotes not so much a theory or a codified set of rules but rather a practice or way of life (*ethos*). As he added (to obviate misunderstanding), self-care in this context is not an emblem of egocentrism or narrow particularism, but rather a practice always conducted in a concrete context—with the result that "this *ethos* of freedom is also a way of caring for others."[16]

From a different angle, the notion of a differentiated ethics not subsumable under universal rules has also been developed by the sociologist Zygmunt Bauman, especially in his *Postmodern Ethics*. Seconding and in part transgressing Foucault, Bauman argues for a "morality without ethical code," in fact for a morality without universalism and foundational banisters. As he writes: "Only rules can be universal. One may legislate universal rule-dictated *duties*, but moral *responsibility* exists solely in interpellating the individual and being carried individually." Sharply put: "One may say that the moral is what *resists* codification, formalization, socialization, universalization." What traditionally had served as universal banisters were the concepts of "human reason" and rational "human nature"—concepts which have lost their cogency in our postmodern times, which have robbed modernity of its "illusions." For Bauman, such disillusionment prompts morality to rupture the "stiff armor" of ethical codes and to "re-personalize" itself, that is, to return to "the starting point of the ethical process": the "primary 'brute fact' of moral impulse, moral responsibility, and moral intimacy" which basically cannot be regulated or prescribed. Despite certain similarities with the Foucauldian approach, one may also note significant divergences. While Foucault's later texts rely on self-care and human autonomy, Bauman resorts to a kind of heteronomy inspired by the teachings of Emmanuel Levinas, namely, to the primacy of "otherness" as stimulus of morality and hence to an "asymmetry" of moral practice. Morality here means a being "for the Other," an "encounter with the Other as face" which begets "an essentially *unequal* relationship." Occasionally, postmodern zeal tempts Bauman to adopt a strategy of reversal or counterenlightenment—a move which Foucault would hardly have endorsed. "From the perspective of 'rational order,'" he writes, "morality is and is bound to be *irrational.*" The enterprise of rational rule-governance always tends to regard the recalcitrance of the moral impulse as "a scandal," as "the germ of chaos and anarchy inside order." Under postmodern auspices, however, morality is finally "free to admit its non-rationality: its being its own (necessary and sufficient) reason."[17]

Apart from postmodern initiatives, moral nonuniversalism or antiuniversalism has also been defended by prominent feminist thinkers in recent times. A widely known and discussed exemplar is the psychologist Carol Gilligan, author of *In a Different Voice*. Reacting against doctrines of moral development wedded to (neo-Kantian) universal principles, Gilligan complained about the widespread "exclusion of women" from the prevalent frameworks of psychological research (an exclusion which was more paradigmatic than purely gender-based). Typically, developmental studies were conducted with young boys and championed a model of moral stages leading from infancy to higher and higher levels of impartiality, fairness, and concern with rule-governed justice. This model was particularly evident in the work of Lawrence Kohlberg—a leading figure in developmental studies—whose theory of six moral stages basically traced a process of increasing decontextualization and universalization. Seen from the vantage of this model, women or girls were largely "deviant" cases whose deviance could only be corrected by their refashioning "out of masculine cloth." For Gilligan, this approach is both empirically skewed and difference-blind—especially blind to differences arising in social contexts which "shape the experiences of males and females and the relationship between the sexes." In modern contexts, numerous factors contribute to differences in identity formation, with male gender identity typically being more tied to abstract, decontextualized rules and female identity to concrete personal attachments. Following other feminists, Gilligan prefers to regard women's presumed "weakness"—their lack of abstract judgment—as a different kind of "moral strength" manifest in the cultivation of responsibilities and the "ability to care." Viewed from this angle, a model of development emerges distinct from that of Kohlberg (as well as Freud and Jean Piaget): one in which morality resides in the "activity of care" rather than the contest over rights and rules and which requires "a mode of thinking that is contextual and narrative rather than formal and abstract."[18]

In a more philosophical vein, a loosely parallel argument has been advanced by the French feminist thinker Luce Irigaray. As she observes in her recent book *Between East and West,* our time desperately needs a differential ethics—one which does not so much cancel universality as rather suffuse general discourse with recognition of diverse idioms or voices. "All attraction," she writes, echoing Gilligan, "is founded upon a difference, an 'unknown' of the desiring subject, beginning with what pushes the boy and the girl, the man and the woman toward each other." What is important and distinctive about Irigaray is that she extends the argument to the global or cross-cultural level. The differential relation between the genders, she adds, can serve as a "relational paradigm" for the ordering of society on all levels; to this extent, respecting the difference of genders "without reducing the two to the one, to the same, to the similar . . . represents a universal way for attaining the respect of other differences." Differential respect of this kind is particularly crucial in our globalizing era where peoples and cultures are thrown together and treated either as separate identities or subsumed under a uniform category—leaving no room for "between-traditions." Western thought, in particular, has traditionally not been very hospitable to differential respect, given the ingrained bent to transform everything "into abstract categories as soon as possible": linguistic rules, legal norms, philosophical and scientific concepts. This background calls for a major rethinking or reorientation, pointing to a different relation to the world and others:

> Where we have learned to control nature, it would be a matter
> of learning to respect it. Where the ideal has been presented to

us as the absorption of the whole in an absolute, it would be a matter of recognizing the merit of insurmountable limits. Where respect for the same stretched, vertically, from the son to the Father-God and, horizontally, to the universal community of men, it would be important from now on to know how to intertwine love of the same and love of the other, faithfulness to self and becoming with the other, a safeguard of the identical and similar for the meeting with the different.[19]

As one should add, Irigaray does not simply applaud differential respect in a general way, but concretely practices it in her personal engagement in cross-cultural relations (at the cusp "between-traditions"). Her book contains thoughtful and probing comments on "Eastern teachings," with a focus on Hindu and Buddhist traditions (including yoga and Tantra); as she tries to make clear, ancient teachings and practices in the East often paid closer attention than is customary in the modern West to the differential entwinement—beyond fusion and separation—of all beings and phenomena.[20] The argument could be extended to the Far East, especially to Confucianism (not discussed in her book). As is well known, Confucian ethics is not rule-governed but relational, and more specifically grounded in five crucial relationships: those of husband and wife, parent and child, older and younger sibling, ruler and minister, and friend and friend. Critics have often charged these relationships as reflecting a rigid hierarchy or mode of subordination; but, although possible as deformations, the latter features do not define their character. As Tu Wei-ming has pointed out, the relations should be seen as a web of "dyadic" linkages—where "dyadic" resonates with Irigaray's differential respect. In each relationship, there are "selves" mutually constituting and respecting each other in their difference or dyadic nexus, which can never be fully stabilized or exhausted. Tu Wei-ming also takes exception to the charge of Confucian complicity in status hierarchy (perhaps even patriarchy). As he notes, the ethical spirit undergirding the five relations is not dependency but mutuality or reciprocity (*pao*). In this connection, friendship is the relation *par excellence* as it is based on mutual trust and care. In fact, in friendship self-care and care for other are in balance:

The authentic approach is neither a passive submission to structural limitations nor a Faustian activation of [inner] freedom but a conscientious effort to make the dynamic interaction between them a fruitful dialectic of self-realization and transformation.[21]

TOWARD A GLOBAL POLITICAL PRAXIS

What the preceding initiatives—whether postmodern, feminist, or transcultural—have thrown into relief are the "deficits" plaguing moral universalism: namely, the de-emphasis of difference and the neglect of concrete motivation and moral self-formation. As one should note, the issue is not simply the slighting of difference as particularity (which, as such, might still be subsumable under universal rules); nor is it the disregard of moral "inwardness" (which still obeys the dualism of inner duty and external constraint). The issue is more serious and has to do with the privileging of moral *theory* over *praxis,* that is, of principles over moral conduct and self-formation grounded in freedom. The notion of *praxis,* however, brings to the fore a domain usually shunned or sidelined by universalist morality: the domain of politics. This domain is unavoidable given the quandaries of moral rules. Even assuming widespread acceptance of universal norms, we know at least since Aristotle that rules do not directly translate into *praxis* but require careful interpretation and application. At this point, eminently political questions arise: who has the right of interpretation? And in case of conflict: who is entitled to rule between different interpretations? This right or competence cannot simply be left to "universal" theorists or intellectuals—in the absence of an explicity *political* delegation or empowerment. These considerations indicate that it is insufficient—on moral and practical grounds—to throw a mantle of universal rules over humankind without paying simultaneous attention to public debate and the role of political will-formation. This caveat is particularly important in our globalizing era where universalism often shades over into the policies of hegemonic and quasi-imperial powers. Viewed from a nonpolitical angle, can universal rules (as theories) not operate indifferently under the aegis of *pax Romana*, of *pax Britannica*, and (perhaps) *pax Americana?*

The sidelining of politics by morality is manifest in many cosmopolitan writings; Nussbaum herself is candid about her priorities. In discussing Kant's debt to Stoic cosmopolitanism, she writes, "I have started from the moral core of their ideas about reason and personhood," while leaving aside the "superficial" aspects of "institutional and practical goals." It was this "deep core" that Kant appropriated in his idea of a "kingdom of ends" which signaled a "common participation in a virtual polity," irrespective of the presence or absence of an actual polity. Paraphrasing the Stoic distinction between a merely local or mundane and a transmundane community, Nussbaum insists that "we should give our first moral allegiance to *no* mere form of government, no temporal power," but rather should give it to "the moral community made up by the humanity of all human beings." Virtualization of politics characterized the behavior of most ancient Cynics. Thus, Diogenes the Cynic is described as an "exile" from his city who paid little heed to "political thought" and adopted a "strikingly apolitical" stance. With the exception of Cicero (more Aristotelian in outlook), most Roman Stoics followed the Cynics' example, even if they held public office. As we know, Seneca was a minister under the emperor Nero—certainly not a model of civic engagement and responsibility. And despite his wisdom and commitment to justice, Emperor Marcus Aurelius showed little or no concern for the political freedom and will-formation of citizens and noncitizens in his far-flung empire. In fact, Stoic theorizing often coincided with the acceptance of oppressive political practices, including slavery. Again, Nussbaum is appealingly candid, as when she writes:

> The Stoics did not and could not conclude, as Kant does, that colonial conquest is morally unacceptable. Cicero tries to moralize the Roman imperial project—but without much success. Seneca certainly could not have uttered such sentiments had he had them, and Marcus focuses on the task of managing the existing empire as justly and wisely as he can, rather than on the question whether he ought not instead to dismantle it.[22]

In contrast to Stoic leanings, modern cosmopolitans—especially cosmopolitan democrats—need not be content with the virtualization of politics and public participation. In this respect, they can draw support from the writings of the later Foucault, especially his linkage of moral self-care and free political *praxis*. An indicated before, Foucault offers a somewhat different account of Stoicism and classical cosmopolitanism. In his *The Care of the Self,* he opposes the bifurcation between participation in a corrupt local polity and withdrawal into a universal realm of ideas. Although late-Roman life was often polarized into the options of participation and retreat, the situation on the ground tended to be more complex and not reducible to a waning of politics in favor of an ethics of withdrawal: "It was a matter of elaborating an ethics that enabled one to constitute oneself as an ethical subject with respect to these social, civic, and political activities, in the different forms they might take." This assessment is buttressed by a reading of late-Roman and Hellenistic records which point not only to the erection of overarching imperial structures, but also to a revitalization of local and urban politics. From this angle, city life with its institutional structures, its interests and struggles, did not simply disappear as a result of the widening context in which it was placed: the people of the Hellenistic period "did not have to flee from 'the cityless world of the great empires' for the very good reason that 'Hellenism was a world of cities'." These comments shed a new light on late-Roman morality—and also on Foucault's own formulation of "care of the self." As he writes, the Stoic notion of self-care is often interpreted as an alternative to civic activity and political responsibility; and— he acknowledges—there were indeed currents recommending that people "turn aside from public affairs" with its troubles and passions. However, it is possible to construe things differently, such that self-care and the art of self-rule "becomes a crucial political factor." In any case, it is not in opposition to public life that self-cultivation places its values and practices: "It is much more concerned to define the principle of a relation to self that will make it possible to set the forms and conditions in which political action, participation in the offices of power, the exercise of a [public] function, will be possible or not possible, acceptable or necessary."[23]

Drawing on both Foucauldian and Aristotelian teachings, Nussbaum's moral (or moralizing) cosmopolitanism has been ably criticized by Peter Euben. Going back to the time of the Cynics and Stoics, Euben carefully weighs the merits and demerits of their teachings. Concurring with Nussbaum, he acknowledges the "impressive contributions" Cynics and Stoics made to "the ideas of human dignity, moral equality, and natural law." Their rejection of parochial customs and status distinctions and their ideal of world citizenship, he writes, have provided "a ground for the critique of slavery, ethnocentrism, and hierarchies of all kinds, critiques that have hardly lost their salience." This, however, is only one side of the ledger; the other is the relative atrophy of political *praxis* among Nussbaum's mentors. Although claiming to follow the Socratic model, Cynics and Stoics tended to lose "the Socratic tension between city as place and philosophy, which in their hands became a simple opposition." In contrast to Socrates and especially to Aristotle, many Stoics dismissed the linkage between public authority and the "voice of the city" in favor of "right reason" as a general principle; in doing so, they encouraged the transformation or streamlining of political philosophy into "moral philosophy and political moralism." This transformation, in turn, had a profound effect on civic freedom as understood by Aristotle—where freedom meant "an experience of acting with others in the public realm" and not simply "the sovereignty of unencumbered individuals who had 'freed' themselves of relationships and public affairs." Euben also notes a certain deceptiveness in Stoic universalism, namely, a political exclusion inhabiting their principle of inclusion. Notwithstanding the espousal of universal citizenship, Stoicism in fact sponsored "a new exclusiveness based on differential commitment to and practice of rationality"—a distinction based on the realization that only "very few exceptional humans could be full members in the [Stoic] community of reason."[24]

These considerations carry over into Nussbaum's account and her attempt to revitalize Stoicism for our time. As Euben points out, cosmopolitanism in Nussbaum's portrayal is basically a posture of "exile," a method of withdrawal from local/parochial attachments or entanglements. To be sure (as indicated above), her outlook does not entirely dismiss local loyalties and cultural differences; however, given her essentialist bent, these features are bound to remain marginal in comparison with "rationally justified" affiliations: "Our 'fundamental' obligations come from what is fundamental about us, and what is fundamental about us is reason." Again, it is not a matter of slighting her moral ideals; for who could object to a desire for "justice, rights, reason, and morality in the world"? Euben's worries go in a different direction. "There is something parochial about this cosmopolitanism," he writes pointedly. "In the broadest terms, what is missing is politics including any political analysis of the nature of her moral critique"—in particular of the danger of a Stoic-like "accommodation to reigning structures of power." In our time, the latter danger is real and pressing, especially in view of widespread political apathy, cynicism, and indifference. Given this situation, Euben offers a recommendation which is nearly the obverse of Stoic exile. As he states, the problem today is that nothing seems to take hold,

> that deeply held preferences are rare, and that only the immediately satisfied self-regarding ones are deemed worth embracing in a system hostile to larger democratic initiatives. Under these circumstances, Nussbaum's cosmopolitan universalism may make things worse by promoting a dialectic between increasing withdrawal and self-righteous interventions.

Unsurprisingly, Nussbaum does not have "much to say about democracy"—a silence which is ominous in our globalizing context where hegemonic power structures may utilize an abstract universalism/moralism as a way of aborting "potentially democratizing commitments." And is there not ample reason to be concerned about hegemonic globalization "especially if, as seems to be the case, the hidden premise of global unity is American popular culture?"[25]

There is much that one can learn from Euben's judicious discussion, especially from his effort to keep morality and politics together (without fusion, but also without separation).[26] In our contemporary globalizing context, what could be more urgent than to cultivate the virtues of cosmopolitanism and the principles of (what used to be called) *ius gentium*? Faced with ethnic conflicts and looming "clashes of civilizations," humankind is called upon to develop a global ethics and civic culture sturdy enough to stem the tide of violence and destruction. To be properly cosmopolitan, this civic culture needs to be as inclusive as possible, that is, to embrace not only people similar to "us" but precisely those who are different or "other"—potentially even those who now are categorized (rashly) as "enemies." At the same time and for the same motives, it is important to remedy the "deficit" of global moralism: its tendential neglect of politics; and the remedy has to be equally sturdy. As indicated before, it is insufficiently moral—in fact, it is hardly moral at all—to celebrate universal values everywhere without also seeking to enable and empower people in their different settings and locations. Although moral norms and theories may be universal in reach, moral *praxis* has a differential texture, especially when viewed from the angle of global justice. Simply put: promotion of justice—that is, the removal of misery and oppression—falls more heavily on the rich and powerful than it does on the poor, the oppressed, and the subaltern. In the case of the latter, nurturing morality—including cosmopolitan virtue—requires first of all an enabling and emancipatory strategy aimed at securing a measure of freedom and self-governance. "Cultivating humanity" thus is a bifocal, moral-political enterprise. Quite possibly, Nussbaum in the end might agree with this conclusion. As she writes, in closing her essay on Kant and cosmopolitanism: at some point it becomes important "to stop contemplating and to act, doing something useful for the common good"[27]—especially (one might wish to add) for the strengthening and empowerment of our common humanity.

On Violence
Post-Arendtean Reflections

In 1970, at the height of the Vietnam conflict, Hannah Arendt wrote her justly celebrated essay "On Violence." The historical backdrop of the essay was grim and turbulent in all domains: in the international arena (the bloody clash between West and East, North and South), in domestic politics, and even on the level of personal life (Arendt's husband died during the same year). What renders her essay so memorable and even "classical"—in the sense of both timeless and timely—is her vigorous defense of politics against its facile and increasingly widespread equation with violence. Without espousing a radical form of pacifism, Arendt's text sought to vindicate the integrity of politics—construed as concerted action or shared exercise of public "power"—in the face of a growing fascination with violence and the progressive colonization of public life by violent strategies and ideologies. As she wrote in a central passage of the text:

> Power and violence are opposites; where the one rules absolutely, the other is absent. Violence appears where [public] power is in jeopardy; but left to its own course it ends in power's disappearance. . . . Violence can destroy power; it is utterly incapable of creating it.[1]

More than thirty years have passed since the publication of the essay; but its timeliness has in many ways increased. Although heralded as the dawn of global harmony and even as the "end of history," the end of the Cold War has not inaugurated a more peaceful era. Released from superpower rivalry, the potential for violence has been reconfigured and diversified along many axes or fault lines. In many parts of the world, inter-ethnic disputes have spawned the scourge of ethnic cleansing, while inter-religious conflicts have repeatedly led to demands for "*jihad.*" At the same time, the process of economic and technological globalization has produced a new form of violence exceeding local and even national confinements: the upsurge of a global terrorism seeking to contest or upstage globally hegemonic institutions. A major victim of this proliferation of violence has been a central feature of public life as conceived by Arendt: the rule of law buttressed by an energetic and vigorously pluralistic "public sphere." In this situation, it becomes an urgent task of political thought to reflect, once again, on the role of political violence and to recapture the basic spirit of Arendt's admonition. The following reflections proceed in three steps. The first part recapitulates briefly the gist of Arendt's argument, while integrating that argument into the broader contours of her work. The middle section shifts the accent to more recent examples of the "literature on violence" and the critique of violence, with special attention given to Bat-Ami Bar On's remarkable study, *The Subject of Violence.* The conclusion returns to and reaffirms an Arendtean conception of politics and public life, while simultaneously cautioning against deceptive proclamations of nonviolence on the part of liberal Western regimes—protestations which, in the view of Maurice Merleau-Ponty, often camouflage an oppressive reality.

ARENDT'S "ON VIOLENCE"

Like all of her writings, Arendt's "On Violence" was not an abstract academic exercise, but written in response to concrete experiences of her time. In the case of this particular essay, the background was the perceived upsurge of the rhetoric of violence in segments of the student rebellion and anti–Vietnam War movement in America and Europe. This upsurge stood in contrast to the more reticent attitude of an earlier generation scarred by the horrors of World War II, a reticence still pervading and even dominating the beginnings of the student movement. As Arendt describes the mood of the period: "This is the first generation to grow up under the shadow of the atom bomb," a generation that inherited from their parents "the experience of a massive intrusion of criminal violence into politics" evident in concentration and extermination camps, in genocide, torture, and the "wholesale slaughter of civilians in war." This battery of memories and impressions had a sobering effect:

> Their first reaction was a revulsion against every form of violence, an almost matter-of-course espousal of a politics of nonviolence. The very great successes of this movement, especially in the field of civil rights, were followed by the resistance movement against the war in Vietnam, which has remained an important factor in determining the climate of opinion in this country.

As Arendt adds, however: "It is no secret that things have changed since then" and that "the adherents of nonviolence are on the defensive."[2]

What was happening was an escalation of rhetoric—sometimes spilling over into practice—spurred on largely by feelings of despair and frustration. As was to be expected, this new shift toward the language of violence was soon countered by the escalation of a counter-rhetoric which denounced the militants as "anarchists, red fascists, Nazis, and, with considerably more justification, 'Luddite machine smashers'." What lent to the last label a measure of plausibility was the fact that modern science and technology had indeed led humankind to the brink of a nuclear abyss—a peril sensed particularly acutely by young people raised "under the shadow of the atom bomb." In Arendt's words, the sciences learned and imbibed by this young generation seemed not only "unable to undo the disastrous consequences of their own technology" but to have reached a stage in their development where (in Jerome Lettvin's phrase) "there's no damn thing you can do that can't be turned into war." These developments together with a series of political calamities—like the war in Vietnam—gave rise to certain apocalyptic leanings, to a radical impatience with liberal normalcy: "It is only natural that the new generation should live with greater awareness of the possibility of doomsday than those 'over thirty', not because they are younger but because this was their first decisive experience in the world."[3]

Adding fuel to such apocalyptic leanings was the "literature on violence" which gained new popularity during this time. In this literature, Arendt's text singles out as chief exemplars the writings of Georges Sorel, Frantz Fanon, and Jean-Paul Sartre—with additional side-glances at prominent catch-phrases (culled from the Far Left and Right). Among these catch-phrases, one which enjoyed wide currency among young rebels was a saying attributed to Mao Tse-tung—"Power grows out of the barrel of a gun"—a saying which, for Arendt, expresses an "entirely non-Marxian conviction" colliding with its ambiance of Marxist ideology. For, although aware of its role in history, violence for Marx was entirely secondary: "not violence but the contradictions inherent in the old society brought about its end." Mao's catch-phrase was seconded by such Rightist figures as Clausewitz and Vilfredo Pareto, for whom politics coincided with warfare or the iron-fisted rule of an elite. None of these figures, however, offered a sustained analysis of, and apology for, violence—a task undertaken by Sorel, Fanon, and Sartre. In the case of Sorel, Arendt detects a strange and perhaps twisted revival of the "life philosophies" of Bergson and Nietzsche with their emphasis on unbounded creativity and forceful life-affirmation. "We all know," she writes, "to what extent this old combination of violence, life, and creativity figures in the rebellious state of mind of the present generation." Sorel's *Reflections on Violence* are cited to illustrate a quasi-Marxist and quasi-Bergsonian defense of class struggle construed entirely "in military terms"—a construal designed to rescue European societies from the "decadence of the middle classes." Only through this type of class struggle, Sorel felt, could the liberal idea of "progress" be replaced by "the image of total catastrophe" when "a kind of irresistible wave will pass over the old civilization."[4]

From a non-European angle, Frantz Fanon's *The Wretched of the Earth* pleaded for a violent struggle of the oppressed against colonial and imperialist domination. In a quasi-Bergsonian or quasi-Nietzschean vein, Fanon presented the "practice of violence" as a creatively galvanizing enterprise capable of binding participants "together as a whole," since "each individual forms a violent link in the great chain, a part of the great organism of violence which has surged upward." In another stunning passage—highlighted by Arendt—the text spoke of the "creative madness" present in violent action operating as a kind of "*élan vital*" brushing aside the cobwebs of established "normalcy." Drawing upon and intensifying Fanon's rhetoric, Jean-Paul Sartre developed violent action into a basic feature of his existentialist philosophy: namely, into a central premise of human freedom and self-creation. In his famous preface to *The Wretched of the Earth*—Arendt notes—Sartre managed to go beyond Sorel and even beyond Fanon himself in escalating the language of rupture and violent discontinuity. His espousal of this language, she writes, shows to what extent Sartre was "unaware of his basic disagreement with Marx on the question of violence," especially when he stated that "irrepressible violence . . . is man recreating himself" and that it is through "mad fury" that "the wretched of the earth" can "become men." She also draws attention to another passage in the preface where Sartre, "with his great felicity with words," had given expression to the "new faith" of the young generation: "Violence, like Achilles' lance, can heal the wounds it has inflicted."[5]

Apart from the legacy of life philosophy (or certain variants of it), Arendt traces the upsurge of violence also to some scientific or pseudo-scientific initiatives: especially the teachings of sociobiology and biological anthropology. Although, in the past, streaks of violence had often been ascribed to elementary forms of human behavior, the linkage of violence and "human nature" has in recent times emerged as a kind of scientific mantra, even giving rise to a new academic discipline called "polemology." As Arendt notes, a "deluge of books on the subject has already appeared," with prominent natural scientists—biologists, physiologists, ethologists, and zoologists—joining in "an all-out effort" to solve "the riddle of 'aggressiveness' in human behavior." In these and related research enterprises, violence and aggressiveness are defined as basic human instincts and claimed to play "the same functional role in the household of nature" as nutritive and sexual instincts in the human life process. The upshot is that violent behavior—with or without provocation—appears as entirely "natural," and hence as morally neutral and incorrigible. Arendt is completely unimpressed by these arguments. "I cannot see," she writes, "how [any of] this could either justify or condemn human behavior. I fail to understand why we are asked 'to recognize that man behaves very much like a group territorial species', rather than the other way around." Her own essay moves in a very different direction. The basic gist of her argument is to show "that violence is neither beastly nor irrational—whether we understand these terms in the ordinary language of the humanists or in accordance with scientific theories."[6]

A major source of the fascination with violence, in Arendt's presentation, can be found in dominant strands of social and political theory, especially in theoretical conceptions of "power" which fail to distinguish the latter from violence. Her essay at this point passes in review some leading social theorists, from John Stuart Mill to C. Wright Mills, who all concurred in equating power with the ability to command or subjugate others. Faithful to utilitarian psychology, John Stuart Mill found two basic inclinations in human nature: the "desire to exercise power over others" and the "disinclination to have power exercised" over oneself. The same outlook was reflected in Max Weber's definition of power as "the chance to assert my own will against the resistance of others"—a definition which echoed Voltaire's dictum that "power consists in making others act as I choose." This "command" conception of power readily shades over into a maxim of violence. Congruent with his construal of power, Weber famously portrayed the "state" as the "rule of men based on the means of legitimate, that is allegedly legitimate, violence." Erecting this approach into a general sociological doctrine, C. Wright Mills declared that "all politics is a struggle for power" and "the ultimate kind of power is violence." Still more recently, Bertrand de Jouvenel—author of the influential book *Power: The Natural History of Its Growth*—declared it to be an incontrovertible lesson of history that "war presents itself as an activity of states *which pertains to their essence*." Quite consistently, de Jouvenel linked this "essence" with traditional views of power from Mill to Max Weber: "To command and to be obeyed: without that, there is no power. . . . The thing without which it cannot be: that essence is command." Having dutifully surveyed this line of literature, Arendt resolutely interjects herself into the discussion:

> If the essence of power is the effectiveness of command, then there is no greater power than that which grows out of the barrel of a gun, and it would be difficult to say in which way the order given by a policeman is different from that given by a gunman. . . . Should everybody from Right to Left, from Bertrand de Jouvenel to Mao Tse-tung agree on so basic a point in political philosophy as the nature of power?[7]

Unwilling to join this disparate consensus, Arendt at this juncture invokes another tradition and a different vocabulary which, she says, is "no less old and time-honored." What surges into view here is the Athenian city-state with its principle of "isonomy" (equality of law) and the Roman Republic with its idea of "*civitas*"—traditions which cherished a concept of power and law not predicated on the "command-obedience relationship" and opposed to the equation of power and law with command. Legacies of this kind were recalled by republicans during the eighteenth century when they tried to establish "governments of law and not of men" and, more specifically, governments based of the consent of the governed. For Arendt, these legacies are by no means obsolete but rather need to be restored and revitalized in our time. Her text at this point reaffirms basic tenets of her own republican political theory with its emphasis on the "*vita activa*" and civic participation in the "public realm." "It is the people's support," she writes, "that lends power to the institution of a country, and this support is but the continuation of the consent that brought the laws into existence to begin with." Under conditions of modern representative government, she adds, "the people are supposed to rule those who govern them" and, in effect, all political institutions are "manifestations and materializations" of this kind of empowerment. By contrast, governmental institutions petrify and become oppressive as soon as "the living power of the people" ceases to uphold them. Here, a crucial distinction between power and violence comes to the fore: whereas power always "stands in need of numbers," violence up to a point "can manage without them because it relies on implements" (that is, the tools and strategies of coercion). Sharply formulated: "The extreme form of power is All against One, the extreme form of violence is One against All."[8]

A central merit of Arendt's text is its contribution to conceptual clarification, accomplished through a series of definitions and semantic demarcations—demarcations which are largely ignored in dominant strands of social and political thought (which is "a rather sad reflection" on the prevailing state of affairs). The key terms distinguished in the text are those of power, strength, force, authority, and violence. For Arendt, these terms denote distinct phenomena, and to treat them as synonyms reveals not only a "deafness to linguistic meanings" but also a "blindness to the realities" of social life—a blindness induced by the "command" theory of politics. As soon as one ceases to reduce public affairs to domination or coercion, however, the "original data" of social life "reappear in their authentic diversity." Most familiar to readers of her earlier writings is Arendt's concept of "power" construed as empowerment or "the human ability not just to act but to act in concert" in the public arena. "When we say of somebody that he is 'in power,'" she elaborates, "we actually refer to his being empowered by a certain number of people to act in their name." By contrast, "strength" designates a property inherent in an object or a person quite independently of any relation to other things or persons. The term "force" points even farther beyond human relationships to anonymous occurrences (such as "force of circumstances" or "forces of nature"). Closely akin to power but lacking in its symmetry or reciprocity is "authority" referring to a consensual hierarchy: "Its hallmark is unquestioning recognition by those who are asked to obey." "Violence," finally, is a mode of nonconsensual control distinguished by its "instrumental character," that is, by its primary reliance on methods or strategies of coercion.[9]

To guard against misunderstanding, Arendt quickly adds that the preceding categories are analytical distinctions which "hardly ever correspond to watertight compartments in the real world." Taken with this proviso, however, the distinctions remain important both for theoretical and practical-political purposes. The temptation to confound power and violence is particularly strong in the case of governmental power, where violence often functions as a means to preserve established structures against foreign enemies or domestic subversives; in this case, it appears indeed as though violence were primary and power "nothing but a façade, the velvet glove concealing the iron hand." That this impression is misleading, however, is revealed in governmental efforts to defeat revolutionaries or subversives: violence here remains effective only as long as governmental orders are in fact obeyed and their legitimacy (as a mode of power) widely accepted: "Everything depends on the power behind the violence." To be sure, in an open contest between violence and power, the former will always triumph, but at an enormous loss: the loss of political empowerment. For this very reason, politics should never be equated with violent coercion. "Violence," Arendt comments wryly, "can always destroy power. Out of the barrel of a gun grows the most effective command, resulting in the most instant and perfect obedience." But "what can never grow out of it is power." All this does not mean that violence can always and completely be banished from the political domain. Under extreme provocation, violence may be warranted for self-defense and "to set the scales of justice right"—provided it is used as a last resort and within carefully designed limitations. Unleashing the full fury of violence, on the other hand, is bound to be destructive and self-defeating: "The practice of violence, like all action, changes the world; but the most probable change is to a more violent world."[10]

ADDITIONAL "LITERATURE ON VIOLENCE"

Violence and coercive power have long been a prominent preoccupation of Western thought. In the view of some, Western civilization as a whole is characterized by a bent toward domination and coercive control, manifest in imperialism and colonial expansion (an assessment which is probably overdrawn as a summary indictment). As indicated before, Arendt's essay passes in review major examples of the Western "literature on violence," starting from the time of Marx and Engels. Undoubtedly, Leftist and Rightist thinkers since that time have been strongly fascinated by the lure of violence—which largely equals the lure of radical upheaval, rupture, and discontinuity. In many ways, what has tended to attract radical thinkers, on both the Left and the Right, to violence is dissatisfaction with bourgeois normalcy, that is, with the steadiness and predictability of routinized public life increasingly dominated by bureaucrats and scientific experts. As Arendt notes, one of the most spirited attacks on bourgeois normalcy was penned by Georges Sorel in his *Reflections on Violence.* In addition to the lines quoted above, it may be appropriate to remember some other passages which vividly reflect the Sorelian "*élan vital.*" In advocating the policy or "myth" of a general strike, his text states: "Revolutionary syndicalism keeps alive the desire to strike in the masses and only prospers when important strikes, accompanied by violence, take place"; hence, "if we wish to discuss socialism seriously, we must first of all investigate the functions of violence in present social conditions." These comments are further underscored in a later passage according to which "proletarian acts of violence" are "purely and simply acts of war; they have the value of military manoeuvres and serve to mark the separation of classes."[11]

While the topic of violence may be readily appealing to politicians or ideologues, the appeal is less obvious in the case of philosophers and social scientists ensconced in more recondite academic discourses. However, here again, concern with routinization and the growing calculability of social life provide powerful impulses for radical protest. The philosophy of Jean-Paul Sartre, cited by Arendt, is a prominent case in point. From his early to his later writings, Sartre's outlook was dominated by the contrast between spontaneous freedom and creative initiative, on the one hand, and social regularity and control, on the other. In his early chef d'oeuvre, *Being and Nothingness,* this contrast was highlighted in the famous chapter on "The Look," which portrayed intersubjective or inter-human relations as a struggle for reciprocal domination or enslavement. As Sartre noted at the time, the other person's look or gaze "constitutes me as a defenseless being for a freedom which is not mine" and to which I am thus "enslaved." Given that the interplay between subjugation and being subjugated can neither be mediated nor resolved, conflict (possibly shading over into violence) was described as "the original meaning of being-for-others" or of inter-human coexistence. In his later *Critique of Dialectical Reason,* Sartre shifted the accent from visual perception to action or social practice—but without modifying substantially the conflictual model. Basically, the "I-versus-You" conflict was translated into an "Us-versus-Them" struggle, with spontaneous freedom and creativity being attributed to a social class. In light of these premises, his preface to Fanon's book—quoted by Arendt—cannot come as a surprise, especially his comment that in the struggle against oppression "irrepressible violence is neither sound and fury, nor the resurrection of savage instincts, nor even the effect of resentment: it is man creating himself."[12]

Whatever its polemical merits, Sartrean existentialism no longer reflects the philosophical mood in the West. Several developments have conspired to erode its popular appeal: foremost among them the Vietnam War and the ensuing student rebellion (especially in France). Partly as a result of these happenings, new intellectual orientations arose in Europe (and, to a lesser extent, in America): perspectives like post-structuralism, postmodernism, and "deconstruction." Basically, what this change involved was a shift from the pathos of human "existence" in the direction of a displacement or "decentering" of human subjectivity and spontaneously creative autonomy. Curiously, despite this radical transformation of philosophical premises, crucial ingredients of Sartre's conflictual model survived the postmodern insurgency. A good example is the work (or rather, some of the works) of Jacques Derrida, probably the foremost post-structuralist European thinker. Already Derrida's early essay on "The Ends of Man" (1969) recommended a radical break with the past (whose vehemence carried overtones of violence). As opposed to the normalcy of routines and even the moderate reform of traditions, the essay privileged another option: the option of changing terrain "in a discontinuous and irruptive fashion, by brutally placing oneself outside, and by affirming an absolute break and difference." Not surprisingly, the name of Nietzsche surfaced at this point, whose ideas elicited at the time an "increasingly insistent and increasingly rigorous" attention in France. Roughly at the same time, Derrida in another essay explored the relation between "violence and metaphysics" and (more specifically) between violence and philosophical language as such. Reacting to the proposal of a purely ethical discourse he asked provocatively whether all discourse is not "originally violent" and whether, in fact, the "philosophical *logos*" (or reason) is not originally "inhabited by war." The only course open in this situation would not be a bracketing but an "*economy* of violence," a pitting of violence against violence. In his words: "Since finite silence is also the medium of violence, language can only indefinitely tend toward justice by acknowledging and practicing the violence within it. Violence against violence."[13]

In subsequent writings, the rhetoric of violence became still more pronounced and occasionally even predominant. This is nowhere more evident than in Derrida's well-known and widely discussed essay "Force of Law: The 'Mystical Foundation of Authority'" (1989). Apart from offering a detailed reading of a text by Walter Benjamin, the essay presents a Derridean account of justice which accentuates the transgression or "deconstruction" of normal routines and social rules. Throughout, strong emphasis is placed on a radical break with calculative rationality, on the rupture or interruption of continuity and established procedures through the intervention of an "outside" force (which ultimately, though ambiguously, is identified with justice). Justice, Derrida writes, "exceeds law and calculation" just as "the unpresentable exceeds the determinable" or given present. Differently put: The "idea of justice" is "irreducible in its affirmative character, in its demand of gift without exchange, . . . without calculation and without rules, without reason and without rationality." To perform its interruptive task, justice requires the exercise of "a decision that *cuts*, that divides," a decision that cannot be reduced to any preceding arrangement. Given this absence of governing precedents, Derrida adds pointedly, we can recognize in the idea "a madness, and perhaps another sort of mystique. And deconstruction is mad about this kind of justice, mad about this desire for justice." The instance of the decision, he repeats, is "a madness, as Kierkegaard says"; and this is "particularly true of the instant of the just decision that must rend time and defy dialectics: it is a madness." Unsurprisingly, the notion of a mad decision is not far removed from, or concurs readily with, the rhetoric of violence. The performance of justice, we are told, "always maintains within itself some irruptive violence" that "no longer obeys the demands of theoretical rationality"; located outside or at the margins of that rationality, irruptive justice entails that not only a violence but "indeed a terrorism and other forms of hostage taking are at work."[14]

What is troubling in Derrida's account—despite its stunningly transgressive élan—is the reduction of justice and violence to an externally irruptive force, to a "mad" or maddening kind of affliction. Treated in this manner, justice and violence are placed not only beyond reason or rational calculation, but beyond the pale of intelligibility and human understanding as such. Leaving aside at this point the issue of justice, the effects of this treatment on violence are disturbing. Although violence, in a sense, is always irruptive and hence never fully transparent, its equation with madness and utter non-transparency strips violence of its experiential dimension: that is, its role as a "cathartic" and transformative agent in human life. It is precisely in this respect that Bat-Ami Bar On's study, *The Subject of Violence: Arendtean Exercises in Understanding,* makes an important contribution by placing the accent on the experience of the victims or "subjects" of violence. As Bar On notes at the outset, Arendt's writings were always deeply imprinted with the agonics of her own life—in a manner which tended to link (without fusing) theoretical reflection and autobiography. In Arendt, she writes, "I found a woman who was a subject of violence [and] who studied violence"—though not simply in memoir fashion. "I tend to trust Arendt's work," she adds, "perhaps because I cannot but read most of it in any other way than as a kind of writing that is fully infused with the personal, especially that part of her work that is about violence." As it happens, much of Arendt's opus deals not with esoteric topics but with the concrete sufferings of the period: the violence of anti-Semitism, imperialism, and totalitarianism; the violence of wars and revolutions; the violence of poverty, exile, and dispossession. In confronting all these phenomena, Arendt did not adopt the stance of a spectator, nor that of an omniscient metaphysician, but that of a victim seeking to come to terms with her traumas. In a quasi-Freudian sense, coming to terms here involves "the 'work of mourning' because it is conditioned by the violence of its time."[15]

In many ways, Arendt's life mirrored the horrors and dislocations of the twentieth century. As a refugee from Germany and as a Jewess, she intensely felt and registered their impact—although always with an alert intelligence and the desire to extend the reach of comprehension to the very brink of the incomprehensible. One of her early essays, titled "We Refugees"—written shortly after her arrival in America—recorded movingly the experiences of displaced persons like herself, that is, the fate of people "who, unprotected by any specific law or political convention, are nothing but human beings." While acknowledging the powerful lure of normalization and quick assimilation into the new society, the essay also described the predicament of refugees (like herself) who were unable or unwilling to forget the abnormal and violent source of their status. Using the term "conscious pariah," Arendt at this point delineated the position of defiantly reflective victims of violence who place themselves at the border between past and present, between integration and exile—victims who "at least nightly . . . think of our dead or . . . remember the poems we once loved."[16] The position of reflective victims was elaborated and fleshed out in many of her subsequent writings, including her 1948 essay on "The Concentration Camps." There, Arendt drew a clear distinction between two kinds of literature on concentration camps written by victims-surviors: on the one side, literature composed in anecdotal or memoir style and reporting an "immediate experience" of inmates; and on the other, more reflective and recollective literature written "consciously for the living" and motivated by an attempt to be "understood at any cost." The essay immediately pointed to the dilemma faced by the second kind of literature: the problem of reflecting consciously on phenomena—like radical violence—hovering on the border of unintelligibility. In Bar On's words, Arendt in that essay

> warns against succumbing to the "great temptation to explain away the intrinsically incredible" and suggests that if any sense can be made of the concentration camps at all, it must be produced through the engagement of the "fearful imagination" of

those who are not simply caught in the experiences of their past but rather dread the possibility of a future that reproduces the horrors of concentration camps.[17]

From the perspective of the literature on violence, the most instructive and revealing text is Arendt's 1953 article on "Understanding and Politics"—an essay on which Bar On concentrates in a chapter on "Shattered Worlds and Shocked Understandings." There, reflecting on grim features of the age (like totalitarianism) and drawing on the teachings of some of her early mentors (like Heidegger and Jaspers), Arendt introduced a basic distinction inside the cognitive domain: that between experiential "understanding" and "scientific knowledge." While the latter type aims at full rational transparency, the former is inherently tentative, open-ended, and infused with an existential subtext: the subtext of personal and social agonies which—although exceeding random whim—can never be rendered fully transparent. In Arendt's account, understanding involves "an unending activity by which, in constant change and variation, we come to terms with, reconcile ourselves to reality, that is, try to be at home in the world." The problem, here again, concerns the meaning of "coming to terms" or "being at home"—for the home in our time is a violent world full of past and present atrocities, that is, an arena of "shattered worlds and shocked understandings." Clearly, "coming to terms" today cannot denote a simple adaptation or accommodation to existing reality—a move which would be both intellectually and ethico-politically untenable since it involves (in Theodor Adorno's words) not a facing up to violence but a tactic of "wiping it from memory." In Bar On's perceptive interpretation, the notion of "understanding" as articulated by Arendt has to be construed as a "very serious kind of 'working through' that must take place and at the same time leads to, at best, only a temporary tentative mastery, the catching of only a 'glimpse' of something that is bound to be undermined" by new experiences and events. Located at the interstices between knowledge and ignorance, between transparency and randomness, understanding also exhibits a built-in duality or tension: by being directed at the same time toward an otherness located beyond the self and a personal catharsis or a "process of self-understanding."[18]

HUMANISM AND VIOLENCE

Given the persistent "shattering" of worlds and "shocking" of understandings in our time, Arendt's writings on violence surely deserve to
be remembered and (still better) to be "worked through" today. In a
period when terroristic violence extends from state-sponsored terrorism to far-flung networks of non-state actors, nothing seems more
urgent than to revive and reaffirm Arendt's distinction between power
and violence, between politics (construed as concerted action) and
warfare (based on the polarization between friend and enemy). From
an Arendtean perspective, nothing is more destructive of politics or
the public arena than resort to radical antinomies or quasi-Manichean
polarities: such as the polarities of subject and object, inside and outside, "us" and "them," light and darkness. In every case, resort to such
antinomies splits asunder the public realm, giving way instead to one-
sided domination and coercive violence. Although there must surely
be room for antagonism and rivalry among political actors, care must
be taken to keep the public arena itself intact. One way to guard
against the latter's erosion is attentiveness to important semantic and
linguistic distinctions—as exemplified in Arendt's differentiation between power, strength, force, and violence. As it happens, her differentiation has not always been heeded by political thinkers—even those
sympathetic to her work—who prefer to use terms interchangeably in
an exercise of semantic largesse.[19]

Apart from the polarities just mentioned there is another important dichotomy which perhaps undergirds all the rest: the antinomy
between continuity and discontinuity, between regularity and rupture, between determinism and contingency or freedom. It is with
regard to this polarity that Arendt's work makes perhaps its most significant intervention: by seeking to rescue politics—or rather "the
political" or "political space"—from both sides of these polar conun-
drums. Basically, her text "On Violence" perceives the danger of violence as arising both from the side of a routinized regularity and
from that of an arbitrary or "mad" irruption. As her critique of Sartre
makes clear, Arendt was suspicious of a notion of freedom construed
as radical and unmediated self-creation; by implication, her suspicion
would likely have extended also to "postmodern" celebrations of

contingency and of the radical rupture or negation of rules. At the same time, and with even greater élan, her work was opposed to the ossification of rules and routines under the auspices of far-flung bureaucracies or "expertocracies"—phenomena which have only been exacerbated since the time of her writing. As she states in her essay, modern bureaucracy is "the form of government in which everybody is deprived of political freedom, of the power to act." This powerlessness is aided and abetted by trends in modern science or pseudo-science—today supported by globalizing hegemonies— which seek to render everything predictable and manageable, thereby assuring that "nothing of importance ever happens" or can happen. For Arendt, this bureaucratically or hegemonically imposed regularity is itself a mode of violent coercion; moreover, it unleashes retaliatory forces which, in turn, are bent on violence: "The greater the bureaucratization of public life, the greater will be the attraction of violence. . . . I am inclined to think that much of the present glorification of violence is caused by severe frustration of the faculty of action in the modern world."[20]

In steering a path between continuity and discontinuity, between regularity and innovation, Arendt's position distantly echoes the outlook of the Dutch humanist Erasmus, whose entire lifework was ensconced in the tension between preservation and rupture. Although working within a long-standing tradition—the tradition of Catholic Christianity—his lifelong endeavor was directed at reshaping and deeply transforming that tradition, an endeavor which, in some quarters, earned him the reputation of being an accomplice of the Reformation (bent on breaking with the past). In the domain of political violence, Erasmus's views also resonate with Arendtean remonstrations and outrage—as indicated in some earlier chapters. Among more recent thinkers, Arendt's position shows a certain "elective affinity" with many of the writings of Maurice Merleau-Ponty. Like Arendt, Merleau-Ponty sought to forge a path between understanding and non-understanding: more specifically, between the transparency of an idealist rationalism (exemplified by Descartes and Edmund Husserl) and the reductionism of an empiricist psychology (exemplified by behaviorism). As he noted in his *Phenomenology of Perception* (of 1945), reductive empiricism cannot account for the emergence of knowledge (beyond sensation), while rationalism or "intellectualism" cannot account for the initial lack of knowledge.[21] The same pathway also guided Merleau-Ponty in his more political reflections, including his explorations of political violence. In the latter domain, the challenge for him was to subject violence to critical scrutiny from the angle of moral-political legitimacy, while at the same time not ignoring its operation out of idealist scruples (which would sideline the task of a serious "working through"). As he observed in his 1947 book *Humanism and Terror,* which has lost none of its relevance: "A regime which is nominally liberal [based on a rational rule of law] can be oppressive in reality," while a regime which "acknowledges its own violence *might* have in it more genuine humanity" by facing up to its task. Hence, the question was not so much of knowing what liberals abstractly "have in mind" but "what in reality is done by the liberal state within and beyond its borders."[22]

For Merleau-Ponty, "working through" the problem of violence required more than good intentions and the self-righteous profession of abstract principles; it demanded above all the sober recognition of the complexity of human actions and of the impossibility to predict and control consequences in a transparent manner. "The curse of politics," he wrote, "is precisely that it must translate values into the order of facts." On the level of political action, however, every prognosis is not merely a rational maxim but a "kind of complicity," with the result that policies cannot be "grounded in principle" alone, but must also comprehend concrete situations and the open-ended character of events. With regard to violence, the contingency of human action poses major problems. A chief danger is that in professing nonviolence one may actually reinforce "established" violence that is "a system of production which makes misery and war inevitable." On the other hand, by acknowledging and participating in the "play of violence" one runs the risk of a "permanent involvement" which would justify "realist" politics. Hence, the crucial task of a humanist politics, for Merleau-Ponty, was "to find a violence which recedes [or vanishes] with the approach of man's future," a future predicated on just and "worked through" human relationships. Such a future, he added, can dawn only when human freedom is no longer worshipped as an abstract idol but as the capacity of concrete human beings to act in the public space.

Thus, *Humanism and Terror* basically seconded Arendt's view of politics as a mode of mutual empowerment and action in concert:

> It is the essence of liberty to exist only in the practice of liberty, in the inevitably imperfect movement which joins us to others, to the things of the world, to our jobs, mixed with the hazards of our situation. . . . [Unfortunately] an aggressive liberalism exists which is a dogma and already an ideology of war. It can be recognized by its love of the empyrean of principles, its failure ever to mention the geographical and historical circumstances to which it owes its birth. . . . Its nature is violent, nor does it hesitate to impose itself through violence.[23]

One of the aspects differentiating both Merleau-Ponty and Arendt from Erasmus is their inattention to religion and problems of interreligious and intercommunal conflicts. It is precisely in this domain that we discover the crucial significance of the lifework of the Mahatma Gandhi—to whom the following chapter is devoted. Placed in the concrete circumstances of pre-independence India, Gandhi found that he had to devote a major part of his efforts to the task of combating inter-religious strife, and especially the intense and often violent rivalry between Hindus and Muslims. In shouldering this task, Gandhi adopted a tactic not far removed from Arendt's (and Merleau-Ponty's) preference for "working through": the tactic of concrete intercommunal engagement which he called "*satyagraha*" (and which can be translated as the enactment of truth and justice or, more simply, as "truth-force" or "soul-force"). A well-known ingredient of *satyagraha* was the practice of nonviolence (*ahimsa*) or minimal use of violence. As one should note, however, both truth-force and nonviolence for Gandhi were not merely abstract mottoes or principles but part of an ongoing struggle: the struggle for social justice and emancipation, that is, for the "future of man" (to borrow Merleau-Ponty's phrase). Above all, the "truth" pursued through *satyagraha* was not an ideology to be imposed unilaterally, but rather a truth or integrity of lived experience—which had to remain attentive or sensitive to the lived experience of others, especially their suffering. Rather than inflicting one's own view on others through coercive means, the "force" of justice requires that one proceed nonviolently and, if necessary, inflict suffering on oneself (through prolonged fasting and austerity) in the hope of awakening the opponent's conscience and humanity. To quote some famous Gandhian passages:

> In the application of *satyagraha*, I discovered in the earliest stages that pursuit of Truth did not admit of violence being inflicted on one's opponent, but that he must be weaned from error by patience and sympathy. . . . Suffering is the law of human beings; war is the law of the jungle. But suffering is infinitely more powerful than the law of the jungle for converting the opponent and opening his ears, which are otherwise shut to the voice of reason. . . . The appeal of reason is more to the head, but the penetration of the heart comes from suffering; it opens up the inner understanding of men. Suffering is the badge of the human race, not the sword.[24]

To be sure, the Gandhian path of nonviolence is steep; its success is not assured. In her essay "On Violence," Arendt raises doubts about the efficacy of *satyagraha* in other historical and political contexts, outside India. "In a head-on clash between violence and power," she notes, "the outcome is hardly in doubt." Thus, if Gandhi's nonviolent resistance had met with a different opponent, the outcome might "not have been decolonization, but massacre and submission." Her skepsis receives powerful support from some recent developments, especially the growing complicity of governments in terrorist activities. Yet, the picture is perhaps less somber than Arendt suggests. It is good to recall that many of the most progressive and humanly empowering changes in the twentieth century have occurred mostly through nonviolent means. Among these changes are: the decolonization of India and of many other countries in Asia and Africa; the civil rights struggle in America (led by Martin Luther King); the abolition of apartheid in South Africa (under the leadership of Nelson Mandela); and the "velvet revolutions" in Eastern Europe (guided by Lech Walesa and Václav Havel). In many of the cited changes, the leading proponents were deeply indebted to the Gandhian legacy and openly acknowledged their debt. So, rather than joining the champions of *realpolitik—*

the defenders of violence and "clash of civilizations"—would it not behoove responsible intellectuals everywhere to join the great humanitarian benefactors of the last century and to champion, whenever and wherever feasible, the course of nonviolence and *satyagraha?* In pursuing this course, they will be boosted by Arendt's famous statement (cited before) that "the practice of violence, like all action, changes the world, but the most probable change is to a more violent world."[25]

CHAPTER SEVEN

Gandhi and Islam

A Heart-and-Mind Unity?

One of the grandsons of the Mahatma recently commented bitterly on the upsurge of communal violence between Hindus and Muslims in India, and especially in his grandfather's native state of Gujarat. The immediate occasion for his comments was the attack on a crowded train near Godhra and the ensuing carnage in many parts of the state. For Rajmohan Gandhi, these events dishonored the basic legacy of the Mahatma, as well as the legacy of many saints and poets in that part of the country. "The Gujarat of Gandhi," he noted, "of the poet Narsi Mehta who spoke of the other person's pain, of the modern Jain saint Rajchandra [who deeply influenced Gandhi], of brothers to the poor like Ravishanker Maharaj and Jugatram Dave . . . stands deeply shaken." The culprits behind the events, in his view, were political and religious agitators who had never accepted the Mahatma's message of nonviolence and interfaith reconciliation: "The truth is that the subcontinent's religious extremists never forgave Gandhi his beliefs and his triumphs." What they particularly detested was Gandhi's "standing up for minority rights, religious freedom, justice, and forgiveness" and his success in "persuading millions on the subcontinent to embrace these values." Angered and frustrated by this success, Rajmohan added, extremists on both sides "put their heads together" and came up with two strategies: "inject hate into Gandhi's Gujarat, and turn Gandhi's healing Ram(a), the Almighty who was also the Compassionate, into an anti-Muslim chariot-riding warrior."[1]

As an antidote to the perpetrated carnage, Rajmohan urged a return to his grandfather's vision of intercommunal harmony and peacebuilding—to what Gandhi himself on repeated occasions had called the goal of a "heart unity" between Hindus and Muslims in India. The following pages seek to explore, once again, the story of India's struggle for independence and, in particular, the role played by Hindu-Muslim relations in this struggle, especially as the latter was carried on under Gandhi's leadership. As will become clear, a central issue during this struggle was the question of priority: whether India's independence (*swaraj*) should have primacy over intercommunal harmony and whether such harmony was in fact a precondition of genuine independence. In the first section, I shall briefly recapitulate the main stages of Gandhi's involvement in the so-called "Muslim question" and his evolving attitude toward the interplay of independence and harmony. The second section will highlight some of the major disputes or bones of contention between Gandhi and prominent contemporary Muslim leaders; a crucial issue at this point will be the dispute between Muhammad Ali Jinnah's formal constitutionalism and Gandhi's grassroots multiculturalism or intercommunalism. The concluding section returns to the contemporary period, in an effort to derive lessons from Gandhi's intercommunal practices both for present-day India and for our steadily shrinking or "globalizing" world.

A STORY OF INTERFAITH ENCOUNTERS

By general agreement, Gandhi played a central—perhaps *the* central—role in India's struggle for independence from British rule. However, the final outcome did not match the initial aspirations. Basically, the country whose freedom Gandhi championed was not the India after partition but the older "Bharata" where Hindus, Muslims, and other faiths had lived together for many centuries. The goal of the freedom struggle, in his view, was to preserve as much of this multi-faith legacy as possible in and beyond the achievement of independence. For this reason, he had to act both as a political leader—organizing an effective insurgent movement against British rule—and as a spiritual leader and interfaith mediator among different religious traditions. It is this combination of talents which, in large measure, accounts for the fascination of his "persona" and the intricate complexity of his actions. Students of Gandhi's life often accentuate his political prowess and the sagacity of his strategic moves, while sidelining his spiritual endeavors (or at least relegating them to an ancillary status). Yet, from Gandhi's perspective, it must have been entirely evident that politics and religious faith cannot be neatly segregated—at least not in a place like the Indian subcontinent marked for centuries as a meeting ground of diverse cultures and beliefs.

As is well known, Gandhi was quite prepared for public service through his legal studies in London and his extensive participation in roundtables and official commissions; and few would deny his efficacy in this arena. However, his religious or spiritual outlook was even more deeply grounded—so deeply as to give a distinctive tuning to his entire life. Part of this tuning came from his family background, another part from his lifelong cultivation of interfaith encounters. For both of his parents, the dominant family tradition was Vaishnava Hinduism, a tradition which emphasized hymn-singing and devotional practices—with only slight attention to orthodox codes and rituals. The center of devotion of Vaishnava faith in Gujarat (then and now) is Lord Krishna, whose teachings are enshrined, above all, in the *Bhagavad Gita*. In terms of that sacred text, there are three pathways or "*yogas*" leading to salvation: contemplation (*jñana*), action (*karma*), and loving devotion (*bhakti*). Among these three pathways, Gandhi resolutely pursued the last two—without entirely neglecting contemplation or reflection. In his well-known self-description, he was a "*karmayogin*," that is, a practitioner of faith—which, in his case, did not mean a mindless activist or busybody, because his actions were always suffused with spiritual devotion (*bhakti*) involving self-restraint and self-transgression in favor of others' needs. In Margaret Chatterjee's words:

> The *Gita* shows the validity of various paths to the attainment of the highest. This suggests that politics too, a human activity which is built into man's living in community, is a valid path. . . . The purification of politics was to be brought about through an infusion of the non-violent spirit into it. There was no [strict] frontier between the things that were Caesar's and the things that were God's.[2]

With its emphasis on devotion and selfless service, Vaishnava Hinduism has always been somewhat close to Islamic faith with its stress on selfless surrender. Above all, the "Sufi" strand in Islamic religion—a strand often deviating from rigidly orthodox canons—was found to be quite congenial to Vaishnava spirituality, and especially to *bhakti* poetry and songs. As the historian Muhammad Mujeeb notes: at least since the end of the fourteenth century "the devotional character of Hindu songs and the appeal which the language made to Sufis brought Hindus and Muslims closer together than any other influence," opening the way "for a mutual appreciation of values."[3] Small wonder that Gandhi's family home in Porbandar had an open-door policy for open-minded Muslims and members of other communities. "Muslims were received as guests in the Gandhi home," writes Sheila McDonough; "the political traditions of diplomatic courtesy [inherited on his father's side] seem to have been imbibed by the child as a self-evident way for a civilized life to be conducted." Childhood experiences of this kind, she adds, must have "encouraged the young Gandhi to think of Muslims, Jains and Parsis as natural friends and supporters in common causes." We also know that he had a boyhood friend, Sheikh Mehtab, who lived close to the Gandhis in Porbandar and who often defended him against bullies at school. In his *Autobiography,* he recollects some of these early experiences and their beneficial effects on him. His father, he recalls, had "Muselman and Parsi friends who would talk to him about their faiths, and he would listen to them always with respect." Often being present at these encounters, such things "combined to inculcate in me a toleration for all faiths."[4]

Following his legal studies in London, Gandhi went to South Africa in order to work as a lawyer for a Muslim business firm whose owner he had gotten to know in Bombay. During his prolonged stay there—some twenty years—he was in contact with a large Indian community, many of whose members were Muslims who originally hailed from Gujarat. Drawing on his childhood experiences, he was able to establish close ties with these Muslims, to the point that he was sometimes treated nearly as a member of the family. What solidified these ties—in addition to mutual respect and sympathy—was the discrimination and oppression suffered by Hindus and Muslims alike at the hands of the white government. As Gandhi reported later, Hindus and Muslims were commonly lumped together by white South Africans in an inferior, subhuman category described variously as "Asian dirt," "semi-barbarous Asiatics," and "squalid coolies with truthless tongues."[5] In response to this treatment, a broad resistance movement was forged, largely under Gandhi's leadership and based on a close alliance between Hindus and Muslims. It was at this point that a kind of "heart unity" came into being, a brotherhood of defiance which could draw inspiration from the respective religious traditions. On the Muslim side, the familiar notion of "righteous struggle" (*jihad*) could serve as a powerful motivating force in the joint Indian insurgency. Looking for an equivalent in the Sanskritic tradition of Hinduism, Gandhi coined the term "*satyagraha*," meaning "enactment of truth" or the resolute commitment to truth and justice irrespective of consequences. In the words of the Muslim writer Abid Husain, reflecting on that critical juncture: encouraged by "the unity of sentiments and purpose" and "the spirit of mutual friendship and trust," Gandhi at the time "launched his first *satyagraha* campaign which was at the same time his first experiment in securing the fraternal cooperation of Muslims . . . for a non-violent struggle that involved the utmost suffering and sacrifice." Different traditions thus could be seen as converging in their practical results. By navigating easily between religious vocabularies, McDonough comments, Gandhi demonstrated his "extraordinary facility in using language to inspire and direct the religious awareness of his hearers." On the whole, the South African struggle fully convinced him of "the validity and importance of mutual understanding and cooperation" among Indians, and especially between Hindus and Muslims.[6]

It was this conviction that Gandhi carried with himself on his return to India during World War I. The conviction was soon going to be put to the test. Not long after his return he began to organize a resistance struggle, called "noncooperation movement," against British domination, a struggle relying in great part on the lessons learned in South Africa. As before, many of his cohorts in this movement were Muslims committed to Indian independence—foremost among them the brothers Muhammad Ali and Shaukat Ali and Maulana Abul Kalam Azad. As it happened, in addition to independence, Muslims in India (and the Near East) were greatly preoccupied at the time with the collapse of the Ottoman Empire, and especially with the fate of the caliphate seen as the last remaining symbol of the Muslim *umma* (community of believers). In order to salvage the caliphate from the Ottoman collapse, Muhammad Ali, Kalam Azad, and others organized the so-called "Khilafat movement," stressing the crucial role of the caliph as protector of the sacred sites in Mecca. Sensing the urgency of the issue, Gandhi wholeheartedly joined the movement, greeting it as an opportunity to demonstrate the needed "heart unity" with his Muslim friends and associates.[7] As we know, the movement came to nothing, mainly due to the decision of the new Turkish leadership to abolish the caliphate. Combined with the upsurge of communal strife in some parts of India (especially Kerala), the demise of the movement had a severely dampening influence on Hindu-Muslim relations throughout the subcontinent. To counteract the deterioration of communal goodwill, Gandhi in mid-1924 devoted a whole issue of his journal *Young India* to the topic: "Hindu-Muslim Tension: Its Cause and Its Cure." As far as the cause is concerned, Gandhi placed it in irritability and in unjust or offensive behavior on both sides. As for the cure, he relied on his South African experience: "I see no way of achieving anything in this afflicted country without a lasting heart unity between Hindus and Muselmans in India." To underscore his conviction and to calm communal hatreds, he embarked on a fast in the house of his friend Muhammad Ali. The final breaking of the fast was celebrated by the recital of passages from the Qur'an and the *Upanishads* and by the singing of both Christian and Vaishnava hymns.[8]

Although calming emotions for a time, the fast did not have the long-term effect that Gandhi hoped for. Despite its overt failure, the Khilafat movement had at least one tangible domestic result: it strengthened the self-confidence of Indian Muslim leaders—many of whom were becoming increasingly suspicious of the National Congress (dominated by a majority of Hindus).[9] The situation was complicated by the rise to prominence of new Muslim voices—like that of Muhammad Iqbal—which, in lieu of interfaith unity, stressed the economic backwardness of Muslims in India and sometimes privileged pan-Islamic aspirations over national independence. One voice which was becoming increasingly influential in the period before World War II was that of Muhammad Ali Jinnah. Although trained like Gandhi at the London Inns of Court, Jinnah nurtured a completely different vision of the future of India and of the Indian Muslim community. A cool-headed rationalist and legalist, he thoroughly disliked Gandhi's penchant for grassroots mobilization and also his intense concern with communal-religious harmony (or "heart unity"). Basically, his inclination was to deal with the British through constitutional negotiation, in the hope of possibly transforming India into an autonomous member within the British Empire or Commonwealth (preferably with separate constituencies for Hindus and Muslims). After assuming leadership of the Muslim League in 1937, Jinnah resolutely pursued his vision—and was supported by many (though not all) Muslim leaders. From this time forward, Hindu and Muslim policies moved progressively in different directions. While Gandhi desperately sought to preserve communal harmony through the shared struggle for independence, Jinnah came to despair of national unity, opting instead for separation or partition. In 1944, a sustained conversation took place between Gandhi and Jinnah on the future of the subcontinent, but nothing was accomplished. In B. R. Nanda's words: "What was Gandhi's hope was Jinnah's fear."[10]

In the end, independence came in a torrent of blood. Even prior to British departure from India, intercommunal violence rocked many parts of the subcontinent. In August 1946, a bloody and destructive riot broke out in Calcutta, followed by Muslim attacks on Hindu villages in East Bengal and Hindu attacks on Muslim villages in Bihar. "From this time until his death by assassination in 1948," McDonough observes, "Gandhi lived his final years in the midst of a sort of hell on earth," for there can scarcely be a worse fate than "outbursts of violence among the very persons one has given one's life to serving." In a desperate effort to quench the flames of violence, the Mahatma during this period traveled on foot to remote, riot-torn villages, ignoring the frailty of his body and the dangers to himself. To quote McDonough again: "The old man who tottered over the logs bridging the main streams in the jungles of Noakhali, and later in Bihar, was in no way confused about his goals: he wanted to communicate with the people in their native places and to teach them to live in peace with each other." Although he finally came to accept the partitioning of the subcontinent, the outcome for him was both a personal disappointment and an unmitigated national tragedy. When, shortly before his death and in the wake of the partition, violence struck Delhi, he undertook his last fast there. During this fast he dictated this message to his secretary:

> Anyone who wants to drive out of Delhi all Muslims as such, must be set down as its enemy number one, and therefore enemy number one of India. We are rushing toward that catastrophy; [but] it is the bounden duty of every son and daughter of India to take his or her full share in averting it.[11]

SOME SUSPICIONS AND CONTROVERSIES

Gandhi's commitment to interfaith and intercommunal harmony was in many ways shared by prominent Muslim leaders. Throughout his life, he enjoyed the friendship or at least close association of influential figures in the Muslim community on the subcontinent. During his early years, these figures included Hakim Ajmal Khan, the first chancellor of the Jamia Millia in Aligarh; Mukhtar A. Ansari, the second chancellor and twice president of the All-India Muslim League; and the brothers Muhammad and Shaukat Ali, organizers of the Khilafat movement. During his later years, friendly ties linked him with Abul Kalam Azad, repeatedly president of the Indian National Congress and later India's first minister of education; Zakir Husain, India's third president; S. Abid Husain, educator and writer; and the "frontier Gandhi" Abdul Ghaffar Khan, leader of the Pathans (or Pashtuns) on the northwest frontier. There are many testimonials attesting to Muslim affection and respect for Gandhi. Thus, a manifesto issued by Hakim Ajmal Khan and Mukhtar Ansari in 1922 stated that "our Hindu brothers . . . are our brothers in all truth, for the Holy Qur'an teaches that the friends of the faith are our brothers"; hence, "let us remain faithful in thought, word and deed, faithful to our cause, to our country, and to the leader we have chosen—Mahatma Gandhi."[12] After the bloody Calcutta riots of 1946, Abid Husain declared: "In Calcutta and Noakhali the fire of hatred was put out with the miraculous power of love by Mahatma Gandhi." And on the eve of independence, Abdul Ghaffar Khan stated: "Mahatmaji has shown us the true path. Long after we are no more, the coming generations of Hindus will remember him as an Avatar."[13]

Despite such testimonials (which could readily be multiplied), Gandhi's relations with Muslims were also troubled by various suspicions and points of contention. Ranking them in ascending order of importance, the following issues stand out: suspicions about Hindu terminology; disputes concerning specific incidents; disputes regarding broader strategies (especially nonviolence); and conflicts over constitutional design and the need for partition. Although sometimes emotionally charged, complaints about Gandhi's occasional "Hindu" rhetoric seem least difficult to settle. As is well known, in order to lift up his countrymen to higher levels of duty and ethical conduct, the Mahatma sometimes invoked the classical image of Ramarajya, that is, the virtuous regime and rulership of Rama. Already during his South African period, he compared the Indian struggle against apartheid with the struggle waged by Rama and his followers against the demon-king Ravana. After his return to India, Rama's virtuous reign was frequently upheld in his speeches as a counterpoise to British oppression and corruption. Combined with other seemingly "Hindu" preferences (like cow-protection and wearing of loin cloth), Gandhi's rhetoric antagonized and alarmed numerous Muslims who perceived it as the opening wedge of a more pervasive and domineering Hindu ideology. On the other hand, some right-wing Hindu leaders—probably against their better knowledge—greeted the rhetoric as a welcome concession to their own program of radical "Hindutva" or Hindu majority rule.[14] However, more thoughtful people on both sides could hardly be deceived by such construals. Philosophically trained Muslims, for example, could hardly overlook the parallel between Ramarajya and al-Farabi's famous portrayal of the "virtuous city." Even without such training, Indians of all shades could readily detect the moral intent behind the rhetoric. An example is Zakir Husain, who, on becoming India's president, stated:

> I have endeavored to follow in my life some of Mahatmaji's teaching . . . and I shall do my utmost to take our people towards what Gandhiji strove restlessly to achieve: a pure life, individual and social, . . . an active and sustained sympathy for the weak and downtrodden, and a fervent desire to forge unity among the diverse sections of the Indian people as the first condition for helping to establish peace and human brotherhood in the world based on truth and non-violence. This is what he called *Ram Raj*.[15]

More aggravating for intercommunal harmony, at least in the short run, were specific communal incidents or events and some Gandhian responses to them. Most prominent among such incidents was the Mappila (or Moplah) rebellion of 1921 in Kerala. The Mappilas were a Muslim community who had long suffered under foreign (Portuguese and British) domination and who also were the victims of a repressive land-ownership system controlled largely by the Hindu majority. Given their experience of oppression, the Mappilas reacted favorably and even enthusiastically to the Khilafat movement and also to Gandhi's noncooperation policy. As things developed, however, reaction went from resistance and noncooperation to outright militancy. Starting in August of 1921, Kerala was shaken by an increasingly violent uprising targeting both the British and the landowning Hindu establishment, an uprising marked by killings, arson, and even forced conversions. In the end, the rebellion was forcibly repressed, with massive costs in human lives for the Mappila community. Apart from widening the gulf between Muslims and the British colonial regime, the events placed a severe strain on Hindu-Muslims relations, even affecting in some eyes the integrity of Gandhi's policies. For some Muslim leaders—including the Urdu poet Hasrat Mohani—the events had tested the Gandhian idea of Hindu-Muslim harmony and demonstrated its futility (given the complicity of many landowners with British authorities). Some others blamed Gandhi directly for the outcome of the rebellion. From Gandhi's side, the situation was relatively straightforward. For one thing, the uprising for him was an isolated incident from which no general conclusion could or should be drawn. For another thing (and more importantly), his sympathies were with the real grievances of the Mappilas, but not with the violent methods used by some of their leaders. To this extent, his criticism of some Mappila actions was not targeting that community, but reflected a general philosophical stance.[16]

Gandhi's attitude toward the Kerala events brings to the fore an issue which is often singled out as a major bone of contention between him and Muslims: the issue of nonviolence or *ahimsa*. As is well known, commitment to *ahimsa* was a central pillar in Gandhi's overall perspective and a loadstar in his public actions. Deriving mainly from Jain and Buddhist sources, observers have often claimed that *ahimsa* is not really indigenous to traditional Hindu culture—and certainly not an integral part of Muslim beliefs. During the struggle for Indian independence, the issue surfaced repeatedly as a dividing line between Gandhian and Muslim practices. Thus, on the eve of the Mappila rebellion, Gandhi's associate Shaukat Ali expressed disagreement quite openly, stating: "I tell you that to kill and to be killed in the way of God are both *satyagraha*. To lay down our lives in the way of God for righteousness and to destroy the life of the tyrant who stands in the way of righteousness, are both a very great service to God." In a more conciliatory manner he added: "We have promised to cooperate with Mr. Gandhi who is with us"; but "if this fails, the Muselmans will decide what to do."[17] In even more forceful terms, Hasrat Mohani defended the Mappila insurgency, including their violent actions, while dismissing *ahimsa*. Muslims who supported Gandhi's idea of nonviolence usually did it for tactical or strategic reasons, not on grounds of moral principle. The friend of his early period, Muhammad Ali, expressed his view of *ahimsa* concisely in 1921 by stating that Gandhi and Muslims both stood for nonviolence, "he for reasons of principle and we for those of policy." Elaborating on this view, he added somewhat later: "I have agreed to work with Mahatma Gandhi, and our compact is that as long as I am associated with him, I should not resort to the use of force even for the purpose of self-defense"— unless there was an overwhelming need to rebuff British oppression.[18]

Although clearly significant, the difference between Gandhi and Muslim leaders on this issue should probably not be overstated. On closer inspection, their respective positions show points of contact and even partial convergence. On the one hand, Gandhi's views were not as categorical or apodictic as is sometimes assumed. Although proclaiming *ahimsa* as a general maxim of action, he was willing to make exceptions in dire emergencies as a last resort to protect lives. While loathe to accept violence as a matter of deliberate policy, he made room for spontaneous retaliation under grave provocation and to relieve unbearable conditions caused by direct assault. As he remarked to Louis Fischer in 1944, he was prepared to go even further and to condone minimal violence if needed to promote economic, especially agrarian, justice.[19] On the other hand, Muslim beliefs do not simply favor violence over nonviolence as a general principle; the reverse is closer to the truth. Although stressing the importance of struggle (*jihad*), Islamic religion in its basic commitments is oriented toward peace (*salam*) and just and peaceful human relations. As is well known, Islamic teachings differentiate between a "greater" and a "lesser" *jihad,* with the former denoting a personal struggle for moral righteousness and the latter involving violent confrontations under exceptional circumstances and for limited purposes (mainly for the sake of self-defense). It was because of the primary emphasis in these teachings on "greater" or "righteous struggle" that Gandhi in some of his campaigns and speeches could use the vocabularies of *jihad* and *satyagraha* as nearly equivalent (as indicated before). At least to some extent, his outlook in this respect was shared by prominent Muslim leaders of the time. To quote Muhammad Ali again (speaking to the National Congress in 1923):

I believe that war is a great evil, but I also believe that there are worse things than war. . . . When war is forced on Muslims, then as a Muselman and follower of the Last of the Prophets I may not shrink but must give the enemy battle on his own ground. . . . [But] when persecution ceases, and every man is free to act with the sole motive of securing divine good will, warfare must cease. These are the limits of violence in Islam.[20]

From a broader, world-historical perspective, the most important factor troubling Hindu-Muslim relations was the dispute between Gandhi and Jinnah over basic policy issues. As mentioned before, Jinnah was a London-trained lawyer with a strong penchant for legal procedures and little or no interest in "heart unity" between different faiths or communities. By contrast, Gandhi sought to cultivate intercommunal harmony and respect as a precondition for the legitimacy and viability of legal procedures and institutions.[21] At least initially, the two leaders strove for the same or a roughly similar goal: namely, India's independence; but they pursued this goal along different paths which in the end radically diverged. Basically, Gandhi hoped for a unified and legally "secular" (or nondiscriminatory) India whose unity was precisely guaranteed by the strength of intercommunal and interfaith interactions on the societal level. On the other hand, Jinnah's vision of the future India was predicated mainly on a procedural maxim which can be described as a "separate-but-equal" formula. This difference in policies brings to the fore more recessed but crucial contrasts involving different views of modernity, and especially different conceptions of a modern liberal political regime. Both sides departed in their own ways from the "mainstream" paradigm of such a regime. For Gandhi, modern liberal institutions were useful for generating a sense of equal citizenship; however, due to a deep-seated distrust of centralized bureaucracies, he aimed to supplement and correct "top-down" legal procedures with "bottom-up" democratic mobilization and intercommunal engagement. Jinnah's departures from the mainline paradigm were even more pronounced—and deeply puzzling. Although supporting the modern conception of the "state" as a contractual artifact, his "separate-but-equal" formula led him to

conflate his liberal proceduralism with deeply noncontractual premises and assumptions: premises anchoring the state in "essentialized"
modes of religion and nationhood. Thus, a liberal-secular leader became in the end the founder of an Islamic or proto-Islamic country.[22]

The conflict between Gandhi and Jinnah can be pursued through
several decades prior to independence; for present purposes the
briefest sketch must suffice. In the early negotiations with the British
regarding representative institutions, the colonial power—with considerable support from Muslims—decided in favor of "separate electorates" which basically divided India along religious-communal lines.
The decision was opposed by liberal opinion both in Britain and in
India precisely because of its violation of liberal principles (one person,
one vote). As Bhikhu Parekh observes, summarizing the opponents'
view: "Under the system of separate electorates, the state reproduced
the divisions of society and, rather than impartially arbitrate between
them [as modern liberalism demands], became an arena of their
conflicts." Moreover, by inscribing religious divisions into the structure of the state, the system "was bound to make Indians abnormally
conscious of their differences and prevent them from developing a
sense of common citizenship."[23] Over the years, separate electorates
became a standing feature of pre-independence India (with new communal identities steadily being added to the system). While firmly
resisted by the leaders of the National Congress, the electoral arrangement was strongly supported by Jinnah as a device to protect the
Muslim minority—a device initially justified on communal-religious
grounds and later, more ambitiously, in terms of nationhood. In a
letter addressed to Gandhi in 1944, Jinnah stated provocatively: "We
maintain that Muslims and Hindus are two major nations by any definition or test of a nation. We are a nation . . . with our distinctive culture and civilization, language and literature, . . . legal laws and moral
codes, customs and calendar, history and traditions." Gandhi found it
relatively easy to debunk this "two-nation" argument by stressing the
many commonalities of language, customs, and historical experiences,
and also by pointing to the possible proliferation of Indian "nationalities" (from Sikhs and Parsis to Christians and tribals). There are indi-
cations that Jinnah himself did not quite embrace his own argument,

except for purely strategic reasons. Once the new state of Pakistan came into being, he abandoned his earlier rhetoric and urged Muslims and Hindus alike to act as "common citizens of the state."[24]

On the eve of India's independence, Gandhi reluctantly and with grave misgivings accepted partition, keenly sensing its dangers and its potential for unleashing massive violence. Despite his deep misgivings about centralized state structures, he also came to accept the need for a formal constitutional order for the country left after partition. In the days before his assassination, he was working on a draft constitution of the National Congress, lending his expertise to this project. But his heart was not fully in it, and he left the details of "nation-building" to such associates as Nehru and Vallabbhai Patel. What mattered to him more at that point, given the prevailing afflictions, were grassroots initiatives and the fostering of intercommunal solidarity. Shortly before his death, he launched an idea precisely designed to foster such solidarity: the transformation of the National Congress into a *"Loka Sevak Sangh,"* that is, a national organization for the service of the people or, better, of the servants of the people. Members of the *Sangh* were to settle in villages and to promote grassroots regeneration. In Parekh's account: they were "to 'awaken' people to their rights, sensitize them to the 'wrongs' done to them, and mediate between them and the official agencies of the state." Acting in this manner, they were "to win over the confidence and trust of the people, build up their strength, and set up a structure of moral authority paralleling the legal authority of the 'official' state."[25] As noted before, Gandhi during this period did not just formulate ideas or proposals, but exemplified their meaning in his practical conduct. Traveling on foot to distant villages and seeking to calm the fury of intercommunal violence was a concrete demonstration of the idea of *"Loka Sevak Sangh,"* showing what it meant for an erstwhile leader of the Congress to be a "servant of the people." In this practical testimonial Gandhi was pretty much alone. Sulking and frustrated by events, the former colonial power simply abandoned the subcontinent without providing any military or police protection for the masses of people trying to cross borders in their scramble for new homes. Nor did the man most responsible for the partition, Jinnah, lift a finger in order to douse the flames of communal mayhem. In the words of

B. R. Nanda: "If Jinnah had toured East Bengal or West Punjab, he might have helped in stopping the rot." However, such a suggestion would have been "laughed away by the League leader; consummate politician as he was, his political instincts rebelled against fasts and walking tours."[26]

LIBERAL STATE AND MULTICULTURALISM

India's struggle for independence is today only a distant memory; however, the issue of intercommunal and interfaith harmony remains as timely and urgent as ever. In this respect, Gandhi's involvement with the "Muslim question" offers numerous lessons for our contemporary era. The dominant tenor of this involvement was not only open-minded tolerance, but something deeper and more existential: affectionate respect and sympathy. As he once wrote in a foreword to *The Sayings of [Prophet] Muhammad:* "There will be no lasting peace on earth unless we learn not merely to tolerate but even to respect the other faiths as our own. A reverent study of the sayings of the different teachers of mankind is a step in the direction of such mutual respect."[27] What this means is that interfaith goodwill depends not only on information and acquisition of knowledge, but on a kind of participation in the inner life and spiritual strivings or aspirations of different faiths. Only through such participation, in Gandhi's view, was it possible to foster the emergence of a genuine and peaceful—though highly diversified or multidimensional—community of well-meaning people everywhere, a kind of ethical-spiritual *umma* or Ramarajya. In Margaret Chatterjee's apt words: "It was Gandhi's belief that there was a mysterious connivance at work between the creative powers in man and the divine forces in the universe. To release, through cooperation and mutual aid, the positive forces in man [humans] was at once to tap the divine source of energy." As she adds: "Religion envisaged as a way of life of the caring individual who participates in a multi-faith community, striving non-violently to establish a just society, would be close to the conception of the founding figures, saints and seers of the different traditions."[28]

Placing the accent on participation in a multi-faith community means to de-emphasize those aspects of religion which tend to divide peoples: theological dogmas or doctrines and external rituals. In the tradition of Sufism and *bhakti* devotion—but also in the tradition of Erasmus and other leaders in the age of Reformation—the core of religiosity is found in personal piety and ethical conduct, that is, in *orthopraxis* rather than *orthodoxy*. This practical aspect of Gandhi's religious outlook is well highlighted by Sheila McDonough when she writes that he conceived of religious life as "primarily personal, that is, of the individual using the images which come to him or to her to illuminate a particular situation." From a Gandhian pespective, religious images and symbols were to be understood "as catalysts which can stimulate direction and purpose in specific contexts." Given this purposive orientation (consonant with his role as a *karmayogin*), McDonough elaborates, there was "a strong element of practicality in Gandhi's make-up which comes out even in his attitude to religious teaching: it is good if it works; otherwise not." Hence, in his intercommunal or interfaith interactions, his invocation of both Hindu and Muslim vocabularies was always directed "towards shaping awareness of the adherents of the two communities in the direction of active involvement in a specific struggle." During his younger years, Gandhi studied intently the works of the Muslim reformer Shibli Numani, whose goal was to regenerate Islamic attitudes, especially in India. Among the heroes singled out in Shibli's writings were such figures as Caliph Umar and Abu Hanifa, who were characterized by "piety combined with the creative ability to devise new ways in the light of new circumstances." In his later years, Gandhi often found himself in a situation similar to that experienced by al-Ghazali, who had deplored the potential for corruption and violence, even among outwardly "religious" people. In McDonough's words: "Ghazali and Gandhi had both concluded that personal religious discipline was an essential basis for the sane and healthy transformation of the wider social order." For his part, Gandhi always interpreted fanatical Muslim violence as a "corrupt understanding of Islam," just as Hindu violence was a "corrupt understanding of Hinduism."[29]

Gandhi's attitudes and practices have relevance far beyond the original Indian context. Of crucial significance are his lessons for modern politics, and especially for the workings of a modern "liberal" regime. According to the mainstream construal of such a regime, liberalism denotes an exodus from "tradition," and especially from particular religious traditions, that is, the adoption of a neutral spectator view vis-à-vis all religious, spiritual, and even ethical beliefs and practices. Although "liberating" people (in a way) from traditional constraints, the adoption of this stance is also enormously debilitating for spiritual *orthopraxis* and ethics: removed from the complex agonies of human bonds, neutral liberals are also exiled (or exile themselves) from the challenges of intercommunal or interfaith engagement and from the travails of ethical-spiritual transformation. In this regard, Gandhi's dispute with Jinnah remains deeply instructive. As has been pointed out, Jinnah—despite his flirtation with Islamic faith and nationhood—preferred to retreat into the realm of legal procedures and formal state structures. Gandhi, by contrast, opted for a grassroots approach seeking to generate goodwill and "heart unity" between different communities. As he admonished his fellow workers at one point: "Islam is not a false religion. Let Hindus study it reverently and they will love it even as I do. . . . If Hindus set their house in order, I have not a shadow of doubt that Islam will respond in a manner worthy of its liberal traditions." At the end of his last fast, he again exhorted his assembled associates that they "should understand the meaning of what they read and have equal regard for all religions"— as had been his own lifelong practice. By doing so, they would be able "to learn from all" and hence "forget the communal differences and live together in peace and amity."[30]

What looms behind Gandhi's encounter with Jinnah is the broad and difficult question of the relation between the modern "state" apparatus and the complex fabric of civil society with its diverse customs and historical sedimentations. As previously indicated, Gandhi did not entirely reject modern state structures; toward the end of his life he even supported in designing the structures of the new Indian government—although he remained deeply suspicious of centralized state power. It was because of this deep-seated suspicion that he wished to supplement formal state authority with (or juxtapose it to) the civil-society based association or movement of the *Loka Sevak Sangh* entrusted with the task of moral and political awakening and ethical transformation. In his conception, the two institutions of the state and the *Sangh* were to be neither entirely divorced nor to be conflated, but to function in a tensional entwinement. The greatest danger resided in their fusion. In Parekh's presentation, the state by its very nature "wielded enormous legal authority and power"; if it were also operating as an institution invested with moral authority, citizens "would not only feel obliged to obey its laws blindly but also entrust it with the custody of their conscience." Hence, for Gandhi, some tension needed to be preserved to allow for constructive critique. While accepting the state as an "essentially *legal* institution," moral and spiritual authority, accruing from "the trust and confidence of the people," belonged in his view to civil-society associations, especially the *Sangh*.[31] Behind the tension between state and society another tension comes to the fore: that between reason (or mind) and heart—in the sense that the state for Gandhi was chiefly governed by legal rationality, while society was the realm of ethics and goodwill. To this extent one might say that Gandhi's recipe for the divisions of modern life was not only a "heart unity" but a "heart-and-mind" unity. This reading would concur with his statement in *Young India* (in 1931): "I have come to the fundamental conclusion that if you want something really important to be done, you must not merely satisfy the reason, you must move the heart also."[32]

In our present globalizing context, the idea of a "heart-and-mind" engagement and cooperation among peoples has particular salience. Faced with recurrent inter-ethnic and inter-religious conflicts— sometimes styled as "clashes of civilizations"—the world desperately needs a strengthening both of global norms and institutions and of intersocietal or cross-cultural goodwill. At the same time, given the upsurge of neo-colonialism and neo-imperialism in recent times, peoples everywhere need to recall Gandhi's suspicions regarding hegemonic state structures—suspicions based on the proclivity of power structures to foster corruption and to obstruct intercommunal cooperation (sometimes by intensifying communal conflicts). A case in point is the situation on the Indian subcontinent following partition: basically, long-standing intercommunal tensions have been reconstituted and intensified by interstate rivalries, with central state structures often fueling communal strife. In the words of Rajmohan

Gandhi, strenuous efforts are needed today to bridge the gaps "that distance Indians from Pakistanis and Bangladeshis," as well as those gaps "that will divide India's Hindus from their Muslim counterparts." In order to overcome these divisions, enlightened "statesmanship in the subcontinent's rulers and wisdom in the populace will be required." Returning to recent events in Gujarat, the Mahatma's grandson eloquently pleaded in favor of a renewed "heart-and-mind" engagement and cooperation:

> Huge tasks beckon: lifting from Gujarat the shroud of terror; restoring to Gujarat's Muslims a sense that their lives count and will be protected; . . . bringing some compensation and healing to the thousands damaged by the inferno; recalling Gujarat's Hindus to their tradition of a calm and honest Hinduism, a Hinduism that feels another's sorrow and does not need an enemy for its sustenance; and presenting alternatives to Gujarat's enraged youth, Hindu and Muslim.[33]

Confucianism and the Public Sphere

Five Relationships Plus One

Rudyard Kipling's famous adage about East and West appears obsolete today. In our age of globalization, the two cultural hemispheres not only "meet" but challenge and interpenetrate each other at a steadily accelerating rate. Not implausibly, this process has given rise to anticipations of a global civil society or civic culture, perhaps even of the rudiments of cosmopolis. Yet, despite such "one-world" visions, the interpenetration of hemispheres has not been entirely mutual or a two-way street. In large measure, contemporary globalization is the result of Western initiatives stretching from the Enlightenment to industrialization to the "information revolution." These initiatives, in turn, can be traced to a deeper trait or tendency inhabiting Western culture: the tendency to transgress or exceed itself, to prefer distance to proximity, new vistas to habitual ways.[1] In a palpable manner, this tendency has manifested itself historically in a steady sequence of expansions: from Alexander to the conquest of the Americas to later colonialism and imperialism. Seen from this angle, contemporary globalization—at least in part—follows a long-standing pattern. Confined to "Westernization," the ongoing process falls short of proper mutuality and, to this extent, still confirms Kipling's adage about the inability of hemispheres to meet.

Apart from its palpable manifestations, the mentioned shortfall surfaces in a number of more recessed cultural and spiritual arenas: including the relations between transcendence and immanence, between universal principles and local customs, between impartiality and concrete engagement. Given the close linkage between globalization and democratization, one cultural arena deserves special attention: the one that has to do with the relation between organized politics and the "life-world," between formal political structures and more informal or personal affairs. In this respect, Western culture has traditionally favored a neat differentiation and even separation: the separation of public from private domains, of uniform legal rules from diversified customs or—in classical terms—of *polis* from *oikos* (or household). By contrast, "Eastern" culture—meaning here prominent traditions in South and East Asia—has (on the whole) preferred to think of human life as a complex web of closely intertwined dimensions, a web in which impersonal and personal relations are mingled and fused, and where politics is seen as playing an important but by no means a privileged or autonomous role. Over the centuries, this difference of perspectives has proved to be a serious stumbling block in the mutual understanding between cultures, often fanning hostile recriminations (proving Kipling's thesis). In the following, an effort will be made to explore and hopefully clarify the difference by focusing on a significant strand in East Asian culture: the legacy of Confucianism. To set the stage for this examination, the opening section recalls prominent features of Western political philosophy from Aristotle to the present, especially features having to do with the distinction between public and private domains. It is against the backdrop of these features that Confucian classical and neoclassical teachings are next profiled, with an emphasis on the so-called "five relationships" (with their mingling of political and nonpolitical roles). By way of conclusion, reflections are offered on the prospects of mutual learning and hence of a possible rapprochement or "meeting" between East and West.

WESTERN POLITICAL THOUGHT: POLIS VERSUS NATURE

For many reasons, and especially for reasons of definitional clarity, Aristotle can rightly be considered the founder of Western political philosophy. To be sure, many of his teachings can be traced to earlier precedents, especially to Plato's *Republic* and *Laws*. In these Platonic texts, we find already an important "dividing line" or division between passions and philosophical knowledge, a division which gives rise to a pyramidal political structure in which reason or knowledge rules over ordinary dispositions; we also find the idea of a general rule of law superseding more localized customs or practices. Building on such precedents, Aristotle opens his *Politics* with a pyramidal design of human associations in which different households and villages coalesce and culminate in the superior and unique association of the *polis* or city. What links these different associations is their orientation toward "some good"; what distinguishes the *polis* from the rest is that it is "the particular association which is the most sovereign of all and, including all the others, pursues its aim [of the good] most fully and is directed toward the most sovereign of goods." Apart from aiming at the highest good, the *polis* also is distinguished by the fact that it is not simply a "natural" association, prompted by natural impulses, but rather one which—without being unnatural—has a moral and legal basis. Notwithstanding his portrayal of "man" as a "political animal," Aristotle does not exclude the role of deliberate design. Although there is "an immanent impulse in all men towards an association of this [political] type," he writes, "the man who first *constructed* such an association was none the less the greatest of benefactors." What emerges in the *polis* or city is the novel dimension of justice and lawfulness. For justice, he adds, "belongs to the *polis*"; in fact, justice "which is the determination of what is just, is an ordering of the political association."[2]

While admitting a certain continuity between household and *polis,* Aristotle's text resolutely underscores their difference. "It is a mistake to believe," we read, "that the 'statesman' [the *politikos* involved in a political association] is the same as the monarch of a kingdom, or the manager of a household, or the master of a number of slaves." Those who hold this mistaken view and assert their similarity maintain that the various roles differ from each other not with a "difference of kind," but only with a difference of degree or of numbers. Thus, someone who controls a few persons as slaves is said to be a "master"; someone who rules over more people is termed the "manager" of a household; and someone who governs a multitude is called a "statesman" [*politikos*] or a monarch. This view, Aristotle objects, "abolishes any real difference between a large household and a small *polis*"; and it also "reduces the difference between the *politikos* and the monarch [meaning someone who rules a kingdom like his household] to the mere fact that the latter has sole and uncontrolled authority, while the former exercises his authority in conformity with [publicly established] rules." Such a view "cannot be accepted as correct" because it neglects the "essential" difference between roles and associations. One aspect of this essential divergence was signaled before by the reference to the dimension of justice and lawfulness inherent in the *polis.* Another crucial feature emerges later in the text when Aristotle contrasts the equality prevailing among members of the *polis* with the asymmetrical or unequal character of relations in other associations. A properly constituted *polis,* he says, is "constructed on the principle that its members are equals and peers" and that they should "hold office by turns"—a principle which insures that no one is permanently superior or inferior and hence that everyone should conduct public affairs for the benefit of all, in accordance with justice: "Those regimes which foster the common benefit are *right* regimes, judged by the standards of absolute justice," while those privileging "the personal interest of the rulers are *wrong* regimes, or *perversions* of the right kinds."[3]

By contrast to the (relative) equality found in cities, all other human associations are marked by asymmetry or forms of super- and subordination. This is clearly the case in the household (*oikos*), which is ruled by the "manager" or *pater familias* and which is made up of three basic relationships: those of husband and wife, parent and child, and master and slave. To these three relations might be added a fourth: that of a king or monarch in a village where the latter is ruled like a larger household. As Aristotle states: A village is simply "a colony or offshoot from a family," and this is the reason "why each Greek city was originally ruled—as the peoples of the barbarian world still are—by kings," for "households are always monarchically governed by the eldest of kin" and villages likewise. In all these associations or group-ings, asymmetry or asymmetrical rulership prevails—which is simply the result of a general principle pervading nature at large. For, leaving aside inanimate matter—the text notes—it is "certainly possible to observe in animate beings the presence of a ruling authority." Thus, the soul rules (or is meant to rule) the body with "the authority of a master," while mind or reason rules over appetite with "the authority of a statesman or a monarch." Now, what holds good in the "inner life" of human beings "holds good outside" as well, meaning that the relation of soul to body carries over into the relation of "man to ani-mals"; likewise, the relation of male to female is "naturally that of the superior to the inferior, of the ruling to the ruled." With regard to the management of the household, Aristotle perceives various shadings of rulership. In general terms, the relation of husband to wife is one of unequal partnership, that of parents to children is like the rule of "a king over his subjects," while the relation of manager to slaves is complete mastery. On the other hand, a *politikos* in a city has only "authority over freemen and equals," that is, rules only periodically as *primus inter pares*.[4]

A central part of the *Politics* deals with the character of the city or *polis* as a "public sphere" inhabited by equal citizens. As Aristotle emphasizes, citizenship is not determined by physical residence or other purely "natural" criteria; nor is it rooted in purely "private" rights, such as the ability to sue or be sued in courts in matters relat-ing to private or personal status (marriage, testation, and the like). Rather, citizenship is anchored in public practices, namely, "sharing in the administration of justice and the holding of public office." As he adds or concedes, this definition applies "particularly and especially to citizens of a democracy," while citizens living under other regimes may only partly fit the description. To accommodate possible variations, the text offers a more general formulation, saying that anyone "who enjoys the right of sharing in deliberative or judicial office [for any period] attains thereby the status of a citizen [*polites*] of his state." Being jointly committed to the goal of justice and lawfulness, citizens in a *polis* are assumed to transgress the narrow limits of private/personal self-interest; to this extent, without sharing ties of kinship, they are linked together by a civic bond or relationship: the bond of friendship (or something close to a friendly disposition). In Aristotle's words, by contrast to people who know only how to rule or how to obey, citizens exhibit a more judicious quality: the "spirit of friendship" which is the proper "temper" of a political community; for where enmity prevails instead of friendship, people "will not even share the same path." As one should note, friendship among equals in the city does not entirely obviate or cancel asymmetrical rulership; for the "freedom" of equal citizens is "naturally" superior both to the unfreedom of noncitizens at home and to unfree "barbarians" abroad. As the text states somewhat harshly, quoting an earlier poet: "Meet it is that barbarous people should be governed by the Greeks—the assumption being that barbarian and slave are by nature one and the same."[5]

In large measure, subsequent political philosophy in the West is a series of variations on Aristotelian themes. On the whole, the breach between public and private domains, between *polis* and *oikos* is maintained and even steadily widened—without affecting the basic subordination of the latter under the former. Under the aegis of Aristotle's pupil Alexander, the structure of the *polis* was changed and expanded into a far-flung empire comprising much of the Middle East. Alexander, Ernest Barker writes, embarked on building an empire "in which he should be equally lord of Greeks and Persians," a move which inaugurated "the idea of the equality of all men—urban or rural, Greek or barbarian—in a *cosmopolis*." What Barker does not mention is that this empire still meant the rule of Greeks (or sufficiently assimilated non-Greeks) over large subordinated populations, while simultaneously bending civic equality to the whim of imperial power. The idea of civic equality in a cosmopolis—or rather, an empire—became later a central tenet of the Stoics, who, according to Plutarch, held that "men should not live their lives in so many civic republics" but "should reckon *all* humans as their fellow-citizens under one order (*cosmos*)," an order coinciding basically with the Roman Empire. During the Christian Middle Ages, this notion of cosmopolis was transformed into the vision of a universal or "catholic" Christendom—although concrete conditions on the ground required many local adjustments. The apex of medieval political thought saw the attempt to combine Aristotle's teachings in the *Politics* with universal Christian aspirations—an attempt which was at the heart of the work of Thomas Aquinas. In the words of Ernest Barker, Thomas's work

> united some of the essential doctrines of the *polis* with the doctrine and practice of cosmopolis. It was through this fusion that there passed into the general thought of the later Middle Ages some of the essential doctrines of the *Politics*—the doctrine that law is the true sovereign, and that governments are servants of the law; the doctrine that there is a fundamental difference between the lawful monarch and the tyrant who governs by his arbitrary will; the doctrine that there is a right inherent in the people, by virtue of their collective capacity of judgment, to elect their rulers and to call them to account.[6]

The onset of modernity brought a number of significant innovations. Among these, the most important was a deepening of the rift between *polis* and *oikos*, now formulated as the distinction between the political state or commonwealth and the "state of nature"; a corollary of this change was the bracketing of the former's lingering naturalness in favor of its constructive design under the aegis of the "social contract." Both moves were dramatically inaugurated by Thomas Hobbes. In the very opening pages of his *Leviathan,* and also of his book on *The Citizen* (*De Cive*), Hobbes takes aim at Aristotle and medieval "schoolmen" following him, and especially at the assumption of the naturalness of politics (captured in the phrase "political animal")—an assumption, he writes, which "though received by most, is yet certainly false and an error proceeding from our too slight contemplation of human nature." Instead of being nature's design, the *polis* or political community for Hobbes is entirely an artifact or artificial construct, which he also calls an "artificial animal"; for by art or design is created "that great Leviathan called a commonwealth or state (in Latin *civitas*) which is but an artificial man" and in which "sovereignty is an artificial soul." The method of construction, however, is by way of contract, through those "pacts and covenants by which the parts of the body politic were at first made, set together and united."[7] Under somewhat changed auspices, Hobbes's initiatives were continued by John Locke—with an opening salvo against naturalness. The waning years of the medieval empire had produced various political ambiguities or confusions; prominent among them was the confusion of *polis* and *oikos* or of political rulership and household management. Prototypically, this merger was defended by Robert Filmer, whose *Patriarcha* equated kingship with the role of *pater familias*. Attacking this equation, Locke's first *Treatise* briskly demolished the notion of "paternal government" or "fatherly authority" in politics, guiding his readers back to the more customary way of forming regimes: "by contrivance and the consent of men making use of their reason to unite together into society."[8]

Locke's second *Treatise* eloquently affirmed the artificiality of the *polis,* its origin in rational design—in a manner which, for all practical purposes, became canonical in modern Western political thought. Taking its cues from Hobbes, the text underscored the bifurcation of nature and commonwealth, stating that "those who are united into one body, and have a common established law and judicature to appeal to . . . are in civil society one with another," whereas "those who have no such common appeal, I mean on earth, are still in the state of nature." The transition from the latter to former condition is the work of deliberate construction, more specifically of a social contract or covenant erecting a common government with a shared rule of law. For, Locke insists, being "by nature all free, equal and independent," nobody can be assumed to be naturally subjected to political power except through "his own consent"—which is done "by agreeing with other men to join and unite into a community for their comfortable, safe, and peaceable living," and by "putting himself under an obligation to every one of that society to submit to the determination of the majority." In keeping with this basic postulate, later sections of the *Treatise* reinforce the distinction between "paternal," "political," and "despotical" power—by claiming that the first (of parents over

children) is granted by nature, while the second is the result of "voluntary agreement," and the last of subjugation and forfeiture (of rights).[9]
As one should add, in the wake of these teachings, Locke's "liberalism"
gave rise to another distinctive feature of modern Western life as compared with classical antiquity: the emergence of a novel "civil society"
wedged between *polis* and *oikos*. Congruent with the emphasis on construction and contractual agreement, this society became the driving
engine in the development of the market economy (or capitalism) and,
concomitantly, in the advancement of modern science, industry, and
technology.

   This is not the place to recount in detail the story of post-Lockean
political thought. Suffice it to say that, although many of Locke's claims
have been challenged—including the idea of a "state of nature"—the
overall structure of his argument has remained largely intact. To illustrate the mixture of continuity and discontinuity, one may wish to
glance briefly at a recent political thinker not usually associated with
the Lockean legacy: Hannah Arendt. Among her many contributions,
Arendt is well known for her vindication of the *vita activa* or active participation in the "public sphere." An opening chapter in *The
Human Condition* deals precisely with the distinction between *polis*
and *oikos* or what she calls the "public" and the "private" realms. In
large measure, this distinction coincides with that between freedom
and necessity or between equal public status and asymmetrical personal relations. As she writes, the distinctive trait of the "household
sphere" is that its members are "driven by their wants and needs,"
especially the need for survival; hence, "natural community" in the
household is "born of necessity." By contrast, the "realm of the *polis*"
is the "sphere of freedom," and since ancient times political thought
has taken for granted "that freedom is exclusively located in the political realm" composed of "equals" or peers. An important innovative feature of Arendt's work is her differentiation not only between
polis and *oikos* (or between "action" and "labor" geared to survival
needs), but also between public action and "work" or instrumental
design—where the latter term comprises both economic production
and the fabrication of technical artifacts. One of her major complaints
about modern politics, in fact, is the growing blurring of differences
evident in the modern "rise of the social," that is, the progressive

colonization of the public sphere first by *"homo faber"* (or construction) and then by *"animal laborans"* (or consumerism). In its classical sense, Arendt insists, politics was never a mere adjunct of "society": "a society of the faithful, as in the Middle Ages, or a society of property-owners, as in Locke, . . . or a society of producers, as in Marx, or a society of jobholders [consumers], as in our own."[10]

THE CONFUCIAN FIVE RELATIONSHIPS

Arendt's complaint about the blurring of domains might also have been addressed to the East Asian context, particularly the legacy of Confucianism. As previously indicated, Asian culture (on the whole) has resisted the neat division or demarcation of domains, preferring to see human and social life instead as a complex web of relationships, as a holistic fabric of elements held together by some kind of inner balance. This difference is particularly important with regard to politics or the "public sphere." Although acknowledging its function, Asian culture has never assigned to politics the commanding height over society that was allotted to it in the Western tradition (even when its supremacy was subordinated to the still more commanding heights of philosophy and theology). In large measure, this command structure had to do with the presumed supremacy of reason over passion, of symmetry over asymmetry, of general rules or principles over particular customs or practices. What renders cultural comparison— including the comparative study of political thought—so difficult is the sea-change that needs to be negotiated: the fact that one is dealing not with isolated elements but with symbolic "ensembles" or clusters—in other words, with holistic language games which cannot simply be collapsed into each other (without being utterly incommensurable).[11]

In classical Confucian teachings, politics is by no means neglected, but is inserted into a larger ensemble: the so-called "five relationships" (*wu-lun*) of husband and wife, father and son (or parent and child), older sibling and younger sibling, ruler and minister, and friend and friend. All these relationships are at a first glance personal relations involving a certain closeness or proximity. As can readily be seen, the first two dyads (husband/wife and parent/child) correspond to two relations in Aristotle's conception of the household or *oikos*. Confucian teachings add a third "household" relation (sibling/sibling) not thematized by Aristotle, while entirely omitting the dyad of master and slave—an aspect which will be taken up a bit later. The only "political" relation is that between ruler and minister—but the relation is not elevated above others and certainly not stylized as a "public sphere" in which reason and equal freedom would rule over passions and private asymmetries. The only general (or at least generalizable) relation is that between friend and friend, more precisely between older and younger friend; but the accent is again on proximity rather than broader public engagement (in the Aristotelian sense of public *philia*). Thus, society in the Confucian view seems to be segmented and highly particularized, in contradistinction to the pyramidal structure of Western politics. Moreover, all five relationships are characterized by asymmetry or a degree of super- and subordination, giving the impression to Western observers of an assortment of quasi-feudal hierarchies. In larger measure, this impression is at the root of the "Orientalist" view of Asian culture as static and confining—predicated on the Western equation of progress and development with growing individual autonomy and rationalization.

Although plausible at first blush, the Orientalist view appears deeply misguided. For one thing, it forces Asian thought into a set of categories not properly germane to it. Although none of the Confucian relationships may be "public" or general in the Western sense, they also are not simply "private" or particularistic (which is merely the reverse side of the same coin). The tendency to "privatize" or particularize Confucian concepts has been ably criticized by Herbert Fingarette in several of his writings, especially in *Confucius—The Secular as Sacred*. As he notes in that text, Western students of the *Analects* may be tempted to place the locus of Confucian conduct in "subjective feelings and attitudes," that is, in private psychological dispositions (in contrast to rational principles). Countering this temptation, Fingarette maintains that the thought expressed in the *Analects* is not at all "based on psychological notions." The point is not that Confucius deliberately meant to exclude reference to "the inner psyche," but rather that the reference "never entered his mind." As an antidote to privatization, Fingarette refers to the role of ceremony or ritual in channeling human conduct—what in the *Analects* is called *li*. Such ceremony, he states, is not simply an external form but a genuine style of life, a style which is both individual and societal, both personal and impersonal or super-personal; ultimately it confers meaning and dignity on human life (even a kind of "sacred dignity"). This aspect also points to the profound relationality or trans-personality of human conduct in Confucius's teachings, a quality eloquently expressed in these lines of the *Analects:*

> You want to establish yourself, then seek to establish others. You wish to advance your standing, then advance that of others. From what is near to you to seize the analogy [i.e., to take the neighbor or other as yourself]—this is the way of *jen* [goodness, humaneness].[12]

As most commentators agree, the feature in Confucius's teachings that most resembles a general or public principle is *jen* or the virtue of goodness or humaneness. According to the eminent Chinese expert Wing-tsit Chan, *jen* in fact should be seen as a general virtue "which is basic, universal, and the source of all specific virtues."[13] Yet, as one must also realize, *jen* is not simply an abstract maxim but always functions in human relationships which are concrete and diversified and shaped, at least in part, by particular customs, ceremonies, or rituals. This complex character of *jen* has been prominently elucidated by Tu Wei-ming, who treats the notion as a "living metaphor," that is, a metaphor for ethical and properly humanized ways of life. "There is no assumption in the *Analects*," he writes, "like the one found in the objectivists' claim that 'all truly reasonable men will always finally agree'" or concur on a general rational principle; rather, it is taken for granted that "reasonable men of diverse personalities will have differing visions of the way" (*tao*) and follow different paths in practicing *jen*. This diversity of paths, however—Tu adds—should not be confused with individual arbitrariness or the pursuit of "projects" suiting private whims. Rather, practicing or cultivating *jen* requires a "continuous process of symbolic exchange through the sharing of communally cherished values with other selves." To the extent that the

Analects recognize a "self" or selfhood, it is a *relational* self or a "self as center of relationships" rather than an "isolable individual" pursuing random goals; accordingly, cultivation of self or "self-realization" is impossible "except in matrices of human converse" or interaction. To this extent, fostering goodness or humaneness is not a "lonely struggle" nor a quest for "inner truth" which would be "isolable from an 'outer' or public realm." Instead of denoting a purely subjective search, *jen* as a basic virtue depends both on self-scrutiny and a "meaningful communal" engagement—which Tu also describes as engagement in a "fiduciary community."[14]

Extending his analysis from the *Analects* to the neo-Confucian period, Tu Wei-ming stresses the continued importance of relationality or trans-personality—despite a steady deepening of inner-directedness coupled with a growing metaphysical universalism (in part due to Buddhist influences). In his view, neo-Confucian thought can best be grasped as a twofold process: "a continuous deepening of one's subjectivity and an uninterrupted broadening of one's sensitivity." Self-cultivation still implies a communal bond, but now entails a series of tensions and paradoxes. In order to fully plumb its inwardness, the self must simultaneously overcome itself and its self-centered structure. Accordingly, to deepen one's subjectivity requires "an unceasing struggle to eliminate selfish and egoistic desires" while also extending one's sensitivity or receptivity to broadening horizons of the world. In Tu's words, the neo-Confucian perspective on fostering goodness/humaneness (*jen*) involves "a dynamic interplay between contextualization and decontextualization"—which can also be described as "a dialectic of structural limitation and procedural freedom" operative at each stage of the ethical quest. Hence, the self as a "center of relationships" finds itself simultaneously in the grip of an ongoing decentering or displacement—which never cancels, however, the limits of time and place. Just as self-cultivation acquires self-overcoming, so cultivation of family and other relations demands a transgression of parochial attachments such as "nepotism, racism, and chauvinism"—and ultimately a transgression of a narrow "anthropocentrism" in the direction of the "mutuality of Heaven and man and the unity of all things" (a mutuality captured succinctly in the famous "Western Inscription" of Chang Tsai in the eleventh century).[15]

From a Western perspective, probably the least appealing aspect of Confucian relationships is their inherent asymmetry or inequality manifest chiefly in the so-called "three bonds" (*san-kang*): the dependency of the son on the father, of the wife on her husband, and of the minister on the ruler. As the sociologist Robert Bellah has chidingly remarked, filial piety and subordination in China "became absolutes," with the model of "familial authority" eventually spilling over into political and all other relationships.[16] Responding to this charge, Tu Wei-ming is at pains to disentangle the salient issues. As he points out, first of all, it is misleading to suggest that the father-son—or, more generally, the parent-child—relationship "provides a model for the other four." Above all, a common mistake made in interpreting traditional Chinese culture—a mistake encouraged by Orientalist leanings—is the tendency to equate the "political" ruler-minister dyad with the father-son relationship (an equation which would replicate the kind of "parental government" extolled by Robert Filmer). What is neglected in this equation is the difference—acknowledged even in classical Confucianism—between "naturalness" and choice, more specifically between natural, kinship-based "affinity" (*ch'in*) and political "righteousness" (*i*). Although conceding a hierarchical element in all five relationships, Tu insists on distinguishing between despotic, whimsical, and self-centered control, on the one hand, and ethical, benevolent, and other-regarding interaction, on the other. In the case of filial piety—widely regarded as the key relation—the father or parent cannot become despotic without forfeiting the "name" or title of parent; hence, "the impression of the father as the socializer, the educator, and thus the authoritarian disciplinarian is superficial, if not mistaken." In terms of Confucian ethics, the father is expected to act "fatherly," so that the son can act in a properly "filial" manner. Differently put: "The son's filiality is conceived as a response to the father's kindness." For this to happen, the father must "set an example for the son as a loving and respectable person before he can reasonably expect his son to love and respect him."[17]

What needs to be remembered, with regard to all five relationships, is the pervasive role of *jen* (in conjunction with *li*): that is, their insertion into a holistic web geared toward humaneness, humanization or self-transformation. Without entirely leveling human bonds, this orientation softens or attenuates whatever asymmetry may prevail. In Tu's words: "The value that underlies the five relations is not dependency but 'reciprocity' (pao)" or mutuality. Specifically, the "filiality" of the son or children is reciprocated by the love and "compassion" of the parent, the loyalty of the minister by the justice and "fair-mindedness" of the ruler, and so on. Preeminently, the aspect of mutuality is exemplified in friendship, which represents "a reciprocal relation of par excellence"; for "it is mutuality rather than dependency that defines 'trust' (hsin) between friends." In a quasi-Aristotelian manner, Confucian-style friendship is not oriented toward an extrinsic goal, such as economic gain or social advantage, but rather toward humanity or mutual humanization. In Tu's view, the core of such a relation is captured in the notion of a "fiduciary community" which is predicated not on domination or manipulation but on trust and reciprocal learning. To this extent, the Confucian "way of the friend" (yu-tao) is closely connected with the "way of the teacher" (shih-tao), for both friendship and the teacher-student relation exist for the sake of personal and transpersonal transformation. The close linkage between friendship and learning or humane transformation is stressed in the very opening lines of the Analects, where we read: "To learn and at proper times to repeat what one has learned, is that not after all a pleasure? That friends should come to visit one from afar, is this not after all delightful?"[18]

FIVE RELATIONSHIPS PLUS ONE?

What emerges from the preceding discussion is an image of Confucianism, and especially of the five relationships, starkly at odds with Orientalist predilections. Above all, the discussion calls into question the tendency of reducing "political" (ruler-minister) relations to a case of filial piety, in a manner replicating Filmer's model; it also challenges the confusion of relationship with dependency or domination. In a broader vein, this challenge undermines the widespread equation of traditional Asian-style politics with "Oriental despotism." (Here it may also be appropriate to recall the absence of the master-slave dyad in the traditional Confucian canon.) To be sure, recognition of the ethical, transformative qualities of Confucianism does not by itself remove the distance separating the latter from the trajectory of Western political thought (outlined above). Occasionally, strong cross-cultural sympathies have tempted scholars to deny or at least minimize this cultural distance; eager to overcome East-West barriers, they were occasionally led to champion a kind of global merger or synthesis neglectful of traditional differences. Thus, in several of their writings, David Hall and Roger Ames have underscored the affinities between traditional Chinese thought and modern Western ideas, especially between Confucianism, on the one hand, and John Dewey's and Jean-Paul Sartre's teachings, on the other. More recently, in a study titled *Democracy of the Dead,* they have detected traces of Western democracy latent in traditional Chinese culture—a finding buttressing their argument that "John Dewey's pragmatic vision of democracy" seems "best suited to engage the realities of Chinese social practice and to support the realization of 'Confucian democracy' in China."[19]

Although well-meaning and engaging, the argument appears precipitous and unconvincing in many ways. Its main drawback is its effect on cross-cultural interaction, where the assumption of synthesis tends to obviate the need for mutual learning. In this respect, Tu Wei-ming seems more forthright when he candidly acknowledges the shortcomings of traditional Asian ways of life—not for the sake of Orientalizing Asia but in order to place differences on the table for open debate and negotiation. Even while acknowledging its ethical virtues, Tu writes, "we cannot ignore the historical fact that Confucian China was unquestionably a male-dominated society." Throughout the centuries, "the education of the son received much more attention than the education of the daughter, the husband was far more influential than the wife, and the father's authority significantly surpassed that of the mother." Generally speaking, the status of women was deplorable in all stages of their development: in their dependency on the father in youth, on the husband in marriage, and on the son in old age. In this and many other domains, neo-Confucianism introduced important changes, especially by cultivating a deepened individuality as well as a potential universalism. If we take this innovation seriously as "a viable persuasion," Tu states, we must criticize an

outmoded Confucian and neo-Confucian ideology "in order to retrieve the deep meaning of its universal humanistic teachings"; even
if neo-Confucian thinkers (like Chu Hsi or Wang Yang-ming) did not
adopt a conscious policy of emancipating women, "their legacy speaks
loudly in favor of such a tendency." All this does not mean an exit from
human relationships in favor of an atomistic individualism. The
"authentic approach" for Tu is "neither a passive submission to structural limitations nor a Faustian activation of procedural freedom but
a conscientious effort to make the dynamic interaction between them
a fruitful dialectic for self-realization."[20]

In our globalizing age, it appears urgent to take up Tu's suggestion
and to explore the dynamic interaction not only between individual
and community but, more broadly, between East and West or between
Confucian teachings and modern Western democracy. To facilitate this
exchange, some concessions need to be made on both sides. On the
side of Asian or Confucian thought, a helpful concession would be
the modification of the traditional five relationships (*wu-lun*) through
the addition of a further, more impersonal relation: that between citizen and citizen in a shared public sphere and under a common rule
of law. Such a relation necessarily transgresses or cuts through the
various "familial" relations and also profoundly modifies the ruler-
minister dyad. In some ways, Confucian thought is already partially
prepared for this concession by virtue of the neo-Confucian innovations highlighted by Tu Wei-ming: especially the deepening of individual subjectivity and the incipient universalization of the framework
of humaneness (*jen*). A further indigenous support for the change can
be found in Asian Buddhism, especially the Ch'an (or Zen) variety,
which for nearly two millennia existed side by side with Confucian
scholarship. In the tradition of Asian Buddhism, the human self as the
"center of [concrete] relationships" tends to be evacuated in favor of
a "no-self" (*anatman*) or an "empty," not contextually limited self
(*sunyata*)—an evacuation which is at the same time the gateway to
liberation and to trans-contextual self-realization. In the words of
Masao Abe, the renowned scholar of Mahayana Buddhism (especially
of Ch'an/Zen teachings), by penetrating to the "negation of negation"
or emptiness, "the ground of human subjectivity is transformed from
mere [empirical] self to the 'no-self', which is another term for the true

self"; emptiness is thus revealed "at the deepest core or at the bottom-less depth" of selfhood. As he adds, with a moral-political edge: "In awakening to the true Self, one breaks through the ego and simultaneously overcomes the source of world evil and historical evil [namely, oppression and exploitation], thereby opening up the true path which enlivens both self and others."[21]

Apart from the support of indigenous Asian traditions, the enlargement of Confucian relations is dictated by important social and political developments in our time. Three such currents deserve special mention. One factor is the change of Asian countries from agricultural to incipiently commercial and industrial societies. An important consequence of this change is the rise of a commercial "civil society" in China and other Asian countries—an aspect which is the topic of widespread scholarly discussion both inside and outside of Asia. For present purposes, it must suffice to say that, as a corollary of modernization, social interactions necessarily transgress local exchange relations in the direction of a large-scale, impersonal market—whose impersonality steadily increases with the advances of globalization. The rise of this market, however, brings to the fore motivations of profit-seeking and capital accumulation which can no longer be contained by the ethics of personal relations thematized in the Confucian canon. It is precisely due to the unleashing of market forces that modern societies—Confucian or otherwise—require the counterweight of a public sphere able to contain or regulate these forces through a common rule of law. Another, equally salient factor is the rise of the modern nation-state and the fact that all Asian societies have been refashioned on the model of Western nation-state structures. With regard to Confucian Asia, this means that traditional segmental or holistic arrangements have been replaced by the pyramidal structure prevalent in Western politics—a change strengthening the hand of governing elites and central bureaucracies. Again, a robust public sphere is required to counterblanace the overbearing and sometimes totalitarian ambitions of nation-state leaders and their officials.[22]

The most important factor speaking in favor of strong "citizen" relations, however, is the character of modern democracy—to the extent that the latter is seen as rule of the people or a regime in which common people are both rulers and ruled. In their capacity as "rulers," common people clearly cannot only relate to particular "ministers," but must cultivate broader, more impersonal relations with each other—which, again, can happen only in a viable public sphere. Much can be learned in this respect from recent discussions of citizenship and democracy in Western literature. As John Pocock observes, commenting on the "ideal" of citizenship from ancient times to the present, active membership in a *polis* is of a special kind: it is a relationship "in which speech takes the place of blood [or kinship], and acts of shared decision take the place of vengeance." Since, in a democratic *polis,* citizens both rule and are ruled, a public sphere is required where "citizens join each other in making decisions" in such a way that each member "respects the authority of the others" and "all join in obeying" the jointly established rule of law.[23] To be sure, in modern democratic politics, the public sphere can only with difficulty be confined to citizens narrowly defined. Given its emphasis on rational equality (as contrasted with "natural" differences and dependencies), the idea of the public sphere necessarily unsettles or contests ethnic as well as nation-state boundaries; its built-in universalizing thrust encourages the progressive amalgamation of civic (or citizens') rights with broader, ultimately cosmopolitan human rights. In the words of Norberto Bobbio, the Italian political philosopher, one can observe a steady widening or univeralizing of public concerns: beginning with the Stoics, it "proceeds through the doctrine of natural law to reach Kantian morals, or a rationalized Christianity, which according to its fundamental maxim means 'to respect the human being as a person'." Ultimately this universalist trajectory points toward "the establishment of an, albeit ideal, *civitas maxima,* or the city for all"—a goal intimated by the Universal Declaration of Human Rights and similar initiatives.[24]

To be sure, tendencies of this kind do not cancel the simultaneous need for more concrete personal relationships situated in space and time. Precisely the universalizing (and transcendentalizing) bent of Western modernity calls for a counterweight mindful of human finitude and of the welter of differentiated loyalties which structure human life. With regard to citizenship and the public sphere, this need is increasingly recognized by Western political theorists otherwise wedded to a (broadly) liberal tradition. Thus, in Gershon Shafir's perceptive account, the Western conception of citizenship expresses "a desire to create comprehensive membership frameworks capable of replacing the weakened communities of traditional society." Yet, even (and especially) today, "the aspiration to recover small and close-knit communities continues to coexist with the new citizenship frameworks," with some prominent thinkers even calling for differentiated or "multiple citizenships" or at least for a closer attunement of citizenship to communal differences.[25] It is precisely at this point that the Confucian legacy of five relationships is bound to prove its continued importance and salience, especially when the accent is placed on its ethical and transformative qualities. Among these relations, the primary role as a bridge-builder between cultural traditions must be allocated to friendship or the friend-friend relationship, particularly if the latter is allowed to broaden and to penetrate into active public life. Here the genuine possibility of an East-West engagement comes into view—an engagement where both sides can freely learn from each other in a spirit of mutual friendship and sympathy. To quote again the opening lines of the *Analects:*

> To learn and at proper times to repeat what one has learned, is that not after all a pleasure? That friends should come to visit one from afar, is this not after all delightful?

Religion, Ethics, and Liberal Democracy
A Possible Symbiosis?

The oral tradition of Islam—the so-called *"hadith"*—contains a statement by Prophet Muhammad regarding religious faith. In response to a question about the basic nature of such faith, the Prophet is reported to have said "self-restraint and gentleness"—which is a surprising statement in many respects.[1] For one thing, the statement does not refer to any specific content of faith, to any religious doctrine or creed. In the language of some contemporary theologians, the saying is not concerned with *orthodoxy*, but rather with a proper mode of conduct or *orthopraxis*. More importantly still, the saying conflicts with an image, popular in the West, of Islam as a basically aggressive or belligerent faith—an image which, among its sponsors, has triggered an equally belligerent Islamophobia. To be sure, the Prophet's statement is not at all surprising if placed alongside central teachings of other world religions. Thus, in Buddhism, the path to liberation/ salvation is said to be paved by self-abandonment or self-overcoming (*anatman*)—an effort which, in turn, ushers forth great gentleness or deep compassion (*karuna*), the willingness to assist "all beings however innumerable they may be." On their part, Christians may recall the so-called "beatitudes" when Jesus praised "the meek or gentle [*mites*], for they shall inherit the earth" and also the "merciful or compassionate [*misericordes*], for they shall obtain mercy." They may also recall the passage in Paul's letter to Timothy where he states that "God did not give us a spirit of timidity but a spirit of power and love and self-restraint."[2]

Sayings of this kind—which could be augmented by many others from different traditions—stand in sharp contrast with politics as practiced in most parts of the world; in fact, an unbridgeable gulf seems to separate the two domains. The gulf is clearly evident in modern Western societies, where the process of "secularization" has tended to expurgate politics of any remnants of religious faith. The trend is particularly pronounced in modern liberal democracies, given their attachment to liberal "neutrality": the doctrine that politics or the public realm must be completely neutral or indifferent vis-à-vis religious (and other substantive) beliefs. In some cases, as is well known, the doctrine has been constitutionally stylized as a "wall of separation" which needs to remain "unimpregnable." The situation is aggravated by the invasion or colonization of the vacant public space by perspectives which are starkly at odds with, and even hostile to, religious as well as ethical teachings. Most prominent among these colonizing inroads is the equation of politics with private business or else with military warfare. Under the auspices of liberal market principles, politics or the public weal tends to be reduced to the dictates of economic self-interest, to the "maximization" of private benefits at the lowest possible cost—with little or no attention being given to ethical or religious concerns. Even more damaging to these concerns is the military colonization of politics. When politics is briskly defined as the confrontation between "friend and enemy," public affairs are placed under the aegis of military campaigns—perhaps with the proviso that "outright" warfare is simply the continuation of politics by other (more violent) means. Similar results derive from the equation of politics with power or struggle for power. When a leading international expert declares power to be "the universal and everlasting essence of all politics," he implicitly grants highest honors to the most powerful—while the sayings of Jesus and Muhammad are effectively expunged.[3]

The point here is not to call into question liberal democracy or the separation of religion and politics—as long as by "religion" one means an established church or an official religious doctrine. Given the diversity of churches and religious creeds in modern societies, the public square can surely not be monopolized by one doctrine or clerical institution. However, things are different on the level of practical conduct. How can a Christian—someone who sincerely follows Jesus's teachings in his everyday conduct—be expected suddenly to forget about these teachings when entering the world of politics? Likewise, how can a Buddhist or a Muslim whose ordinary life is governed by self-restraint and compassion be assumed to switch suddenly in politics to rampant self-interest and belligerence? Strictly applied, liberal doctrine in this respect seems to lead to a Jekyll-and-Hyde existence, in any case to large-scale social schizophrenia. The danger is all the greater given the "democratic" component of liberal democracy: the fact that ordinary people at large are assumed to be the ultimate rulers and hence to function both as rulers and ruled, as politicians and private citizens. Particularly in democracies, there is an urgent need to synchronize modes of conduct: that is, to encourage and enable people to apply congruent standards in their public and private lives, both as rulers and as ruled. Earlier phases of Western political thought still exhibited a strong concern with the moral character of "rulers," a concern manifest in an extensive literature dealing with the proper education of "princes." The present chapter, in its first section, reviews one prominent treatise taken from this literature: Erasmus's *The Education of a Christian Prince,* a text which will be compared briefly with similar writings found in other cultural traditions. The second part turns to a discussion of Erasmus's text by a leading contemporary democratic theorist (Norberto Bobbio) who concludes, regretfully, that some of its teachings are not applicable to "real-life" politics. By way of conclusion, I attempt to show that the teachings are indeed applicable to, and even required by, democratic politics, using as my chief witness the Mahatma Gandhi, whose lifework illustrates the linkage of self-rule and compassion.

ERASMUS ON THE EDUCATION OF RULERS

Nurturing the moral character or fiber of rulers is a vital need at all times and places; yet, it is often disparaged for various reasons. For one thing, skeptics may refer to the absence or shortage of agreed-upon norms of conduct—a point which derives some plausibility from the evidence of cultural variations. However, the same skeptics are prone to protest, irrespective of cultural differences, whenever their own rights or personal interests are unfairly curtailed—and they will do so not merely on the basis of dislike, but on moral grounds. Another point frequently heard is that moral conduct cannot be legislated or imposed (so to speak) from "on high"—which again has some plausibility given the difference between properly motivated conduct and legally sanctioned or coerced behavior. However, the real issue here is not legislation of morals but rather persuasion and education—an endeavor which is bound to be all the more effective if accompanied by the exemplary conduct of teachers. A further point often raised concerns the presumed traditionalism of the topic: the aspect that much of the literature in this field is tailored to the education of monarchs, princes, and other potentates. In a time of liberal democracy, one hears, this focus is basically obsolete—an objection which is profoundly mistaken. Precisely in a democracy where ordinary people are the ultimate rulers, the conduct and moral character of these rulers cannot be viewed as irrelevant. In fact, great vigilance on this score is needed at all times. Wherever the rulers of a regime are unjust, violent, or corrupt, the welfare and even survival of populations are in jeopardy; in a democracy whose rulers exhibit the same character traits, the fate of minorities and dissenters is inevitably at risk.

In the traditional literature on the training of rulers—the so-called "mirror of princes" literature—Erasmus's *The Education of a Christian Prince* (*Institutio principis Christiani*, 1516) stands out for its simplicity and its eloquent but sober style. In this treatise, Erasmus does not seek to propagate radically new or unfamiliar moral standards; many of the views expressed can be found in earlier texts on the subject (stretching from antiquity to the Renaissance). On this score, his treatise is sometimes criticized as being conventional and insufficiently innovative. However, this criticism is hardly judicious. The book and its moral instructions were addressed to actual, not imaginary princes, that is, to political rulers or professional politicians—who, by and large, can be assumed to be slow learners. Confronting such rulers with unheard of or unfamiliar principles would scarcely make a dent in their behavior; by contrast, the chances of education are improved if instruction appeals to customary moral teachings and especially to principles which political rulers, in their better moments, might themselves approve or at least seem to cherish. Erasmus was not unaware of the advantages of the latter approach and deliberately adopted it in his political writings. As he noted in one of his letters, it was his belief that

> no other way of correcting a prince is as efficacious as offering the pattern of a truly good prince under the guise of flattery to them, for thus do you present virtues and disparage faults in such a manner that you seem to urge them to the former while restraining them from the latter.[4]

The historical context of the treatise was turbulent and fraught with grave dangers. As previously indicated, this was the time of the emerging European nation-states, with powerful national monarchies competing for preeminence. In addition to political rivalries, the age was ripe with religious, social, and economic conflicts—which, a century later, would throw Europe into a paroxysm of destruction. At the time of the book's first appearance, Spain was ruled by Philip I, to whose son, Prince Charles—the future Emperor Charles V—the text was dedicated. In England, Henry VIII was at the helm—an impetuous and headstrong ruler (to whom Erasmus, nonetheless, dispatched one of the first copies). France was under the reign of Francis I and Germany governed by a variety of princes. Barely a year after the book appeared, Charles was at war with Francis I. During the ensuing decades, England was steadily preparing for its decisive battle with

Spain. In this context, educating political rulers was surely an uphill battle. As Thomas More wrote to his friend Erasmus: "How I wish Christian princes would follow good instructions! Everything is upset by their mad follies."[5] Mindful of this sobering situation, Erasmus starts his book by appealing immediately to the most illustrious teachings on rulership, especially to Plato's *Republic* and the *Laws,* which commend the greatest diligence in the training and education of rulers. In these writings, he says, Plato "does not wish them to excel all others in wealth, in gems, in dress, in statues and attendants, but in [philosophical] wisdom alone"—where wisdom does not mean being adept in disputing about abstract principles but rather having a mind "free from the false opinions and vicious predilections of the masses" and acting accordingly. Being free of false opinions and vicious impulses means not to be under their tyrannical sway—which also is a safeguard against becoming a tyrant or a ruler obsessed with lust for power or dominion. As Erasmus adds, addressing himself to Charles and other European rulers: "If you want to make trial of yourself with other princes, do not consider yourself superior to them if you take away part of their power or scatter their forces, but only if you have been less corrupt than they, less greedy, less arrogant, less wrathful, less headstrong."[6]

As can be seen, Erasmus was not opposed to competition as such, to a genuine "agon" about excellence, but to unjust and senseless power plays. To be able to switch from the latter to the former type of contest, political rulers have to undergo training aimed at fostering self-restraint and self-overcoming—a training which was at the heart of traditional teachings about virtue and character formation. Following the classical canon, Erasmus maintains that rulers should be people who excel in "the requisite kingly qualities of wisdom, justice, moderation, foresight, and zeal for the public welfare." In conformity with Seneca, the text distinguishes between three kinds of excellence or nobility—of which only the first one is truly admirable. This top kind is displayed in "virtue and good actions"; the second type reflects hearsay acquaintance with virtue, while the last one relies on kinship and the genealogy of wealth: "It by no means becomes a prince to swell with pride over this lowest degree of nobility, for it is so low that it is nothing at all, unless it has itself sprung from virtue." For a

Christian ruler, in particular, training in virtue and self-overcoming involves sharing not in the glory but in the cross of Jesus. What is this cross? Erasmus asks, and responds: "I will tell you: follow the right, do violence to no one, plunder no one, sell no public office, be corrupted by no bribes." A ruler adhering to these maxims is bound to be not a scourge but a boon and a blessing to people. In the words of Plutarch, such a ruler has exalted and nearly divine qualities, for "his goodness makes him want to help all; his power makes him able to do so." Employing similar language, Erasmus's text compares a good ruler more to a "divine being" than an ordinary mortal; for such a ruler is "sent by God above to help the affairs of mortals by looking out and caring for everyone and everything," holding the life of others "more dear than his own," even "at great risk to himself." Upon the moral qualities of such a ruler "depends the felicity of the country."[7]

Given the title of Erasmus's text, his admonitions are addressed first of all to the typical rulers of his time, that is, to "princes" or monarchs. In fact, in agreement with the dominant opinion of his age, Erasmus tended to view kingship or monarchy on balance to be superior to other regimes—provided the qualities of the ruler were adequate for the task. Lacking these qualities, however—he agreed—monarchy was in grave danger of sliding into tyranny. The basic difference between these regimes resided in the ruler's treatment of the common people; for whereas a good prince treats the well-being of citizens as his paramount concern, a tyrant turns everything to "his own personal gain," thus subjugating and abusing his people. Moreover, the prince's goodness cannot remain a private judgment, but must be endorsed as such by the common people, that is, elicit the "consent of the governed." For "what is it which alone makes a prince," Erasmus asks pointedly, "if it is not the consent of his subjects?" In another bold statement, reminiscent of the Stoics, the text affirms that "nature created all men equal, and slavery was superimposed on nature—which fact even the laws of the pagans recognized." Christian people, in any event, cannot accept any ruler as absolute master, much less as slave master—because they recognize as their master only Jesus (whose lordship, however, is not based on subjugation, but on justice and grace). Heeding the teachings of the ancients as well as the example of Jesus, a good ruler must avoid being harsh, cruel, arrogant, and oppressive, and instead cultivate the virtues of kindness, equity, and mercy. The character traits which, in Erasmus's view, are "farthest removed from tyranny" are the qualities of "clemency, affability, fairness, courtesy, and kindliness," to which might be added "integrity, self-restraint, seriousness, and alertness." Again, Plato is invoked as a reliable witness who, in his *Republic*, demanded "a quiet and mild nature in a prince" and stated that "men of sharp and excitable nature are suited to a military career," but "entirely unfit for government."[8]

Although addressed to a "Christian prince"—specifically Prince Charles—Erasmus's instructions are not narrowly confessional or even narrowly religious in character. On this score, as a learned "humanist," Erasmus differed markedly from some of the religious reformers of his time who, reviving the older quarrel between Athens and Jerusalem, opted resolutely in favor of the latter. As he observes sharply: "To be a philosopher and to be a Christian is synonymous in fact; the only difference is in the nomenclature." This statement concurs entirely with his view of the meaning of Christian faith—a conception which was far removed from doctrinal orthodoxy and basically centered on inner disposition, practical conduct, or *orthopraxis*. "Who is truly Christian?" the text asks, and responds: "Not he who is baptized or anointed, or who attends church. It is rather the man who has embraced Christ in the innermost feelings of his heart, and who emulates Him with his pious deeds." In their practical conduct, princes or political rulers need to emulate the teachings of Jesus and the ancients— and not seek an alibi in the distinction between political affairs, on the one hand, and philosophy and religion, on the other. Notwithstanding certain occupational differences, rulers like other people—and more so because of their preeminence—should cultivate the qualities of equity, kindness, and self-restraint, rather than "slide back into the ways of Julius [Caesar] and Alexander the Great." Moreover, the virtues of equity and kindness must be practiced by rulers not only toward their own subjects or citizens, but also—and with particular diligence— toward outsiders or strangers. Again, Plato serves as witness:

> Although the prince must ever try to see that no one suffers any harm, still, according to Plato, in the case of strangers he should be even more careful than in the case of his own subjects to see

that no harm befalls them; for strangers are deprived of all their friends and relatives and hence are more susceptible to mishaps. For this reason, they are said to have Jupiter as their special protector, who in this capacity is called *Xenius* [the wayfarer's god].[9]

Given his nondenominational and truly ecumenical outlook, Erasmus's observations on rulership can be readily compared with prominent views originating in different religious and cultural settings. In the context of Islamic civilization, it seems appropriate to turn briefly to the great al-Farabi (870–950)—both because of his closeness to Plato and Aristotle and because of his effort to reconcile his religion with classical philosophical teachings (or Athens with Mecca). Among al-Farabi's numerous writings, the most pertinent here is a treatise called *Aphorisms of the Statesman* (*Fusul al-Madani*), which seems to present his own views on rulership (rather than merely commenting on the ancients). Morally commendable rulership is defined in the text as the practice and continuous cultivation of virtues whose goal or result is the well-being and happiness of all inhabitants. "The true king [or ruler]," al-Farabi states, "is one whose aim and purpose . . . are such that he affords himself and the people of the city true happiness, which is the end and gist of the royal craft." The most prominent and important quality in a good ruler and a "virtuous city" is justice or equity, especially when the latter is joined with kindness, friendliness, and compassion. As the text states emphatically: when the segments or parts of the city are "united and bound together by sympathy," the city will be "controlled and maintained by justice and the actions of justice. . . . Justice follows upon sympathy." These standards are entirely incompatible with a rulership geared toward self-enhancement or self-glorification, that is, toward political domination and conquest. Although military action may sometimes be justified for limited purposes and as a last resort, just rulership must never be identified with warfare as such. Thus, if a ruler makes war "for nothing else but for the sake of conquest," he engages in unjust war; similarly, "if he makes war or kills to appease rage, or for the pleasure he takes in sheer victory," he commits an injustice and forfeits the claim to just rule.[10]

Similar sentiments can also be found in East Asian traditions, especially in the long history of Confucian teachings. Among the many sayings ascribed to Confucius, one may recall the one about rulership, where he stated that a good ruler "loves his people" and a wise ruler "knows or understand them." At another time, the sage listed three requisites of good rulership: trust of the common people, adequate food, and sufficient weapons. When asked which of the three, if need be, he would forgo first, he responded "weapons," and which to forgo second, he said "food": "For from old, death has been the lot of all men; but a people that no longer trusts its rulers is lost indeed." Despite modifications in detail, the sage's teachings were preserved intact through the centuries, finding a particularly strong resonance during the so-called "neo-Confucian" revival at the time of the Sung dynasty. A prominent theme in this revival was the emphasis on self-restraint (or "self-rectification") as a requisite of good rulership—a theme which was developed in a number of texts dealing with the "Learning of Emperors and Kings" (or similar titles). Among neo-Confucian scholars, a particularly impressive figure was Chen Te-hsiu (1178–1235), who lived in the interval between al-Farabi and Erasmus. Following in the footsteps of Confucius, Chen stressed the importance of combining knowing and loving (or "mind and heart") and of placing both in the service of justice or equity. The basic standard of good rulership in his view could be summed up in this motto: "To cultivate fully one's mind-and-heart, and to be fair-minded or equitable. In developing fully his mind-and-heart, the ruler will have no reason to be ashamed; if he is fair-minded, he will not be guilty of favoritism." On another occasion, Chen expressed the standard in these couplets:

> Discipline the self by incorruptibility.
> Pacify the people by humaneness (*jen*).
> Preserve the mind by impartial equity.
> Perform your duties with diligence.[11]

NORBERTO BOBBIO'S IN PRAISE OF MEEKNESS

Classical teachings of this kind are no longer in vogue and have become nearly apocryphal in our time. Even people specializing in the study of politics are rarely, if ever, acquainted with traditional texts on rulership. As previously indicated, politics and political rule today tend to be equated with business affairs or with power plays, that is, with the pursuit of economic self-interest or else with a struggle for power which treats opponents as "enemies" (in a quasi-military sense). Even political philosophers—the supposed guardians of a long tradition—often dismiss concern with the qualities of rulership, either because of an excess of moral skepticism or because of a misguided attachment to liberal "neutrality" (as stated before). Fortunately, neglect is not universal and one can find voices remonstrating against the prevailing state of affairs. For present purposes, attention will be focused on a prominent contemporary voice: the Italian political philosopher Norberto Bobbio. What makes the choice of Bobbio appealing is both his immense erudition and his deep concern with the fate of liberal democracy, demonstrated in his numerous publications as well as his public life.[12] On both philosophical and political grounds, his credentials as a defender of liberal democratic principles and practices are unimpeachable and widely recognized. At the same time, he has never hesitated to hold up to democrats or democratic rulers the unflattering "mirror of princes," that is, the basic ethical standards of rulership and just conduct. While not explicitly predicated on religious grounds, his observations on this theme largely concur with past teachings, or at least mesh with them on the level of *orthopraxis*.

One of Bobbio's most recent writings is titled *In Praise of Meekness: Essays on Ethics and Politics*. As the subtitle indicates, the book struggles with the basic issue of the relation between moral standards and politics, an issue which has been vexed throughout history but has reached unprecedented acuteness in recent times due to the experiences of totalitarianism and genocide. In a central chapter devoted to the topic, Bobbio discusses a broad spectrum of possible positions ranging from rigid "monism" all the way to rigid "dualism"—where "monism" means either the reduction of politics to ethics or of ethics to politics, and "dualism" the thesis of an unbridgeable gulf. For a number of reasons, Bobbio finds himself unable or unwilling to subscribe to the first kind of monist coincidence; one of the chief reasons is precisely the rise of liberal democracy with its differentiation between religion and politics, church and "state" (which carries over into the distinction between private and public domains and the espousal of individual freedom of conscience). At the same time, he holds no brief for the collapse of ethics into power politics or for the doctrine of liberal neutrality predicated on a radical gulf. What emerges from his deliberations is a highly nuanced mode of mutual correlation which, while respecting individual freedom, does not release democratic politics into moral indifference. As Bobbio writes, with a glance at fashionable defenses of *realpolitik:* "An efficient government is not of itself a good government"—the latter being defined by the moral end of rulership, that is, the well-being of the governed. An efficient government may also be corrupt, where corruption—in line with venerable teachings—means that a ruler "has placed his personal interest before the collective interest, personal benefit before the common good." Wanton pursuit of "power for its own sake" is likewise corrupting, because it transforms a mere means into a final goal. Thus, even in liberal democracies, political action—which is "free or presumed to be so"—"does not escape the judgment whether it is right or wrong."[13]

One of the writers repeatedly mentioned in Bobbio's book is Erasmus, and especially his *Education of a Christian Prince*—a testimony to his own broadly humanist leanings. Although close to the Renaissance thinker in many ways, Bobbio is hesitant to endorse the former's text wholeheartedly—mainly (it seems) because of an apprehension of appearing politically naïve or idealistic. In introducing Erasmus at one point, he refers to the German historian Gerhard Ritter, who argued that there were two basic tendencies at the beginning of the modern age: one was the "realist current" represented by Machiavelli and the other the "idealist" strand typified by Thomas More, who portrayed "the republican Utopia in which perfect peace rules with perfect justice." As Bobbio adds, apparently endorsing the argument: "It must not be forgotten that Machiavelli wrote *The Prince,* regarded as the unsurpassed example of realist politics, at the same time as Erasmus wrote *The Education of a Christian Prince,* which is considered a similarly perfect example of idealist politics." Likewise, when presenting his spectrum of positions on the ethics-politics relationship, he offers Erasmus's text as an exemplar of the "monistic" variety which levels politics into ethics—contrasting this type sharply with Machiavelli's reverse monism. Almost a contemporary of Machiavelli's

The Prince, he writes, "Erasmus's Christian prince is the reverse of the demonic face of power." The virtues extolled by Erasmus as standards of rulership are light-years removed from Machiavelli's robust and realist notion of *virtú:* the former's "exclusively moral virtues have nothing to do with virtue understood in the Machiavellian sense."[14]

As stated, the contrast is somewhat puzzling. For one thing, it lacks the kind of nuances which Bobbio otherwise commends and exemplifies. Surely, Erasmus was not unaware of the need of a prince—Christian or otherwise—to wield power and authority to preserve order and lawfulness in the country; moreover, his text made room for military action abroad, provided the latter was carried out for defensive purposes and as a last resort. At the same time, though not a traditional moralist, Machiavelli was not entirely averse to pronouncing moral judgments—as Bobbio recognizes. Despite all his justifications for political behavior deviating from common morals, he says, "a tyrant remains a tyrant" even for Machiavelli. Although asserting that, in the interest of public safety, considerations of "kind or cruel" must be set aside, he still "denounced Agathocles as a tyrant for 'ill using' his cruel actions."[15] The contrast, however, is more puzzling still for another reason: the theme announced in the book's title, namely, the "praise of meekness." As it happens, Bobbio's praise of this disposition—his *"elogio della mitezza"*—is one of the finest tributes paid to religious and classical virtues in recent political-philosophical literature. In introducing the disposition, Bobbio immediately refers to Jesus's Sermon on the Mount, and especially to the "beatitude" which states "Blessed are the meek (*mites*) for they shall inherit the earth." He also points to classical teachings about virtues, noting that meekness is "certainly an ethical virtue" (as distinguished from intellectual or "dianoetic" virtues) and, in fact, belongs among the "cardinal" virtues. In the same context, he refers again to Erasmus's *The Education of a Christian Prince,* commenting that, in that text, we find "the supreme virtues of the ideal prince: clemency, kindness, equity, civility, benevolence, as well as prudence, integrity, sobriety, temperance, vigilance, generosity, and honesty"—qualities which clearly bear an affinity with meekness.[16]

Importantly, meekness for Bobbio is not simply a private feeling or idiosyncrasy, but rather a social attitude implying a relation to fellow beings. In this respect, he distinguishes meekness from "mildness," which is more a "personal" attribute or private character trait. By contrast, he writes, meekness is a "social virtue"—in the sense in which Aristotle differentiated personal virtues, such as courage and moderation, from the highest social virtue of justice; it involves "a positive inclination toward others," whereas courage and moderation are "only positive attitudes toward oneself." Although clearly implying an "inward inclination" or inner disposition, meekness in Bobbio's portrayal "radiates only in the presence of the other"; more specifically still, a meek person is someone "needed by others to help them defeat the evil within themselves." In this connection, he refers to another Italian philosopher, Carlo Mazzantini—like him a teacher at the University of Turin—whom he singles out for his perceptiveness and "deep philosophical vocation." In discussing meekness, Mazzantini advanced a remarkable thesis or proposition which underscores its social quality: namely, the thesis that meekness is "the only supreme power," a power which consists in "letting the other be himself" (a phrase clearly resonating with Heideggerian "letting be"). "Note," Bobbio elaborates, "how the word 'power' is used to designate a virtue that reminds one of the opposite, that is, powerlessness, but mind you: not resigned powerlessness." As one can see, meekness—again in a quasi-Heideggerian vein—is identified neither with impotence or passive surrender nor with an aggressive will to power, but rather, with a kind of "power-free" potency. Here is a citation from Mazzantini, together with Bobbio's comment:

> "A violent person has no power, because by using violence he disempowers those who wish to give of themselves. Whereas power rests in those who possess the will that does not yield to violence, but is expressed through meekness." "To let the other be himself," therefore, is a social virtue in the intrinsic and original meaning of the term.[17]

To profile further the quality of meekness, Bobbio contrasts it with a number of counter-terms. The opposites of meekness, he writes, are "arrogance, haughtiness, and domination." Arrogance here means an "exaggerated conception of one's merits" which justifies (or pretends

to justify) the abuse of power. Haughtiness, in turn, is a "showy arrogance," a way of "flaunting one's supposed virtues" in a blatant and
impertinent way. Compared with the preceding terms, domination or
aggressiveness is "even worse," because it consists in "the abuse of
power, not only feigned but effectively exercised." Aggressive individuals, Bobbio observes, exhibit their domineering nature in manifold ways—"for instance, as if swatting a fly or squashing a worm";
they exercise their power over others through "all kinds of abuse and
outrage, or acts of arbitrariness and, when necessary, ruthless domination." To avoid misunderstanding, the text quickly adds that, in
opposing such outrage, meekness does not simply coincide with sub-
missiveness or passive compliance. While a submissive person is someone who "abandons the struggle due to weakness, fear, or resignation,"
meek persons "do not yield" or submit because they basically repu-
diate and transgress the rules of the game governing domination.
Being non-submissive, meek persons are also calm, serene, and even
cheerful—the latter because "they are inwardly convinced that the
world to which they aspire is better than the one they are forced to
inhabit." To this extent, Bobbio affirms, a meek person can be depicted
"as the precursor of a better world" who anticipates that world by
"effectively exercising the virtue of meekness" in daily living—as the
herald of an "ideal city" where "the kindness in customs becomes universal practice." Such kindness in customs also involves simplicity and
charity or compassion—the first serving as the precondition of meekness and the second as its likely consequence.[18]

   In light of this affirmation and even celebration of meekness, the
reader is bound to be surprised and chagrined by the conclusion Bobbio draws for politics. After glimpsing an exalted vision of social life,
what is one to make of this harsh statement: "Meekness is not a political virtue; rather it is the most apolitical of virtues"? As he elaborates
further: "In the predominant meaning of politics, that is, the Machiavellian or the updated Schmittian version, meekness is exactly the
opposite side of politics." In this connection, Bobbio draws a distinction between two sets of virtues: "strong" or "high-class" virtues, on
the one hand, and "weak" or low-class, on the other. Strong or high-
class virtues—like courage, daring, and prowess—are "typical of the
powerful" and cultivated by those who have the task of "governing,

directing, commanding" people and of "creating and maintaining nation-states." By contrast, weak virtues—like simplicity, gentleness, and meekness—are "inherent to private, insignificant or inconspicuous individuals"; they characterize that section of society where "the poor, the humiliated and hurt" are situated, that is, all those people "who will never become rulers, who die without leaving any other trace of their presence on this earth than a cross in a cemetery bearing their name and a date." As Bobbio adds bluntly, summarizing this point: "In the political or even democratic struggle . . . the meek have no part."[19] What, the reader may ask, is happening here? How can the meek be unyielding and defiant and even possess a supreme, but non-domineering "power" (in Mazzantini's sense)—and yet play no role in political life? How can they exhibit a "social virtue" and even herald or anticipate an "ideal city"—if that city can never be a *polis*, or if its public significance is absent or indefinitely postponed? After all, are "insignificant" common people not precisely called to be the "rulers" in a democracy understood as people's rule? Is Bobbio here not leading us back into the dilemma of liberal democracy and liberal "neutrality" mentioned at the outset: that is, into the gulf between ethical standards and political indifference (or worse: immorality), into the schizophrenia of private versus public conduct?

DEMOCRATIC ORTHOPRAXIS AND KARMAYOGA

These questions are clearly at the heart of contemporary political life, especially life in a liberal-democratic regime. As previously indicated—and as Bobbio would rightly insist—the solution cannot be found in a simple fusion or synthesis, that is, in the merger of ethics and politics or of morality and public legality. In a liberal democracy wedded to individual freedom, ethical standards can no longer be erected into a public dogma or official creed—at least not beyond certain limited constitutional safeguards. To this extent, liberal democracy remains heir to the central principles of Western modernity: freedom of conscience, freedom of faith, noncoincidence of religion and politics ("church" and "state"), morality, and legality. Moreover, it would be extremely odd and even counterproductive if some of the discussed virtues—like meekness or gentleness—would be erected into political ideologies, into instruments of public domination and (conceivably) oppression. The very nature of these virtues seems to run counter to and undermine any such attempt. From this angle, Bobbio's concluding observations appear in a new and more favorable light—but only if politics is identified with sheer power politics or the pursuit of unfettered self-interest (in a "Machiavellian" or "Schmittian" vein). But why grant the latter a monopoly in the political domain? Could one not conceive of a politics where Bobbio's preferred virtues—and the virtues/beatitudes of Jesus and the ancients—would function not as oppressive masters but as vigilant servants and custodians of public conscience? In this case, these virtues would not simply be "apolitical," but remain politically relevant as counterweights to oppressive tendencies, as guideposts of an ongoing democratic struggle: that is, as guideposts of a critical *orthopraxis*.

Curiously, Bobbio himself provides clues pointing in this direction. Tucked away in a footnote of his text, we find a reference to another fellow Italian, Aldo Capitini, who is described as a "defiant philosopher" and "liberal-socialist thinker" whose opposition to political domination—especially fascist domination—was both morally and religiously inspired. He contended, the note states, that there was a need "to go beyond the contrast between capitalism and communism," and "to use non-violence and non-cooperation as the basis" for this struggle; in this respect, "he was deeply influenced by Gandhi's thought and actions."[20] Despite its brevity and obscure location, one can hardly fail to recognize the direct import of this reference. By all accounts, Gandhi was one of the foremost practitioners of those "weak" virtues highlighted by Bobbio: gentleness, meekness, kindness, compassion. At the same time, he was a champion of those "insignificant or inconspicuous individuals," of all "the poor, humiliated and hurt" people shunted aside and trampled upon by the powerful. Neither his engagement for the poor nor his cultivation of "weak" virtues, however, kept Gandhi away from politics or from involvement in political struggle. Like the "meek" described by Bobbio, he was non-submissive and unyielding, as well as calm and frequently cheerful; but he was particularly unyielding when dealing with abusive and oppressive political power. In his struggle for India's independence,

Gandhi did not shrink from inserting himself in the thick of politics—but a politics of a different kind, carried on in a different register, at odds with and in defiance of sheer power politics. As he stated at one point:

> Politics pervades all our activities; [and] I am not talking of retirement from politics in this broad sense. . . . But power politics should be kept out [of our proceedings]. We are taking that step not out of cowardice, but for the sake of self-purification. That is the way of non-violence. I know that in this country all constructive activities are part of politics; in my view this is true politics. [But] non-violence can have nothing to do with the politics of power.[21]

In his entire lifework, Gandhi provided crucial lessons for modern liberal democracy: the lesson of being involved in politics without being corrupted by power-lust and self-seeking, and the lesson of how to cultivate moral and religious virtues without erecting them into public dogmas or official creeds. Apart from being a moralist in the footsteps of Ruskin and Tolstoy, Gandhi was also a deeply religious person in a broadly ecumenical sense but with special attachment to his native Vaishnava tradition; in the language of that tradition, he was above all a *karmayogin,* that is, one committed to purified action or *orthopraxis.* In this capacity, his entire life-conduct exemplified the great teachings of the *Bhagavad Gita,* especially these lines: "Set your heart on work (*karma*), but never on its reward. . . . Do your work in the peace of *yoga,* free from selfish desires, unmoved by success or failure." And these: "Offer to me all your works and rest your mind on the Supreme. Free from vain hopes and selfish thoughts, and with inner peace, conduct your struggle or fight." Deep religious commitments of this kind, however, never prompted Gandhi to sponsor an "established" religion or a religious "establishment" in India. Throughout his life he opposed the idea of an independent India governed by "Hindus" alone (an idea which today is promulgated as "Hindutva"). The guiding principle here was the distinction between public doctrine and practical conduct, between official dogma and *orthopraxis.* As he stated a few months before his assassination: "If I were a dictator, [organized, official] religion and the state would be separate. I swear by my religion; I will die for it. But . . . the state has nothing to do with that." The situation was different on the level of practical conduct—where religion really is put to the test. If you were to watch my life, he added, "how I live, eat, sit, talk, behave in general—then the sum total of all this is my religion." Such religiosity, for Gandhi, offered hope for the future—a future when religion would no longer be reduced to "a Saturday or a Sunday affair" but "lived every moment of one's life": "Such religion, when it comes, will rule the world" (though not in the manner of power politics).[22]

Even more than in his own lifetime, Gandhi's exemplary conduct provides a beacon for our troubled period—a time when Gandhian-style virtues are almost entirely eclipsed by selfish interests and power plays (now under the auspices of neoliberalism and the struggle for planetary control). Under the aegis of globalized markets, democratic politics is almost everywhere surrendered to the dictates of economic advantage—dictates which usually privilege the rich over the poor, the affluent and arrogant over the "humiliated and hurt." At the same time, under the impact of ethnic cleansing, terrorist acts, and campaigns against terrorism, politics is steadily being assimilated to warfare—with the result that the age-old longing for cosmopolitan peace is perverted into global militarism or militarization (now extending itself into outer space).[23] In this situation, Gandhi's approach—his option not for an exit from politics, but for another kind of politics grounded in nonviolence (*ahimsa*) and ethical action (*karmayoga* and *satyagraha*)—retains more than ever its instructive value. So does Bobbio's embrace of meekness and related traditional virtues. As Bobbio makes it quite clear, his choice should be seen as "a reaction to the violent society in which we are forced to live." This reaction, he adds, is not the result of a naïve belief that human history "has always been idyllic"; rather, it derives from the unprecedented magnitude of possible violence, from the accumulation of weapons of mass destruction which can "destroy the earth many times over." This destructive potential, moreover, is not restricted to superpowers (or the only remaining superpower), but through a kind of contagion is steadily disseminated around the globe: "What terrifies me is those dreaded megatons combined with the persisting will to power," a will which spreads from great powers to smaller states and even to private agents—such as "the lone assassin, the small terrorist group, or someone who throws a bomb into a crowd, or in a bank, a crowded train . . . where it can cause the death of the largest possible number of innocent peoples."[24]

Probably the most significant lesson of Gandhi's lifework has to do with the quality of politics in a modern liberal democracy. As indicated, Gandhi's conduct combined open-minded fairness with religious faith, liberal tolerance and commitment to freedom with ethical *orthopraxis.* To this extent, his conduct exemplified the qualities extolled by Erasmus in his instructions to a Christian prince: wisdom, justice, kindness, and zeal for the public good. These instructions, in turn, harken back to the teachings of the "divine" Plato, who commended a "quiet and mild nature" in princes (while relegating people with "excitable" tempers to a military career). As stated before, these teachings are particularly important in a liberal democracy where ordinary people are the rulers—and hence are expected to display the qualities or virtues of rulership championed by Erasmus and the ancients. These virtues cannot be legislated or dogmatically imposed, but only be cultivated in a slow learning process, aided by good example, which gentles and transforms behavior. Such a learning process is at the heart of the future "ideal city" envisaged by Bobbio in his "praise of meekness"—a city where "kindness in customs becomes universal practice."[25] Given the immensity of possible destruction in our time, this future deserves to be cherished and fondly anticipated. To return to a point made earlier: unjust, vicious, or violent rulers place the welfare and even survival of populations at risk; by contrast, just and kind rulers are a boon and a blessing to people. In the words of Erasmus: on the good qualities of rulers "depends the felicity of the country"—we might add today: the felicity and survival of our world.

CHAPTER TEN

Homelessness and Pilgrimage
Heidegger on the Road

Ours is an age of massive population movements, an age of migrants, refugees, expatriates, and exiles. Wars, genocides, and ethnic cleansings have taken their grim toll. In many parts of the world—from Africa to the Middle East to South Asia—vast numbers of people have been displaced, uprooted, and made homeless. This situation is a concern not only for demographers, but also for philosophers and socially engaged intellectuals in general. In his famous "Letter on Humanism" (of 1947), Martin Heidegger ventured the statement that "homelessness today is becoming a global destiny."[1]

In this statement, Heidegger referred not only to the millions of people uprooted by the Second World War, but also—and perhaps principally—to a kind of "world alienation" steadily assuming global proportions. Far from referring to a happy journey or vagrancy, "alienation" here has the sense of agony or loss—an agony stimulating the search for a proper home or abode. In the following, my accent will be on this twilight zone of home and no-home, place and no-place. In addition, the presentation will also honor other twilight zones or border crossings by moving between modernity and classical antiquity, between Heidegger and India, between East and West, and between philosophy and poetry.

HEIDEGGER AND ANTIGONE

In his *An Introduction to Metaphysics*—first presented as a lecture course in 1935—Martin Heidegger discusses the human condition or what it means to be "human." To elucidate this condition, he turns to the first chorus from the *Antigone* of Sophocles (verses 332–375). The chorus begins with these lines: "*Polla ta deina kouden an/thropou deinoteron pelei.*" In the English translation of Ralph Manheim the opening verses read:

> There is much that is strange [*deinon*], but nothing
> That surpasses man [humans] in strangeness.
> He sets sail on the frothing waters
> amid the south winds of winter
> tacking through the mountains
> and furious chasms of the waves.

Later on in the same chorus we find these lines, which might be rendered as follows (varying slightly Manheim's translation):

> Everywhere journeying, getting nowhere,
> [or: Passing everywhere, without passage; Greek: "*pantoporos
> aporos*"]
> he comes to nothing . . .
> He wends his way between the laws of the earth
> and the sacred justice of the gods.
> Rising above his place [or city], devoid of place [or city; Greek:
> "*hypsipolis apolis*"],
> he for the sake of adventure takes
> nonbeing for being, thus losing
> his place in the end.[2]

Commenting on the opening verses of the chorus, Heidegger translates the Greek term "*deinon*" as "*unheimlich,*" meaning "unhomely" or "not-at-home," and he writes: "We are taking the strange, the uncanny (*das Un-heimliche*) as that which casts us out of the 'homely,' that is, the customary, familiar, habitual, secure. The unhomely (*Unheimische*) prevents us from making ourselves at home, and therein it is overpowering." As he adds, "man" is stranger than and even strangest (*deinotaton*) among all beings, not only because he passes his life among unfamiliar things but because he departs from or transgresses his own customary or familiar limits, thus "moving in the direction of the unhomely in the sense of the overpowering." Turning to the lines beginning with "Passing/journeying everywhere, getting nowhere (*pantoporos aporos*)," Heidegger elaborates: "Everywhere man makes himself a path; he ventures into all realms of being, of the overpowering power, and in doing so he is flung out of all paths. Herein is disclosed the entire uncanniness of this strangest, uncanniest (*deinotaton*) of creatures." Coming finally upon the third "salient phrase" of the chorus (*hypsipolis apolis*), Heidegger notes that "*polis*" is usually translated as city or city-state. But he adds: "This does not capture the full meaning. *Polis* means, rather, the place (*Stätte*), the there (*Da*) wherein and as which historical being-there (*Da-sein*) is." Differently phrased: "The *polis* is the historical place (*Geschichtsstätte*), the there *in* which, *out of* which, and *for* which history happens."[3]

So far the chorus from *Antigone* and Heidegger's commentary. These comments do not arise from nowhere. Almost a decade earlier, in *Being and Time* (1927), Heidegger had already presented human being as *Dasein,* as "being-there," more specifically as "being-in-the-world." Against this background, his comments on *Antigone* clarify what he means by being-in-the-world, that is, they spell out *how* we are "in the world." As he states in *An Introduction to Metaphysics:* "The uncanniest of beings (human *Dasein*) is what it is because, fundamentally, it cultivates and guards the familiar [the homely], only in order to break out of it and to let what overpowers it break in. Being [*das Sein*] itself hurls *Dasein* into this breaking-away," into the unhomely, thereby "driving it beyond itself to venture forth toward Being." What the *Introduction* here guards or cautions against is a careless or absent-minded reading of *Being and Time,* and especially of the phrase "being-in-the-world," a reading which would portray "world" simply as an empirical receptacle, a spatial container into which *Dasein* happens to be placed. To be sure, a careful or attentive reading of *Being and Time* renders this construal entirely impossible. Heidegger's text contains a radical critique of "world" seen as an external space, especially along the lines of Descartes' *res extensa* into which the *cogito* happens to be inserted (in the manner of Gilbert Ryle's "ghost in the machine"). As the text clearly states: "Neither is the space *in* the subject [as an a priori category] nor is the world *in* the space [as a container]. Rather, space is disclosed by the worldliness or in-the-world-being of *Dasein.*" Elsewhere in *Being and Time,* Heidegger characterizes the status of *Dasein* by saying that *Dasein* is what is "nearest" to us (most familiar, most homely) and at the same time what is "farthest," most distant (unhomely) from us, namely in its exposure to (the transcendence of) Being—a characterization which again ruptures or deconstructs any simple spatial construal of *Dasein's* worldliness.[4]

About two decades after *Being and Time,* Heidegger was at pains to clarify further the meaning of "world" and "being-in-the-world." As we read in his "Letter on Humanism": "In the phrase 'being-in-the-world', 'world' does not in any way imply earthly as opposed to heavenly being, nor the 'worldly' [mundane] as opposed to the 'spiritual.' For us, 'world' does not at all signify [ontic] beings nor any [ontic] realm of beings but rather the openness of Being." Reiterating points made earlier, Heidegger circumscribes *Dasein* again as "ek-sistence," as a mode of being characterized by "ek-stasis," that is, by its standing out into "the openness of Being." This standing out is not an individual choice or arbitrary whim, but rather is constitutive of the very character of *Dasein* as it is molded (or "thrown") by Being itself as a creature of "care." As the "Letter" adds: " 'World' is the clearing of Being into which man stands out on the basis of his thrown condition. 'Being-in-the-world' designates the nature of human existence with regard to the open dimension out of which the 'ek' of ek-sistence unfolds." Despite many later readjustments or shifts of emphasis, Heidegger remained basically faithful to these formulations throughout his life. In one of his late writings titled *Art and Space (Die Kunst und der Raum,* of 1969), he still insisted that the place or location of *Dasein* is not an empirical (ontic) container or receptacle. In his words: "The place (*der Ort*) is not located in a pre-given space understood in the sense of physical-technical spatiality. Rather, the latter emerges only out of the happening of places of a region"—a happening conceived as the "gathering" interplay of place and openness, of placement and displacement (of place and no-place/emptiness).[5]

To be sure, it would be quite misleading to claim that Heidegger's thought was stationary and that there was no development or steady transformation in his thinking. If nothing else, such a claim would run counter to his famous and much-belabored "turning" (*Kehre*). Yet, caution is required when approaching this difficult topic. The "turning" is misrepresented and basically misunderstood if it is seen as an abandonment or "turning away" from something in favor of an entirely new trajectory. On closer inspection, what actually happened was more a reformulation of earlier intimations in more adequate or appropriate language; seen in this light, turning involved Heidegger's more resolute "turning toward" his own distinctive path of thought.[6] This is not the occasion to elaborate this theme (on which there is extensive literature); some brief hints must suffice. About seven years after *An Introduction to Metaphysics,* Heidegger returned to Sophocles' *Antigone,* continuing and modulating his earlier reflections. The occasion was a lecture course offered in 1942, in the midst of World War II, on one of Hölderlin's great hymns, "Der Ister" (the Danube). In this hymn, Hölderlin the poet presents the river as a metaphor of human life, of human journeying and wayfaring in the world. In Heidegger's words, the river is "the site (*die Ortschaft*) of the dwelling of historical human existence on earth."[7] To illustrate the meaning of journeying, Heidegger—in interpreting the hymn—turns again to Sophocles' *Antigone,* but now with a slight change of accent: in the sense that the stress is no longer put entirely on displacement (*hypsipolis apolis*), but on the entwinement of place and no-place, and more particularly on the possibility of finding a dwelling place in no-place or journeying.

Turning to the first lines of the chorus Heidegger renders "*deinon*" again as "*unheimlich,*" that is, as unhomely or not homelike, adding that, taken in this vein, "the word of Sophocles that man is the most uncanny creature signifies that man is in a unique sense alienated or not at home and that homecoming (*Heimischwerden*) is his pervasive concern." One should note here the somewhat novel thought of "homecoming." In Sophocles' tragedy, the opening lines of the chorus apply with particular force to Antigone herself, whose course of action entails a complete estrangement from her home or native city. As she herself states in the dialogue with her sister Ismene, Antigone is prepared "*pathein to deinon touto*"—to suffer the full measure of uncanny estrangement. As Heidegger comments, the phrase "*pathein to deinon*" indicates that uncanniness (un-home-ness) is not something fabricated by humans but rather something that happens or befalls us, that makes or transforms humans into "what they are or can be" (and thus constitutes their humanity). Although implying suffering, *pathein* denotes not merely passive endurance but the readiness to shoulder or undergo a genuine learning experience ("*das eigentliche Erfahren*"). Seen from this vantage, Antigone is neither a tragic heroine bent on asserting her individuality, nor is she a religious martyr resigned to pliant passivity; instead, she undergoes the estrangement/displacement inherent in the human condition, and she does so in an exemplary fashion. Moreover, in pursuing her course, Antigone does not simply go to her doom. Although estranged/displaced from the place of her city, her action honors a dwelling place beyond mundane power which ultimately redeems her death. In Heidegger's words: "Her dying is a homecoming, but a homecoming in and through estrangement/displacement. . . . What if the most deeply estranged, farthest removed from everything homely, were to emerge as the domain guarding at the same time the closest connection with the home?"[8]

In his lecture course on Hölderlin, Heidegger is intent—perhaps more intent than in previous writings—on differentiating uncanniness and journeying from sheer vagrancy, adventurism, or nomadism. For Heidegger, journeying is not *mere* errancy from place to place guided by aimless curiosity. As depicted in the chorus, he observes, "man is not an adventurer (*Abenteurer*) bent on nomadic homelessness; rather, sea, land, and desert are domains which man diligently traverses . . . to find a home somehow." In Heidegger's view, the adventurer may be strange, exotic, and "interesting," but he is not uncanny or unhomely in the sense of *deinon*. The adventurer is indeed abroad or "not at home," but merely in the mode of escapism or self-indulgent denial. Heidegger turns at this point again to the phrase "*pantoporos aporos.*" In his commentary—or his new reading of the phrase—*pantoporos aporos* designates now a creature bent on exploring everything, on pursuing all kinds of thrills or stimulating excitements, but whose adventures fail to yield a sustained learning experience. For the genuinely uncanny person, by contrast, home and not-home, place and no-place, are not simply opposites but closely intertwined: homelessness or not-home here means an experienced lack or felt need (for home), in the sense that journeying abroad becomes a gateway to a "homecoming," the no-place a gateway to a dwelling place. Differently phrased: an intimation of homecoming pervades and sustains the journey abroad, in the mode of a "present absence" or of "presencing" in the mode of absence. As Heidegger writes, placed in the midst of (ontic) beings, human *Dasein* faces the constant possibility or temptation to be "oblivious or forgetful of Being"; but *Dasein* alone among beings also has the intrinsic capacity to relate to or care for "Being as such."[9]

As one should note, the "home" sought and found in homecoming is not a place located somewhere else in empirical space-time, but rather something like a promise (or "promised land")—a promise which also does not point simply to a no-place or a place outside of space-time, but rather inhabits the journey or search from beginning to end. Returning to Hölderlin's hymn "Der Ister," Heidegger comments:

> Place (*Ortschaft*) and journey (*Wanderschaft*)—emblematic of the poetic nature of streams or rivers—are related to the impending homecoming into one's own, and this in the special sense that self-discovery and finding oneself are not the easiest, most natural thing, but remain the most difficult task—a task that is entrusted to the poet's care. . . . Homecoming into one's own implies that, for a long time and perhaps always, human existence is not at home; and this, in turn, implies that man ignores, rejects, and denies—perhaps must deny—the site of home [*das Heimische*]. Homecoming for this reason is a transit through otherness [or not-home, *das Fremde*].[10]

AN INDIAN PILGRIMAGE

Heidegger's observations on journeying and homecoming, and especially on the intimate connection between journey and home, between no-place and place, can be (and have been) interpreted in many different ways. For present purposes, one line of exegesis will be explored. As one may plausibly claim, Heideggerian journeying bears a distinct affinity with the traditional notion or practice of pilgrimage. Like Heidegger's wayfarer, the pilgrim is not simply a vagrant or vagabond aimlessly moving from place to place. Nor is the pilgrim an adventurer or global tourist seeking exotic thrills for the sake of self-indulgence or self-stimulation. Rather, the pilgrim like the wayfarer undergoes a challenge; he/she is engaged in a quest which involves hardship and exposure to unfamiliarity or strangeness (*pathein to deinon touto*). But the quest is not pointless: the pilgrim also seeks a dwelling place in the midst of dislocation or no-place. Still, in some interpretations or instances, the nature of pilgrimage tends to be curtailed or reduced to a simple movement from one place to another, from a place of departure to a place of arrival. In this case, the place of arrival is a sacred place and the sole purpose of the pilgrim's journey, with the result that the journey itself becomes purely incidental or ancillary to the goal. In our age of jet travel, one could imagine a streamlining or near-collapsing of pilgrimage into an efficiently managed instant arrival. Some pilgrimages in the West have taken on this connotation; in India too, some pilgrimages seem geared entirely to the place of arrival, the holy site which is the eagerly anticipated destiny of the journey. However, there are exceptions.[11]

Here it must suffice to illustrate the proper sense of "pilgrim's progress" with the help of one example taken from the Indian context. What is significant about this example is the fact that, in this instance, the pilgrim's journey *is* in a way a sacred site, that journeying or displacement is perceived as revelatory of a dwelling place or homecoming. The pilgrimage happens in the state of Maharashtra, and it is undertaken by the so-called Warkaris, who undertake periodic journeys to the holy city of Pandharpur and there to the temple of Vithoba (Vitthal), who is worshipped as a "*swarup*" (original form) of

Vishnu-Krishna. As many observers have remarked, the point of the Warkaris' journey is not simply to get to or arrive at Pandharpur; rather, the accent is on the journey more than on the point of arrival (or on the journey *as* the point of arrival). Differently phrased: sacredness is not an extrinsic end beyond, but rather the very heart of, the pilgrimage; that is, Pandharpur inhabits or indwells the journey from beginning to end. In the words of Philip Engblom, a leading student of Indian pilgrimage, the Warkaris' journey is "more than just a means to attain the goal of *darshan* of Vitthal in Pandharpur"; it carries significance in itself "as a spiritual discipline." As Engblom explains, the term "Warkari" comes from the root "*wari*," which means journeying or "coming and going." Hence, a Warkari is basically or constitutively, and not just incidentally or occasionally, a wayfarer or pilgrim. However, the character of this wayfaring or journeying needs to be carefully noted. Although not governed by an external goal or destination—and insofar "going nowhere"—the Warkaris' journey is not just a pointless vagrancy or drifting, but rather displays (as Engblom says) a kind of "discipline" by being undertaken as an act of devotion (*bhakti*). To this extent, the Warkari is a *homo viator* (in the sense of Gabriel Marcel), a wayfarer whose main concern is the search for the proper "way" or the proper manner of being "on the way" or "on the road."[12]

This kind of search is manifest in the general conduct of the Warkaris—which is not monastic or a form of mystical escapism but an ordinary-life conduct, though one suffused with an ear for the more-than-ordinary or divine. Here the influence of one of the great poet-saints of Maharashtra, himself an early Warkari, can be seen: the influence of Jñanadev or Jñaneshwar, author of such poems as *Amritanubhava* and *Jñaneshwari* (his commentary on the *Bhagavad Gita*). A simple man and—in the words of James Edwards—an "outcaste Brahmin," Jñanadev (together with some fellow poets) has left an indelible imprint on Warkari pilgrimage. In the account of Eleanor Zelliot, there were three main features of the poet's life that carried over directly into the Warkari movement: "implicit criticism of Brahmanical narrowness [or high-caste elitism]; egalitarianism in spiritual matters; and family-centered life." For a genuine pilgrim, criticism of clerical or priestly elitism is inevitable, because such elitism implies that the sacred is empirically managed by a privileged caste and localized at a given place (in space-time). This criticism quite naturally entails, or lends aid and support to, spiritual egalitarianism and cultivation of ordinary life. All these features were fully embraced by Jñanadev's close friend, Namadev, himself a great poet-saint. Under Namadev's direct guidance, the Warkari movement gathered in its fold an impressive company of saints, poets, and ordinary people, a company which—as Zelliot writes—reflected "almost the complete range of the populace of Maharashtra" at the time.[13] In later periods, the movement counted among its members Eknath, the householder Brahmin; the Shudra poet-saint Tukaram; and also a number of Muslims, most importantly Sheikh Muhammad, the Sufi *bhakta* and saint. In this respect, as one can see, Warkari pilgrimage resembles a moving or mobile Gandhian *ashram,* in its crossing of caste barriers, in its social as well as religious nonexclusiveness, and in its involvement in ordinary-life practices.

A DWELLING PLACE?

Having been transported to India, to a particular historical setting in Maharashtra, readers may feel that we have strayed or journeyed far afield indeed from our starting point: namely, Heidegger's philosophy. Moreover, hearing about pilgrims and pilgrimage, they may object to the insertion of specifically "religious" motifs into a purely philosophical and largely nonreligious discourse. These objections or reservations might be warranted if the excursion to India had appealed to an "organized" religion or established church armed with a panoply of theological doctrines or dogmas; they seem less plausible and perhaps unwarranted if religion is taken (as it is here) in its unassuming etymological sense as a form of "bonding" or reconnecting. Bonding of what? Returning to Heidegger one might say: bonding of human existence, of *Dasein,* with the other side of the human which calls *Dasein* into its humanity, into its very being. We know from *Being and Time,* that it is "conscience" (*Gewissen*)—located in the heart—which issues or transmits this call or exhortation (of Being). Roused by this call, *Dasein* is propelled into a search, into a journey through alienation and homelessness to find a proper home (which allows it "to be"). This search is not far from Warkari pilgrimage (as portrayed above). Moreover, that Heidegger himself was a perennial wayfarer is evident in his persistent invocation of "ways" or "paths" in his writings and in reference to his thought as a whole: *"Feldwege,"* *"Holzwege," "Wege nicht Werke."*[14]

By way of conclusion, it seems appropriate to return to the theme of homecoming, which for Heidegger—especially the later Heidegger—is a gateway to a genuine human "dwelling," a dwelling "on the earth under the heaven." About a decade after his lectures on Hölderlin's "Der Ister," Heidegger (in 1951) turned his attention again to the poet, this time reflecting specifically on the lines ". . . poetically man dwells . . ." (*". . . dichterisch wohnet der Mensch . . ."*). The phrase occurs in one of Hölderlin's late poems, which begins: "In lovely blueness blooms the steeple's metal roof . . ." (*"In lieblicher Bläue blühet mit dem metallenen Dache der Kirchturm . . ."*). In commenting on "poetic dwelling," Heidegger brings the phrase in contact with some preceding lines according to which "man" (*Dasein*) "not unhappily measures itself against the godhead" (or the divine). Thus, he notes, the godhead or the divine is the "measure" by which humans "measure out or define their dwelling, their sojourn on the earth beneath heaven (or the sky)." Of course, measure or measuring here does not refer to a tape measure or a quantitative measuring rod. Rather, measuring, finding the right measure or balance, is here said to be the work of poetry—where poetry does not mean sentimental effusion but responsiveness to language and its "call" of Being. As Heidegger states: "Poetry is measuring; in poetry takes place what measuring basically means." Measuring means here a willingness to measure oneself against the divine—not in the sense of hostile opposition, but in the sense of taking one's measure from, of allowing oneself to be measured by, the divine. In doing so, humans are able to live, as mortals, on this earth, but under the heaven or the divine. In this manner humans "dwell," and more precisely, they "dwell poetically."[15]

In pursuing Hölderlin's lines further, Heidegger also reflects on the meaning of "godhead" (or the divine) as used by the poet. His comments immediately make it clear that this meaning is far removed from the dogmas of organized religion, and also from a simple pantheism (or immanentism) which would submerge God in natural phenomena. In Heidegger's reading of Hölderlin, the godhead reveals itself in the world precisely by hiding its inscrutable mystery; it is precisely in the worldly disclosure that concealment or sheltering occurs. Taking his cues from another line in the poem which reads "Is unknown the godhead?" he writes: "The god(head) as such or in itself is unknown for Hölderlin, and it is just in *this unknown quality (als dieser Unbekannte)* that it is the measure for the poet." Thus, God is unknown and yet is the measure nonetheless. Moreover, the unknown God, the *deus absconditus,* must precisely "by showing Himself as the one He is, appear as the one who remains unknown." Hence, "God's very manifestness . . . is mysterious." For the poet, the manifestness of God shows itself preeminently in the sky or heaven (*Himmel, ouranos*), the dark blueness of the sky. (One may recall here the opening lines: "In lovely blueness blooms . . .") Thus Heidegger continues: "The measure consists in the manner in which the God who remains unknown [*absconditus*] is revealed (made manifest) *as such* by the sky. God's appearance through the sky consists in a disclosure that lets see what conceals or shelters itself." As previously indicated, this appearance is "the measure against which (or by which) *Dasein* measures itself," thereby achieving its proper mode of dwelling on this earth under heaven or under the sky.[16]

This dwelling, as we know now, is a "poetic dwelling," where the two terms mutually reinforce and illuminate each other. Dwelling—for Hölderlin and for Heidegger—is genuine only in a poetic manner, and poetry is genuine only as a mode of dwelling. Poetry, Heidegger writes, "is the basic capacity (*Grundvermögen*) for human dwelling. But *Dasein* is capable of poetry only to the degree that its very being is given over or devoted to that which, in turn, enables and lovingly favors (*mag*) humans and thus needs their being." The comments on "*mögen/vermögen*" (liking, favoring, enabling) lead Heidegger in the end back to some lines in the same poem which were only partially quoted before. The lines read:

> . . . As long as friendliness (*Freundlichkeit*)
> in purity still stays with his heart, man
> not unhappily measures himself
> against the godhead. . . .

As Heidegger notes, Hölderlin says in his preferred idiom "with or at his heart" (*am Herzen*), not "in his heart" (*im Herzen*). "At his heart," in Heidegger's exegesis, means that friendliness has "arrived at the dwelling place of humans, arrived as the call of the measure to the heart in such a way that the heart turns to give heed to the measure." As long as this arrival of friendliness endures, so long *Dasein* is able to measure itself not unhappily against the godhead. And when this measuring happens, then poetry also can happen, and then humans are able to "dwell poetically and properly humanly (*menschlich*) on this earth."[17]

These words of the poet, as interpreted by the philosopher, bring us back to the opening reflections of the present chapter, reflections triggered by our global situation at the beginning of the new millennium. As indicated there, Heidegger spoke at one time of homelessness as a "world destiny," of alienation or loss of home rapidly assuming global dimensions. And how can one question or deny his statement given the dark shadows clouding our time: the shadows of brutal terrorism, of ecological devastation, and of possible nuclear holocaust? However, there are also redeeming rays of light illuminating our landscape, rays clearly pinpointed in Hölderlin's verse: "As long as friendliness / in purity still stays with his heart . . ." ("*So lange die Freundlichkeit noch / am Herzen, die Reine, dauert . . .*"). As long as this verse still radiates its intrinsic measure, so long humankind may still find a home and dwell "properly humanly" on this earth under the sky. Since, to illustrate the search for home, we previously made an excursion to India, it may be appropriate now to close with a passage from a great Indian text: the *Brihadaranyaka Upanishad*. The passage is quoted by Raimon Panikkar, in a book devoted to a similar search for home, called *A Dwelling Place for Wisdom*. The passage reads:

> The heart is truly *brahman*. . . . The heart is its dwelling place (ayātana), its space (akasha), its basis (pratishta). . . . The heart is the dwelling place of all being, the basis of all beings; all beings rest (find their dwelling) in/at the heart.[18]

Appendix
Lessons of September 11

Remembering September 11 is painful, like the memory of any great personal loss or misfortune. Remembering those events means not just recollecting a historical date, but re-experiencing a wound or major injury. Hence, thinking of that day involves inevitably a sense of mourning and grief. Mourning for what or whom? First of all, of course, for the thousands of people killed in New York and Washington, for (and with) their families and friends, for lives destroyed or shattered. But mourning reaches still deeper and farther. Like a bolt of lightning, September 11 suddenly illuminated an otherwise hazy or obscure landscape: the condition of humanity or of our "global village." Dashing comforting illusions, the lightning revealed profound fissures and cleavages in that village—cleavages brimming with hatred, resentment, and unmitigated fury. For, what else but the deepest hatred (or else the deepest despair) could have unleashed upon the world the images of horror that September 11 imprinted on the collective memory of humankind? And here is the cause for a wider, global grief in our time: grief over the festering, near-mortal wounds afflicting humanity at large.

As was to be expected, the events of that day produced a storm of emotional reactions around the world; they also triggered an avalanche of learned commentaries offered by pundits of international affairs. Although often insightful, these commentaries frequently were still deeply embroiled in the drama of the events and their aftermath—too deeply to allow room for reflective judgment. The following reflections do not directly address or analyze the drama of September 11; they presuppose what is publicly known about the events. Instead, the effort is to adopt a more long-range perspective: to ponder the possible implications or consequences of the events and thus to derive lessons for the future. The discussion will proceed in three steps. First, I want to reflect on the broader implications of September 11 for the United States and its overall position in the world. Next, I shall turn my attention to Islamic civilization or the Muslim world and indicate what general consequences follow for Muslims from that day. Finally, I will shift the focus to the broader international arena, in an attempt to garner some lessons for contemporary inter-civilizational relations and for the future life in our global village.

WHITHER AMERICA?

Great human calamities happen in a specific time and place. Given the targets of the September attacks, their effects were most keenly and most painfully felt in the United States—notwithstanding an outpouring of sympathy and good wishes from around the world. In a nearly uninterrupted series of news broadcasts, Americans were informed, during the following days and weeks, of the magnitude of the disaster: the steadily rising death toll, the valiant efforts of firefighters, and the dwindling hopes of finding survivors in the wreckage. The immediate reaction was a mixture of sadness and angry outrage. But pervading these sentiments something else was at work: a deep sense of

bewilderment and surprise. How could this calamity have happened—
here in America, of all places? Were we not living in a reasonably well-
adjusted and peaceful world—now after the end of the Cold War and
the disappearance of a competing superpower? Thus, more perhaps
than the rest of the world, September 11 struck America as a thunder-
clap disclosing something that had been excised or repressed before:
namely, the vulnerability of the country in the midst of a relentlessly
globalizing world. What dawned on most Americans—even if only
dimly—was the realization that globalization is here to stay, that our
globe is finite, and that America is part of this finite world.

The surprise experienced by Americans may itself be surprising to
non-Americans. Here again, time and place demand their due. It is
difficult to overestimate the role and continued relevance of isolationism (sometimes linked with "exceptionalism") in American history
and politics. Right after the founding of the new nation, the leading statesmen declared it to be the guiding principle of the country
to keep out of "foreign entanglements" (both in Europe and the
non-European world). Of course, this declaration did not prevent
the country from meddling deeply in Central and South American affairs; but this was seen as occurring in the "Western Hemisphere" and
hence in America's backyard. Apart from occasional skirmishes,
America was not drawn into major foreign wars until the twentieth
century—and then only in response to major provocation. During the
Second World War, it took the shock of Pearl Harbor to lure America
out of its isolationist retreat. Subsequently, the "iron curtain" erected
during the Cold War had the effect of shielding an enlarged Western
Hemisphere—now styled "the free world"—against contamination
from a hostile, external (and "un-American") world. After the end of
the Cold War, the triumphant upsurge of American liberalism (especially market liberalism) around the world promised a new and still
more efficient kind of "containment": namely, the containment and
eventual obliteration of all modes of life incompatible with, or re-
calcitrant to, liberal market principles. Pursued as Westernization or
"Americanization," globalization thus has a strange and paradoxical
effect: namely, by drawing a curtain between West and non-West
(Americans and non-Americans) and hence restoring isolationism/
exceptionalism under global auspices.

Little insight is required to see that this paradox is laden with grave dangers. For some time, prudent observers have pointed to the hazards afflicting our contemporary world—perils arising from the growing rift between North and South, between rich and poor, between developed and undeveloped societies. Nearly a decade before September 11, a leading expert of international affairs had warned of looming "clashes of civilizations," especially clashes between (what he called) "the West and the rest."[1] Even without expertise, any traveler in the "rest" of the world in recent years could have sensed the perils evident in mounting frustration and despair. Acknowledgement of these conditions—it is important to stress—in no way means to excuse or justify the atrocities of September 11; however, neglect is equally unwarranted. Immediately after the September attacks, some observers still pointed to underlying reasons or "causes" of the debacle; subsequently, however, such references were eclipsed or sidelined by the "war on terrorism." Addressing a large audience at the University of Notre Dame (on September 13), Baroness Shirley Williams—a member of the British House of Lords—urged her listeners "not only to think of retaliation" but to face the difficult question of "how one deals with the sources of terrorism." Among these sources she listed the "excessive inequalities" prevailing in our world, evident in the fact that the income of the poorest 20 percent of the world's population is one-sixtieth of that of the wealthiest 10 percent. Her account could be supported by figures released by the World Bank in its *World Development Report 2000,* according to which the average income in the richest twenty countries is today thirty-seven times the average in the poorest twenty—a gap that has doubled in the past forty years.[2]

Again, social and economic inequities of this kind cannot serve as a warrant for terror; however, they should induce sobriety and a responsible reflection on future prospects. Here, possible lessons of September 11 come into play—for one should always derive something good even from bad events. It is not deriving good from bad, however, if one persists in fostering conditions which have led or contributed to bad results; this would mean evading or failing the lesson—which admittedly is a difficult one. The difficulty resides in the fact that the lesson involves a major change or modification: from national self-interest, narrowly construed, to a shared or common interest. In some ways, this seems to go against the grain of American self-understanding. From the beginning, Americans have always been on the move *away* from something: first from the Old World to the New World, then in America from the East to the Western "frontier," and with the vanishing of the territorial frontier, from Earth to new frontiers in outer space. A major political thinker of the twentieth century has called this attitude "world alienation."[3] America also is called, or calls itself, the "land of the free"; but traditionally freedom has mainly meant a freedom *from* something: from foreign entanglements, from governmental politics, and from societal bonds. This fact explains also why, in America, liberalism and democracy have always been in tension, if not at war with each other—given that democracy inevitably means some kind of shared political enterprise. Moreover, America's self-definition as "land of the free" suggests that people elsewhere are basically unfree (after the model of the "Greek vs. barbarian" dichotomy). And does this bifurcation not lend a semblance of legitimacy to the rule of the former over the latter?

The learning required in our globalizing age is hard and taxing (though not unmanageable with goodwill). The prospects are not improved by a deep-seated American hankering for "unilateralism" (an updated version of isolationism). Although occasionally sharing in international ventures, American policy-makers in recent years have increasingly shown a preference for exodus or "going it alone." America has refused to ratify the Kyoto Treaty on global warming, has boycotted plans for the establishment of an international criminal court, and has unilaterally abrogated the Anti-Ballistic Missile (ABM) Treaty of 1972 in favor a National Missile Defense system which would transform the country into "fortress America." In an essay published shortly after September 11, retired Rear Admiral Eugene Carroll denounced these moves as "unilateralism amok." As he writes soberly:

> Every nation has a fundamental right and duty to provide for its own security. However, in today's interdependent world that right is circumscribed by a requirement not to pursue security through measures which reduce the security of other nations. This caveat applies specifically to the United States which today seeks its security in the form of a global military hegemony

maintained by nearly 250,000 combat ready troops continuously deployed on foreign seas and soil. In the jargon of current U.S. security policy this is known as "forward presence," but in historic terms it is better described as gunboat diplomacy.

Admiral Carroll also points to the extraterrestrial ambitions of U.S. security policy: the effort to turn space into a new battleground by developing laser and "kinetic kill" weapons systems to be deployed in battle stations in space (whereby populations can be annihilated via remote control). "We cannot create a Maginot line in the sky," he demurs, "which will shield us from the consequences of our global military activities nor can we disengage politically or economically from an interdependent world community."[4] The recent war against Iraq has amply demonstrated the American preference for military unilateralism, as well as the dangers of this preference for global (and regional) cooperation deriving from the collusion of unilateralism with possible hegemonic-imperial designs.

WHAT KIND OF MUSLIM POLITICS?

The September 11 attacks were not simply an American affair; they also sent shock waves around the world—including those parts of the world inhabited mainly by Muslims, that is, the "*dar al-Islam*" or world of Islamic civilization. In fact, one can say that, outside America, the effects of the debacle were nowhere more intensely felt or gave rise to more agonizing self-scrutiny than in Islamic societies wedged between fondly cherished, premodern traditions and the realities and pressures of modernization. If, as previously indicated, September 11 was a wake-up call for America (regarding its place in the world), the day was equally a wake-up call for Muslims regarding their role in a rapidly changing global context. Again like a lightning bolt, the day suddenly cast a spotlight on an otherwise hazy landscape in the Near East and beyond, revealing a world in the grip of inner turmoil and profound disarray. The revelation posed a challenge, and presented a lesson, to Muslims everywhere, but especially to Muslims living in the

Near East: the challenge of reimagining or reconstructing the *dar al-Islam,* and the lesson that terrorism is not the way.

Given the circumstances, condemnation of terrorism was expectedly most vocal in America (and the West). However, condemnation was by no means geographically confined: apart from a few isolated voices, Muslims around the world soon joined the chorus of anti-terrorist declamations. Leading Muslim clerics in Egypt, Iran, and other parts of the Middle East publicly and in stern language denounced the September 11 attacks, declaring them to be blatantly incompatible with Islamic religion and indeed with any conceivable standards of ethics. Statements by high-ranking clerics were quickly echoed by statesmen and politicians in the Muslim world. Barely a month after the attacks, an emergency meeting of the Organization of Islamic Conference (OIC) convened in Doha, the capital of Qatar. In the final statement adopted at that meeting, the delegates of Muslim countries strongly and unanimously "condemned the savage acts of terrorism which targeted the United States and which resulted in gross human losses from various nationalities and great destruction and damage in New York and Washington." The statement also emphasized that such acts of terrorism "contravene the teachings of divine religions and moral and human values" and, in particular, "run counter to Islam's tolerant heavenly message which opposes injustice and oppression" and which "champions peace, harmony, tolerance, and respect among people."[5] Not surprisingly, similar condemnations of terrorism were also forthcoming from Muslim leaders in America and the West—prompted in part by genuine religious conviction and in part by fears (not entirely unfounded) of violent retaliations against Muslims in that part of the world. Partly in an effort to counteract the danger of reprisals, the American government stepped into the breach by drawing a sharp dividing line between moderate and peaceful Muslims, on the one hand, and violent Islamic terrorists, on the other.

No doubt, the drawing of this boundary was important on pragmatic grounds (to protect innocent lives); it also seems religiously defensible. Surely, in purely religious terms, Islam cannot be defined as a terrorist doctrine—any more so than (say) Christianity or Hinduism. From a religious faith perspective, one need not quarrel with the OIC statement when it speaks of "Islam's tolerant heavenly message which opposes injustice and oppression." This recognition, however, does not go to the heart of the issue. The problem is that— even though in itself a message of peace—it is the *religion* of Islam which today is widely invoked and used as a mobilizing force by Islamic militants and terrorists. Here a basic difference or asymmetry between America and the Islamic world comes to the fore—a difference which is located on a strictly *political* plane. From the American or Western side, the war on terrorism—especially the war in Afghanistan—has never (or very rarely) been portrayed as a religious campaign, as a war of Christianity against Islam. The reason is that, in the West, religion is on the whole no longer a politically motivating force; at least since the Peace of Westphalia (1648), international politics has been conducted on the basis of national interest (*raison d'etat*) and national security—motives which are distant from religion (and sometimes even distant from ethics). To put matters differently: politics in the West is basically "secularized"; in international affairs, nationalism and national interest commonly suffice as mobilizing political agencies. What is the character of *political* agency in the Islamic world? What resources can Muslims draw on in the attempt to build a viable *political*—and peaceful—*dar al-Islam?* Here September 11 disclosed a glaring political "deficit": the absence of a constructive political vision—outside or apart from the political use or abuse of religion.[6]

In a nutshell: this construction is the challenge and the lesson presented to Muslims by the September 11 attacks. Constructing a viable political order, no doubt, is a formidable task—given the trials and tribulations of Islamic history and the deep fissures dividing Muslim societies today. In a recent book titled *What Went Wrong?* the Middle East pundit Bernard Lewis explored the historical sources of the contemporary malaise, putting the blame mostly (though not wholly) on the doorstep of Muslims: particularly their unwillingness or inability to join modern Europe in its headlong rush from Renaissance and Enlightenment to industrialization and the information age. Although containing kernels of truth, the picture seems overdrawn. For, in fairness, can one ignore the great calamities which have historically befallen the Muslim world, from the destructive Mongol invasions to colonialism and imperialism? Can one simply forget the facts that Moghul rule in India was cut short by British colonial expansion, that the Ottoman Empire was dismembered by the Allied powers after the First World War, and that these powers subsequently parceled out the Middle East among themselves (as League of Nations "mandates")? Can one also forget that the same powers implanted a new nation-state within the perimeters of the Muslim world and later interfered in numerous ways in the affairs of that world? Under democratic auspices— seeing that democracy rests on consent—should all these actions not have been sanctioned by the consultation and consent of the governed in that region? Against this background, Lewis appears somewhat callous when he blames Muslims for most of their problems and when he counsels them simply to "abandon grievance and victimhood."[7] One would have hoped for a more evenhanded and sympathetic treatment of the historical adversities and misfortunes of other people.

What is right about Lewis's account is that the task of building a viable political order rests first of all on Muslim shoulders. No one can hand self-government or self-rule to other people. Lewis is also right in saying that "grievance and victimhood" are not sufficient for the task and that it is time for Muslims to "settle their differences and join their talents, energies and resources in a common creative effort." In our globalizing age, the creative political vision required in that part of the world has to be modern and democratic—which does not mean that Muslims need to forget about their faith. Surely, there are different ways of being secular and modern ("secular" England, for example, boasts an established church); there are also different ways of conceiving democracy (we customarily distinguish between parliamentary, presidential, liberal, and social-democratic forms, to mention just a few). There is no reason why Muslims cannot design their own version of democratic self-rule—provided they respect the basic premises of democracy (which are human liberties and rule of law). These premises might be preserved, for example, if religion were cultivated in ordinary lives and civil society—without seeking to grasp the reins of governmental power and control. Again, the task of construction is first of all a Muslim responsibility—although, in our interdependent world, it cannot and need not be theirs alone. America and the West can and should help in this construction, partly through direct encouragement and partly through omission of detrimental acts. Clearly, the task is not furthered if Western powers and their allies inflict injustice and oppression on Muslim peoples—behavior which only strengthens the hand of extremists triggering an escalation of violence.[8] Somehow, the cycle of violence needs to be broken, and it can and should be done first of all by the more powerful party in the dispute (being better able to take the moral lead). Through such cooperative effort, the *dar al-Islam* could be restored and be transformed from an outcast or pariah into a valued member of the global community.

WHAT KIND OF GLOBAL ORDER?

By way of conclusion, I want to reflect briefly on the condition of international politics in the aftermath of September 11. In many ways—to use currently fashionable vocabulary—the international arena hovers precariously between "clash" and "dialogue" between civilizations. Stated in different and more customary terminology, the arena is wedged between internationalism and transnationalism, that is, between traditional interstate politics and an emerging transnational or global politics (possibly guided by a hegemonic superpower). This situation is risky and hazardous because of the lack of historical precedents and clear guidelines. There have been frequent assertions in recent times, by experts and nonexperts alike, concerning the imminent demise of nation-state politics; but the alternative is far from obvious or readily intelligible.[9] The hazards of the situation are particularly evident in the case of war or military conflict, because of uncertainties regarding rules of engagement. Traditional interstate warfare—although deplorable and destructive—had at least the advantage of being hedged in by relatively well established rules governing the beginning and the conduct of war (*ius ad bellum, ius in bello*). No such established rules are available in the case of domestic or civil warfare—whether the latter occurs inside a nation-state or in the nascent cosmopolis. Historical experience teaches that civil wars tend to be marked by particular savagery and brutality—because combatants are protected neither by civil nor by international rules or norms.

The hazards of contemporary international politics were clearly brought out into the open by September 11 and its aftermath: the so-called "war on terrorism."[10] From the beginning, this war was ambivalent and amorphous. The initial attacks were launched not by a state but by a private "warlord" and his followers (although they may have enjoyed the protection of a regime). The American response was swift, but also ambivalent. In the press and the media, the response was firmly proclaimed as a "war"—evident in the rhetoric of the "war on terrorism" or "America's new war." But a war against whom? Against a public regime or state (say Afghanistan and later Iraq)? In that case, the normal rules of warfare applied (*ius ad bellum, ius in bello*). Or was it a military action against a private band of outlaws or terrorists? In that case, the action hovered in a legal vacuum—since neither international norms nor domestic civil laws (of America or Afghanistan) could be invoked. The hazards of the situation were further illustrated in later phases of the military campaign, when large numbers of Taliban and other enemy fighters were captured. Given the repeated designation of the campaign as a "war," one could with reason expect that fighters captured in that war would become "prisoners of war" (POWs) entitled to the protection of familiar international conventions. When the United States suddenly chose the term "detainees," it seemed to indicate that the campaign had not been a "war" after all, but rather something like a global police action or a global "domestic" conflict (akin to a global civil war). But what are the rules authorizing or regulating such action?

In this respect, September 11 brought into the open a global political "deficit": the lack of norms and institutions mediating, or bridging the gap, between trans- and internationalism, that is, between the emerging globalism and the traditional system of nation-states. Here a major global lesson comes into view: the need to build viable institutions and multilateral conventions able to remedy the dangers implicit in the mentioned legal vacuum or no-man's-land. Such mediating institutions—today in short supply—could be of a regional or functional type; but regionalism has special advantages because of its democratic potential (its closeness to the people in the area) and its tendency to curb absolute or unilateral political power (which inevitably corrupts those who wield it). History teaches that power cannot be contained by wishful thinking but only by a constellation of lateral institutions—an insight which has found application in the doctrine of the "separation of powers" and the old European practice of "balance of power." A promising example of a functioning regional institution today is the European Union; other more fledgling examples exist in South Asia and the Far East. In their effort to restore or redesign the *dar al-Islam,* Muslims might take some cues from the European Union—not for aggressive or bellicose purposes but for the sake of cultivating a peaceful regional system of rule governance (preserving diversity in unity).[11] Within a stable and tolerant Muslim commonwealth, the danger of terrorism would be minimized and could be handled mainly through internal mechanisms. The task, as anyone can see, is enormous; but the alternative is the morass of terrorism and the "wars" it triggers. The issue is not one of optimism or pessimism, but of active engagement. I, for one, am unwilling to abandon the promise contained in Immanuel Kant's vision of "perpetual peace"—even if we are only able to advance inch by inch toward this goal.[12]

Preface

1. Alasdair MacIntyre, *After Virtue: A Study in Moral Theory* (Notre Dame, IN: University of Notre Dame Press, 1981). As he writes there (p. 2): "We possess indeed simulacra of morality, we continue to use many of the key expressions. But we have—very largely, if not entirely—lost our comprehension, both theoretical and practical, of morality."

2. Erasmus, *The Handbook of the Militant Christian,* in John P. Dolan, ed., *The Essential Erasmus* (New York: Mentor Book, 1964), p. 93.

3. Erasmus, *The Complaint of Peace* (1517), in Dolan, *The Essential Erasmus,* p. 197.

4. *The Complaint of Peace,* p. 203.

CHAPTER ONE.   Peace Talks: An Enduring Complaint

1. Erasmus, *The Complaint of Peace* (1517), in John P. Dolan, ed. and trans., *The Essential Erasmus* (New York: Mentor Book, 1964), pp. 177–178. For a slightly different translation see Erika Rummel, ed., *The Erasmus Reader* (Toronto: University of Toronto Press, 1996), pp. 288–289. In the following, I combine the two editions and translations.

2. *The Essential Erasmus,* pp. 179–180.

3. *The Essential Erasmus,* pp. 187–188, 192, 197, 200–201.

4. *The Essential Erasmus,* pp. 182–183; *The Erasmus Reader,* pp. 295–297.

5. *The Essential Erasmus,* pp. 182–185; *The Erasmus Reader,* pp. 295, 297–299.

6. *The Essential Erasmus,* pp. 185, 188, 191; *The Erasmus Reader,* pp. 299–302.

7. For some of the pope's statements see *South Bend Tribune,* January 1, 2001, p. 1, and July 28, p. 1.

8. His Holiness the Dalai Lama, *Ethics for the New Millennium* (New York: Riverhead Books, 1999), pp. 203, 205–206.

9. See Bo Wirmark, *The Buddhists in Vietnam: An Alternative View of the War,* ed. Joseph Gerson (Brussels: War Resisters' International, 1975), p. 32; Thich Nhat Hanh, *Vietnam: Lotus in a Sea of Fire,* with a foreword by Thomas Merton (New York: Hill and Wang, 1967), and *Love in Action: The Nonviolent Struggle for Peace in Vietnam* (Paris: Vietnamese Buddhist Peace Delegation, n.d.); also James H. Forest, *The Unified Buddhist Church of Vietnam: Fifteen Years of Reconciliation* (The Hague: International Fellowship of Reconciliation, 1978), p. 12.

10. See especially Christopher S. Queen and Sallie B. King, eds., *Engaged Buddhism: Buddhist Liberation Movements in Asia* (Albany, NY: State University of New York Press, 1996). The book deals in some detail with such figures or movements as A. T. Ariyaratne in Sri Lanka, Buddhadasa Bhikkhu and Sulak Sivaraksa in Thailand, Thich Nhat Hanh in Vietnam, and Soka Gakkai in Japan.

11. See in this context Daniel Berrigan and Thich Nhat Hanh, *The Raft Is Not the Shore: Conversations Toward a Buddhist/Christian Awareness* (Boston: Beacon Press, 1975).

12. John Howard Yoder, *For the Nations: Essays Public and Evangelical* (Grand Rapids, MI: Eerdmans Publishing Co., 1997), p. 235; see also his *The Politics of Jesus,* 2nd ed. (Grand Rapids, MI: Eerdmans, 1994). Compare also Stanley Hauerwas, *The Peaceable Kingdom: A Primer in Christian Ethics* (Notre Dame, IN: University of Notre Dame Press, 1983), and John Paul Lederach, *Building Peace: Sustainable Reconciliation in Divided Societies* (Washington, DC: United States Institute of Peace Press, 1997).

13. See Yoder, *For the Nations,* pp. 51–53. See also Stefan Zweig, *Jewish Legends,* ed. Leon Botstein (New York: Marcus Wiener, 1987), and Arthur A. Cohen, *The Jew: Essays from Martin Buber's Journal "Der Jude"* (Tuscaloosa, AL: University of Alabama Press, 1980).

14. Chandra Muzaffer, *Rights, Religion and Reform: Enhancing Human Dignity Through Spiritual and Moral Transformation* (London & New York:

Routledge Curzon, 2002), p. 357. See also his *Human Rights and the World Order* (Penang: Just World Trust, 1993).

15. Hannah Arendt, "On Violence," in *Crises of the Republic* (New York: Harcourt Brace Jovanovich, 1972), p. 177.

16. Walter Benjamin, "The Work of Art in the Age of Mechanical Reproduction," in *Illuminations,* ed. Hannah Arendt, trans. Harry Zohn (New York: Harcourt, Brace & World, 1968), pp. 243–244. Compare in this context also Albert Camus, *Resistance, Rebellion, and Death* (New York: Vintage, 1961).

17. *The Erasmus Reader,* p. 319.

18. This chapter gains particular importance in view of the widespread neglect of international law by major powers in our time, and by the willful and cynical manipulation of international institutions (like the United Nations) for great power purposes. In this respect, Rawls's notion of a "law of peoples" is significant because it points to a time when peoples will rein in and hold accountable their rulers.

19. As Merleau-Ponty wrote in 1947 (in a passage full of forebodings): "Communism is often discussed in terms of the contrast between deception, cunning, violence, propaganda, and the respect for truth, law, and individual consciousness—in short, the opposition between political realism and liberal values. Communists reply that in democracies cunning, violence, propaganda, and *realpolitik* in the guise of liberal principles are the substance of foreign or colonial politics and even of domestic politics. Respect for law and liberty has served to justify police suppression of strikes in America; today [1947] it serves to justify military suppression in Indochina or in Palestine and the development of an American empire in the Middle East. The material and moral culture of England presupposes the exploitation of the colonies. . . . Thus there is mystification in liberalism." See *Humanism and Terror: An Essay on the Communist Problem,* trans. John O'Neill (Boston: Beacon Press, 1969), p. xiii.

20. Confucius, *Analects* 1:1; see *The Analects of Confucius,* trans. Arthur Waley (New York: Vintage Books, 1989), p. 93. As I have been told by experts, the idea of a "sixth relationship" had actually been broached by some Chinese intellectuals in the early part of the twentieth century. Compare in this respect Yang Xiao, "Liang Qichao's Social and Political Philosophy," in Chung-ying Chen and Nicolas Bunnin, eds., *Contemporary Chinese Philosophy* (London: Blackwell, 2002), pp. 17–36.

21. See Norberto Bobbio, *In Praise of Meekness: Essays on Ethics and Politics,* trans. Teresa Chataway (Cambridge, UK: Polity Press, 2000). This reference is a welcome occasion for me to express my profound gratitude to Professor Bobbio, who, despite his many other duties, took me under his wings when I was a fledgling postgraduate student at the Institute of European Studies in Turin in the late 1950s. One of my earliest published essays was devoted to his thought: "Studie über Norberto Bobbio," *Archiv für Rechts- und Sozialphilosophie,* vol. 42 (1956), pp. 403–428.

22. Indicative of Heidegger's "turning" is a study he wrote at the beginning of the Second World War where he points to the looming prospect of "limitless wars (*grenzenlose Kriege*) furthering the unconditional empowerment of power." In the same study he denounces the warmongers of his time as "global master criminals" who "can be counted on the fingers of one hand." See *Die Geschichte des Seyns,* ed. Peter Trawny (*Gesamtausgabe,* vol. 69; Frankfurt-Main: Klostermann, 1998), pp. 44, 78; also my "Resisting Totalizing Unformity: Martin Heidegger on *Macht* and *Machenschaft,*" in *Achieving Our World: Toward a Global and Plural Democracy* (Lanham, MD: Rowman & Littlefield, 2001), pp. 189–213.

CHAPTER TWO.   A War against the Turks? Erasmus on War and Peace

1. Samuel P. Huntington, "The Clash of Civilizations?" in *Foreign Affairs,* vol. 72 (Summer 1993), pp. 22–49. See also Sheldon S. Wolin, "Fugitive Democracy," in Seyla Benhabib, ed., *Democracy and Difference: Contesting the Boundaries of the Political* (Princeton: Princeton University Press, 1996), pp. 31–45; and my "Beyond Fugitive Democracy," in *Achieving Our World: Toward a Global and Plural Democracy* (Lanham, MD: Rowman & Littlefield, 2001), pp. 71–89.

2. Erasmus, *The Praise of Folly* (*Moriae encomium,* 1511), in John P. Dolan, ed., *The Essential Erasmus* (New York: Mentor Book, 1964), pp. 94–173.

3. Erasmus, "On the War against the Turks," in Erika Rummel, ed., *The Erasmus Reader* (Toronto: University of Toronto Press, 1990), pp. 316–319.

4. *The Erasmus Reader,* pp. 318–319. Erasmus adds a further restriction on the beginning of warfare (or *ius ad bellum*), one particularly congenial to our democratic (or democratizing) age: Christian princes "must not resort to

this most dangerous of expedients without the consent of their citizens and of the whole country" (p. 320).

5. *The Erasmus Reader*, pp. 317, 321–322.

6. *The Erasmus Reader*, pp. 318, 320. Contemporary readers may be reminded here of genocides in Europe, of the "dirty wars" and disappearances in Latin America, and of episodes like My Lai in Vietnam (to name just a few examples).

7. *The Erasmus Reader*, pp. 317, 323–325. To be sure, the aim of conversion still falls far short of genuine recognition. However, Erasmus's comments on this point may have been dictated by political prudence.

8. *The Erasmus Reader*, pp. 329–330, 332. Erasmus in this context (p. 332) mentions a further suspicion nurtured by some—that, under the guise of war, one or the other European ruler might aim at world domination: "The idea of universal monarchy, at which certain princes are supposed to be aiming, frightens some." While not fully sharing this fear, the preferred solution for Erasmus—given "human frailty"—resided in "a number of modest dominions, linked together by the bonds of Christianity" or ethical-religious standards.

9. Erasmus, *The Complaint of Peace* (*Querela pacis*, 1517), in Dolan, ed., *The Essential Erasmus*, pp. 177–204.

10. See *The Adages of Erasmus*, selected by William Barker (Toronto: University of Toronto Press, 2001), pp. 317–356 (Adage IV, i, 1). According to Barker, the proverb appeared as a single sentence in the collection of 1500, but expanded into the longest essay by 1515.

11. *The Adages of Erasmus*, pp. 319, 321–322.

12. *The Adages of Erasmus*, p. 323. The *Adages* contain a very brief entry on the saying "*homo homini lupus*" (man is a wolf to man) and a much longer essay on the parallel saying "*homo homini deus*" (man is a god to man). See pp. 37–41 (Adage I, i, 69 and I, i, 70). For Thomas Hobbes's invocation and privileging of the former proverb see *De Cive or The Citizen*, ed. Sterling P. Lamprecht (New York: Appleton-Century-Crofts, 1949), p. 1 (Dedicatory Letter). Compare also *De Cive*, chapter 1, pp. 21–30; and *Leviathan*, Part I, chapter 13 (London: Everyman's Library, 1953), pp. 63–66.

13. *The Adages of Erasmus*, pp. 324–325.

14. *The Adages of Erasmus*, pp. 319–320. (The citation has been corrected for gender bias.) For some recent trends in "philosophical anthropology"

pointing in a similar direction see, e.g., Helmuth Plessner, *Die Stufen des Organischen und der Mensch, Einleitung in die philosophische Anthropologie* (2nd ed.; Berlin: de Gruyter, 1965); *Conditio Humana* (Pfullingen: Neske, 1964); and *Laughing and Crying: A Study of the Limits of Human Behavior*, trans. James S. Churchill and Marjorie Grene (Evanston, IL: Northwestern University Press, 1970); also my "Social Role and 'Human Nature': Plessner's Philosophical Anthropology," in *Beyond Dogma and Despair* (Notre Dame, IN: University of Notre Dame Press, 1981), pp. 69–93.

15. *The Adages of Erasmus*, pp. 319, 328. As Erasmus adds (p. 350): "If you examine the matter more closely you will find that almost all wars between Christians have arisen either from stupidity or from malice. A few youths, with no experience, have been influenced by the bad example of their forbears and of stories which fools have spread from foolish books. Then they have been encouraged by the call of flatterers, goaded by lawyers and theologians, with the consent or connivance of bishops, perhaps even at their demand." On the notion of "experience" compare Martin Heidegger, *Hegel's Concept of Experience*, trans. J. Glenn Gray and Fred D. Wieck (New York: Harper & Row, 1970); Hans-Georg Gadamer, *Truth and Method*, 2nd rev. ed., trans. Joel Weinsheimer and Donald G. Marshall (New York: Crossroad, 1989), pp. 346–362.

16. *The Adages of Erasmus*, pp. 350–352.

17. *The Adages of Erasmus*, p. 353. For interpretations of Erasmus as basically a precursor of Enlightenment rationalism and secular liberalism compare, e.g., Roland Bainton, *The Reformation of the Sixteenth Century* (Boston: Beacon Press, 1952); Preserved Smith, *Erasmus* (New York: Harper & Bros., 1923); and Johan Huizinga, *Erasmus of Rotterdam* (London: Phaidon Press, 1952).

18. How far Erasmus was removed from any kind of fanatical or "fundamentalist" militancy can be gleaned from a concluding passage in the *Handbook* where he warns readers against falling "into the clutches of those superstitious religious who, partly for their own advantage, partly out of great fervor, but certainly not out of any definite knowledge, 'wander about seas and deserts'. If they ever get their hands on a man returning from vices to virtue, then by outrageous arguments, blandishments, even threats, they drag him into the monastic life." See *The Handbook of the Militant Christian*, in Dolan, ed., *The Essential Erasmus*, p. 92.

19. *The Essential Erasmus*, pp. 13, 28, 37. As one should note well, Erasmus's aim was not to condemn theorizing or philosophizing as such—one

of his basic efforts was precisely to elucidate the "philosophy of Christ"—but rather to challenge a purely abstract speculation completely divorced from practical conduct. He valued reason and philosophy, but not as a substitute for piety and praxis. This outlook is captured in his well-known motto *"eruditio et pietas"*: learning *and* piety, not one in place of the other.

20. *The Essential Erasmus*, pp. 64, 68–69.

21. *The Essential Erasmus*, pp. 26–27. On the issue of faith vs. works one may note a recent conciliatory breakthrough in the debate between Catholic and Protestant (Lutheran) theologians—a breakthrough very much in the spirit of Erasmus's *Handbook:* the "Joint Declaration on Justification" signed on October 31, 1999, in Augsburg, the same city where the Peace of Augsburg between the confessions had been signed in 1555. (Students of comparative religious studies may also note the similarity between Erasmus's approach and what in the Hindu tradition is called *karmayoga.*)

22. *The Essential Erasmus*, pp. 273, 287–288.

23. *The Essential Erasmus*, pp. 381, 386. For Erasmus's letter see P. S. Allen, ed., *Opus Epistolarum Desiderii Erasmi Roterdami* (London: Oxford University Press, 1951), vol. VI, p. 76; cited in English translation in *The Essential Erasmus*, pp. 327–328.

24. *The Essential Erasmus*, pp. 15–16.

25. Perhaps, one way to deal with this problem might be to treat the "oneness" of God not as a numerical oneness but in the sense that God or the divine (however defined) is "the one," that is, more important than anything else in the world.

CHAPTER THREE.   The Law of Peoples: Civilizing Humanity

1. John Rawls, *The Law of Peoples, with "The Idea of Public Reason Revisited"* (Cambridge, MA: Harvard University Press, 1999), p. vi.

2. I refer here loosely to the categories differentiated by Jürgen Habermas in his "On the Pragmatic, the Ethical, and the Moral Employments of Practical Reason," in *Justification and Application: Remarks on Discourse Ethics,* trans. Ciaran P. Cronin (Cambridge, MA: MIT Press, 1994), pp. 1–17.

3. Quoted from O. F. Robinson, *The Sources of Roman Law: Problems and Methods for Ancient Historians* (London: Routledge, 1997), p. 2.

4. H. F. Jolowicz, *Roman Foundations of Modern Law* (Oxford: Clarendon Press, 1957), p. 38. As he adds (p. 39): "When in A.D. 212 the Roman citizenship was extended to all (or nearly all) the free inhabitants of the Empire, this would have meant logically the complete (or almost complete) disappearance of all law other than Roman [*ius civile*], if the personality principle had been rigidly applied. In fact, however, we know enough to say that this result did not follow immediately, whether because the principle was not sufficiently recognized, or because of the *de facto* resistance put up by the provincials . . . to an attempt to change their law by a stroke of the pen." For further details regarding the interaction between *ius civile* and *ius gentium,* and especially the role of "praetorian" legislation, see Robinson, *The Sources of Roman Law,* pp. 39–42.

5. Cicero, *De legibus,* Bk. 3, chapter 22:33.

6. These passages are found in the first book of the *Digests,* which, together with the *Institutes* and the *Codex Justiniani,* form the *Corpus Juris Civilis.*

7. A. Passerin d'Entrèves, *Natural Law: An Introduction to Legal Philosophy* (London: Hutchinson's University Library, 1951), pp. 24–26.

8. As it appears, Justinian himself was particularly insistent on adding the dimension of natural law to the compilation. See Robinson, *The Sources of Roman Law,* p. 26. Compare also Jolowicz's comment that "in Justinian's day it was not only theoretically, but in large measure practically true that one system applied throughout the Empire to all its subjects." *Roman Foundations of Modern Law,* p. 39.

9. Compare in this regard the comments of Max Harold Fisch in his "Introduction" to *The New Science of Giambattista Vico,* trans. Thomas G. Bergin and M. H. Fisch (Garden City, NY: Anchor Books, 1961), pp. xxx–xxxv.

10. Quoted from d'Entrèves, *Natural Law,* p. 33.

11. Regarding the so-called "reception" of Roman Law on the Continent, especially the work of the so-called "glossators" and "post-glossators," see, e.g., Hermann Kantorowicz, *Studies in the Glossators of Roman Law* (Cambridge, UK: Cambridge University Press, 1938), and Hermann Lange, *Römisches Recht im Mittelaltur* (Munich: Beck, 1997).

12. Antonio T. Serra, *Die Grundsätze des Staats-und Völkerrechts bei Francisco de Vitoria* (Zürich: Thomas Verlag, 1947), p. 15 (my translation). Compare also James B. Scott, *The Spanish Origin of International Law: Francisco*

de Vitoria and His Law of Nations (Oxford: Oxford University Press, 1934). The main other members of the Spanish School were Domingo de Soto (1495–1560), Luis de Molina (1535–1600), and Francisco Suárez (1548–1617).

13. Francisco de Vitoria, *The First Relectio on the Indians,* thesis 19; in Ernest Nys, ed., *De Indis et De Jure Belli Relectiones* (Washington, DC: Carnegie Institution, 1917), p. 125. Compare also Nys's comments on Vitoria and his relation to Las Casas (p. 85): "In 1519 another solemn discussion took place before the young king, Charles V, in which Diego Columbus, viceroy of the Indies, took part. Bartolomé de Las Casas made himself there the devoted advocate of the oppressed, and thus inaugurated the long series of devoted services which won for him the glorious name of defender of the liberty of the natives of America. In his *Relectiones* Francisco de Vitoria repudiates all theories, whether based on the alleged superiority of the Christians, or on their right to punish idolatry, or on the mission which might have been given them to propagate the true religion."

14. On Vitoria's relation to Erasmus see the comments of Nys, ed., *De Indis et De Jure Belli Relectiones,* pp. 77–81. Nys (p. 79) quotes from a letter written by Juan Luis Vivès to Erasmus where Vivès describes Vitoria as "a Dominican, a theologian of Paris, a man of genuine reputation, in whom much confidence is placed; more than once he defended you at Paris before numerous theologians; from his childhood he has occupied himself with literature; he admires you, he adores you. He is a teacher at Salamanca, where he holds what is called the primary chair."

15. Nys, ed., *De Indis et De Jure Belli Relectiones,* pp. 131, 134, 135, 157 (First Relectio, second section).

16. Nys, ed., *De Indis et De Jure Belli Relectiones,* pp. 151, 153; Antonio T. Serra, *Die Grundsätze des Staats-und Völkerrechts,* pp. 49–50. In a subsequent note (p. 51), Serra comments on the combination in Vitoria's work of *ius gentium naturale* and *ius inter gentes* (or *ius gentium voluntarium*), stating that this position differs both from the later "rationalist school" of international law (Pufendorf and Thomasius) and the legal positivism of the nineteenth century: whereas the former only "recognized natural [rational] law," the latter only accepted "positive law" based on human will. On this point, Bernice Hamilton seems to go astray when she writes that, for Vitoria, the law of nations (*ius gentium*) "should be classified with positive human law rather than with natural law, in spite of the fact that the jurists held the opposite

opinion." See her *Political Thought in Sixteenth-Century Spain* (Oxford: Clarendon Press, 1963), p. 99.

17. Nys, ed., *De Indis et De Jure Belli Relectiones*, pp. 168, 170–171, 173, 187. Vitoria even made provision for "conscientious objectors," stating (p. 173): "Subjects whose conscience is against the justice of a war may not engage in it whether they be right or wrong."

18. Lassa Oppenheim, *International Law: A Treatise*, vol. 1: *Peace*, 6th ed., ed. H. Lauterpacht (London: Longmans, Green & Co., 1947), pp. 85–86. J. L. Brierly is more circumspect when he writes: "Few books have won so great a reputation as the *De jure belli ac pacis;* but to regard its author as the 'founder' of international law is to exaggerate its originality and to do less than justice to the writers who preceded him; neither Grotius, nor any other single writer, can properly be said to have 'founded' the system." See his *The Law of Nations: An Introduction to the International Law of Peace*, 6th ed., ed. Sir Humphrey Waldock (Oxford: Oxford University Press, 1963), p. 28.

19. Brierly, *The Law of Nations*, p. 28.

20. In the words of James Brown Scott: In addition to being a lawyer, Grotius was also "a theologian, and was so eager to unite the sects to the Church universal that even in our day it is disputed whether he was a Protestant or Catholic at heart." See his "Introduction" to Hugo Grotius, *De Jure Belli ac Pacis Libri Tres*, vol. 2, trans. Francis W. Kelsey (Oxford: Clarendon Press, 1925), p. xix.

21. Grotius, "Prolegomena," in *De Jure Belli ac Pacis*, p. 18.

22. Grotius, *De Jure Belli ac Pacis*, pp. 38, 42, 44. In Brierly's words: "It is important, Grotius tells us, to keep the notions of the law of nature and the law of nations (to adopt a mistranslation of *ius gentium* which its new meaning makes almost necessary) distinct; but he is far from doing so himself." *The Law of Nations*, p. 30.

23. Grotius, *De Jure Belli ac Pacis*, pp. 13, 38–39. Departing from Thomistic teachings, the book only made allowance (p. 45) for "volitional divine law" based on divine will, bypassing the notion of "eternal law" (reflecting divine reason). See Oppenheim, *International Law*, vol. 1, p. 89. Passerin d'Entrèves seems to be largely on target when he writes: "Reason to the Roman lawyer was perhaps only another name for experience. For the medieval philosopher it was the gift of God. In both cases the evidence of reason had to be implemented, and indeed confirmed, by some other evidence—of fact or faith. But

now the evidence of reason is in itself sufficient. . . . [Grotius] proved that it was possible to build up a theory of laws independent of theological presuppositions. His successors completed the task." See *Natural Law*, pp. 49, 52.

24. In Grotius's words: "I have made it my concern to refer the proofs of things touching the law of nature to certain fundamental conceptions which are beyond question; so that no one can deny them without doing violence to himself. For the principles of that law . . . are in themselves manifest and clear, almost as evident as are those things which we perceive by the external senses. . . . With all truthfulness I aver that, just as the mathematicians treat their figures as abstracted from bodies, so in treating law I have withdrawn my mind from every particular fact." *De Jure Belli ac Pacis*, "Prolegomena," pp. 23, 30. The parallel with Descartes' "clear and distinct" ideas is striking.

25. Strangely, the "Prolegomena" state (p. 20) that, confronted with the "utter ruthlessness" of warfare, some people "have come to the point of forbidding all use of arms to the Christian whose rule of conduct, above everything else, comprises the duty of loving all men. To this opinion sometimes John Ferus and my fellow-countryman Erasmus seem to incline, men who have the utmost devotion to peace in both church and state." One wonders how diligently Grotius had read the works of his fellowcountryman.

26. Grotius, *De Jure Belli ac Pacis*, pp. 171–175. Grotius (p. 174) also refers to Cicero when he says "not less rightly": "Who has ever established this principle, or to whom without the gravest danger to all mankind can it be granted, that he shall have the right to kill a man by whom he says he fears that he himself later may be killed?" The passage clearly rejects the right of preemptive warfare or killing.

27. *De Jure Belli ac Pacis*, pp. 560–562.

28. *De Jure Belli ac Pacis*, pp. xxxix, 20. The book, published in 1625, was dedicated to Louis XIII of France. In his dedication (p. 5), Grotius appealed to the king with these words: "The peoples of Christian lands are so bold as to ask of you something further: that, with the extinction of warfare everywhere, through your initiative peace may come again, not only to the nations but also to the churches, and that our time may learn to subject itself to the discipline of that age [of the early church] which all we who are Christians acknowledge in true and sincere faith to have been Christian."

29. Oppenheim, *International Law*, vol. 1, p. 87. More circumspectly, Brierly comments: "It is usual in estimating the work of Grotius to speak of

its remarkable and instantaneous success; and if it is a proof of success that within a few years of its author's death his book had become a university text-book, that it has often since been appealed to in international controversies, that it has been republished and translated scores of times, and that every subsequent writer treats his name with reverence, however widely he may depart from his teaching, then Grotius must be accounted successful. But if by success is meant that the doctrines of Grotius as a whole were accepted by states and became part of the law which since his time has regulated their relations, then his work was an almost complete failure." *The Law of Nations,* p. 33.

   30. See Oppenheim, *International Law,* vol. 1, pp. 90–95; also Brierly, *The Law of Nations,* pp. 34–40.

   31. Immanuel Kant, "Perpetual Peace: A Philosophical Sketch," in Hans Reiss, ed., *Kant's Political Writings* (Cambridge: Cambridge University Press, 1970), p. 114. To be sure, Kant's treatise relied basically on "philosophers' law" and made little or no reference to actual *ius gentium.* This emphasis is also evident in the "secret article" attached to the treatise (p. 115): "The maxims of the philosophers on the conditions under which public peace is possible shall be consulted by states which are armed for war." The same emphasis is present in "The Metaphysics of Morals" where Kant exhorts "jurists" to abandon "empirical principles for a time and look(s) for the sources of these judgments in the realm of pure reason" (p. 132).

   32. Rawls explicitly differentiates his approach from that of Kant, but the distinction remains somewhat hazy. As he writes: "I should say the following [vis-à-vis Kant]: at no point are we deducing the principles of right and justice, or decency, or the principles of rationality, from a conception of practical reason in the background. Rather, we are giving content to an idea of practical reason and three of its component parts, the ideas of reasonableness, decency, and rationality. The criteria for these three normative ideas are not deduced, but enumerated and characterized in each case. . . . Although the idea of practical reason is associated with Kant, political liberalism is altogether distinct from his transcendental idealism." Rawls also distinguishes the "law of peoples" and modern "natural law," but in a somewhat misleading way, claiming that natural law was thought to be "part of the law of God" (which is not unequivocally true for Grotius and his successors). See Rawls, *The Law of Peoples,* pp. 86–87, 103–104.

33. *The Law of Peoples,* pp. 37, 91–94. In large measure, Rawls's arguments concur with recent restatements of the traditional "just war" theory. Compare in this regard, e.g., John Joseph O'Connor, *Conditions for a Just War* (New York: Pro Ecclesia, 1999); Jean Bethke Elshtain, ed., *Just War Theory* (New York: New York University Press, 1992); Michael Walzer, *Just and Unjust Wars* (New York: Basic Books, 1977).

34. Rawls, *The Law of Peoples,* pp. 53, 95–96, 101. Regarding conduct in war, Rawls also critiques (p. 102, note 26) the excessive use of airpower in recent wars, calling such airpower "a great temptation to evil" because of its unpredictable effects on civilian populations. Challenging the "new-speak" of "collateral damage" he states tersely: "Proper military doctrine declares that airpower must not be used to attack civilians."

35. *The Law of Peoples,* pp. 54–70. As in his other writings, Rawls uses the term "liberalism" in a broad and moralistic way (often identifying or confounding it with "democracy" or "constitutional democracy"). This usage is dubious given the fact that "liberalism"—especially in its "neo-liberal" variety—often has economic and social consequences (of inequality and exploitation) which can hardly be termed "just" or "well-ordered." On the other hand, "outlaw states" seem to have no rights at all and to be subject to attack at will. As Rawls notes, in a harsh phrase (p. 103): "Certainly war is a kind of hell; but why should that mean that normative distinctions cease to hold?" That view is entirely at odds with the traditional *ius gentium,* which granted to all individuals and societies—just or unjust—the right of self-defense.

36. *The Law of Peoples,* pp. 25, 28–29, 105. As he adds (p. 105): "The statesman must look to the political world and must, in extreme cases, be able to distinguish between the interests of the well-ordered regime he or she serves and the dictates of the religious, philosophical, or moral doctrine that he or she personally lives by." The notion of "supreme emergency" exemptions goes back to Michael Walzer, *Just and Unjust Wars,* pp. 255–265.

37. Rawls, *The Law of Peoples,* pp. 6–7. The text (p. 10) explicitly appeals to Kant's "Perpetual Peace" and his idea of *foedus pacificum.*

38. Richard Falk, "The World Order between Inter-State Law and the Law of Humanity: The Role of Civil Society Institutions," in Daniele Archibugi and David Held, eds., *Cosmopolitan Democracy: An Agenda for a New World Order* (Cambridge, UK: Polity Press, 1995), pp. 170–171, 178–179.

CHAPTER FOUR. A Global Spiritual Resurgence? Some Christian and Islamic Legacies

1. J. Matthew Ashley, "Contemplation in Prophetic Action: Oscar Romero's Challenge to Spirituality in North America," in *Monseñor Oscar Romero: Human Rights Apostle* (Notre Dame, IN: Helen Kellogg Institute for International Studies, 2000), pp. 25, 30. As Ashley notes, the phrase "spiritual marketplace" was coined by Wade Clark Roof. For a similar assessment see Peter Toon, *What Is Spirituality? And Is It for Me?* (London: Daybreak, 1989), who writes (p. ix): "Spirituality has become an 'in' word. Inside and outside the churches people are talking about it—or at least using the word. Publishers are listing a growing number of volumes under the heading 'Books on Spirituality'."

2. See Hans Küng and Karl-Josef Kuschel, eds., *A Global Ethic: The Declaration of the Parliament of the World's Religions* (New York: Continuum, 1995), pp. 36, 101. Muller also quoted the remark by André Malraux that either the third millennium will be "spiritual" or there will be no third millennium.

3. Regarding the meaning of "spirit" in different traditions see, e.g., the article on "Soul, Spirit," in Keith Grim et al., eds., *The Perennial Dictionary of World Religions* (San Francisco: Harper & Row, 1989), pp. 699–702.

4. See Plato, *Republic,* Book IV, 435b–441c. In modified form, the tripartition persists in Kant's three critiques and, still more recently, in the sociological (Weberian) distinction of the three "value spheres" of science, ethics, and aesthetics (or art).

5. On the Chinese tradition of *hsin* see especially Wm. Theodore de Bary, *Neo-Confucian Orthodoxy and the Learning of the Mind-and-Heart* (New York: Columbia University Press, 1981).

6. See Philip Sheldrake, "What Is Spirituality?" in Kenneth J. Collins, ed., *Exploring Christian Spirituality: An Ecumenical Reader* (Grand Rapids, MI: Baker Books, 2000), pp. 26–30. In Sheldrake's words (p. 27), it would be most fruitful "to study the 'mysticism' of the Fathers as the very *heart of their theology.*" Compare also Jordan Aumann, *Spiritual Theology* (London: Sheed and Ward, 1980).

7. Martin Luther, "The Freedom of a Christian," in Timothy F. Lull, ed., *Martin Luther's Basic Theological Writings* (Minneapolis, MN: Fortress Press, 1989), pp. 344–346. Compare also Bengt Hoffman, "Lutheran Spirituality," in Collins, ed., *Exploring Christian Spirituality,* pp. 122–137.

8. Charles Taylor, *Sources of the Self: The Making of the Modern Identity* (Cambridge, MA: Harvard University Press, 1989), pp. 512–513. From an explicitly Christian perspective Sheldrake writes: "I would suggest that what the word 'spirituality' seeks to express is the conscious human response to God that is both personal and ecclesial." See his "What Is Spirituality?" in Collins, ed., *Exploring Spirituality*, p. 25. Compare also Karl Rahner's comments: "It has been said that the Christian of the future will be either a mystic or no longer a Christian. If we mean by mysticism not peculiar parapsychological phenomena but rather a genuine experience of God arising from the heart of existence, then the statement is correct and its truth and depth will become clearer in the spirituality of the future." See Rahner, "In Sorge um die Kirche," in *Schriften zur Theologie*, vol. 14 (Einsiedeln: Benziger, 1960), p. 375.

9. As Wolfgang Böhme writes: "Christian mysticism [or spirituality] cannot be grounded entirely in 'inner' experience or reflect a pure inwardness. There must also be an impulse from beyond, an appeal in some kind of mundane form." See Böhme, ed., *Zu Dir Hin: Über mystische Lebenserfahrung, von Meister Eckhart bis Paul Celan* (Frankfurt-Main: Insel Verlag, 1987), p. 12. For further definitional clarifications see Walter Principe, "Toward Defining Spirituality," in Collins, ed., *Exploring Christian Spirituality*, pp. 43–59; and Alister E. McGrath, *Christian Spirituality: An Introduction* (Oxford: Blackwell, 1999). For a broader comparative perspective see Eliot Deutsch, *Religion and Spirituality* (Albany, NY: State University of New York Press, 1995).

10. In some versions of gnosticism, dualism or "dyotheism" is greatly attenuated in favor of an ascending scale of insight available to a select group. What links the various branches of gnosticism is mainly the stress on "*sophia*" or intellectual illumination leading to knowledge of the divine. In the Indian tradition, the two modes of spirituality discussed in this chapter correspond to the pathways of "*jñana*," on the one hand, and "*bhakti*" and "*karma*," on the other.

11. On gnostic traditions and teachings see especially Hans Jonas, *The Gnostic Religion* (Boston: Beacon Press, 1963); *Gnosis und spätantiker Geist*, 2 vols. (Göttingen: Vanderhoeck & Ruprecht, 1934–35); Gilles Quispel, *Gnosis als Weltreligion* (Zürich: Origo, 1951). In view of the tendency to hermeticism, Eric Voegelin's association of gnosticism with modern political mass movements appears odd and unconvincing; see his *Science, Politics and Gnosticism* (Chicago: Regnery, 1968).

12. The following presentation stays largely on an ecumenical level, thus bypassing denominational differences. For a discussion of "Orthodox," "Anglican," "Methodist," "Evangelical," and similar forms of Christian spirituality see Collins, ed., *Exploring Christian Spirituality*, Part 3, pp. 93–226.

13. Emil Brunner, *Die Mystik und das Wort* (Tübingen: Mohr, 1924), p. 387; cited in Böhme, *Zu Dir Hin*, p. 12.

14. At that time, Christian gnosticism often took the form of "docetism," a doctrine according to which Jesus was only seemingly human and his death on the cross only an apparent death, but actually an illusion.

15. See Malcolm Barber, *The Trial of the Templars* (Oxford: Cambridge University Press, 1994), p. 46; Trevor Ravenscroft and Tim Wallace-Murphy, *The Mark of the Beast* (London: Sphere Books, 1990), p. 53; Tim Wallace-Murphy and Marilyn Hopkins, *Rosslyn: Guardian of the Secrets of the Holy Grail* (Shaftesbury, UK: Element Books, 2000), pp. 103–104.

16. Otto Uttendörfer, *Zinzendorfs religiöse Grundgedanken* (Herrnhut: Bruderhof, 1935), p. 161; cited in Dietrich Meyer, "Christus mein ander Ich: Zu Zinzendorfs Verhältnis zur Mystik," in Böhme, ed., *Zu Dir Hin*, p. 213.

17. In fact, the symbolism can be traced back even further to Jewish "wisdom" literature in which God and humankind were seen as linked in covenantal love.

18. Thomas à Kempis, *The Imitation of Christ* (New York: Penguin, 1952); also *De imitatione Christi* (Paris: Duprey, 1860), vol. 2, p. 38; cited in Josef Sudbrack, "Christliche Begegnungsmystik," in Böhme, *Zu Dir Hin*, pp. 142–143.

19. Gerhard Ebeling, *Die Wahrheit des Evangeliums* (Tübingen: Mohr, 1981), p. 207. Similarly Wolfgang Böhme observes: "Love is possible only when there is a Thou or You *toward* whom we can move, who addresses us, and with whom we can have a 'loving dialogue'. . . . Hence, the divine You remains the reference point, which militates against a [gnostic or pantheistic] submergence or disappearance in the cosmos [or in nothingness]." See *Zu Dir Hin*, p. 11. Böhme also cites Martin Buber's rejection of a cosmic union or fusion, which, for Buber, only reflected human conceit and self-aggrandizement; *I and Thou*, trans. Ronald G. Smith (Edinburgh: T & T Clark, 1958), pp. 109–123.

20. For the passages from John of the Cross see Sudbrack, "Christliche Begegnungsmystik," in Böhme, *Zu Dir Hin*, pp. 146–148. As Sudbrack comments (pp. 148, 150): "There is here no fusion with the godhead, no expansion

of consciousness to cosmic dimensions, no insinuation of ultimate convergence, nor any submergence in private subjectivity. . . . With indisputable clarity John of the Cross stresses the unbridgeable distance from God on the level of knowledge and sensation, while finding a possible union only through active love." (I bypass here John's and Sudbrack's linkage of loving with "willing.") Compare also Marilyn M. Mallory, *Christian Mysticism—Transcending Techniques: A Theological Reflection on the Teaching of St. John of the Cross* (Amsterdam: Van Gorcum, 1977).

21. Teresa of Avila, *The Autobiography of St. Teresa of Avila* (Rockford, IL: Tan Books and Publ., 1997), cited by Sudbrack in *Zu Dir Hin,* pp. 152–153. In Sudbrack's view (pp. 151, 153), it is impossible to understand Teresa's life and work without attention to the congruence of devotion to God and care for humans, of contemplation and commitment to social responsibility. Ultimately, the "encounter with Jesus" was for her the "touchstone" of spirituality. See also Sudbrack, *Erfahrung einer Liebe: Teresa von Avilas Mystik als Begegnung mit Gott* (Freiburg: Herder, 1979).

22. Josef Zapf, "Die Geburt Gottes im Menschen: Nach Johannes Tauler," in Böhme, *Zu Dir Hin,* p. 89. Compare also Georg Hofmann, ed., *Johannes Tauler: Predigten* (Einsiedeln: Johannes Verlag, 1979).

23. For the above see Dietrich Meyer, "Christus mein ander Ich," in Böhme, *Zu Dir Hin,* pp. 214–215, 217, 219. In Meyer's words (p. 225): Zinzendorf's spirituality involves "union with Christ as personal encounter and friendship." For him, this personal relation is primary, in contrast to any kind of "mystical fusion." Compare also Meyer, *Der Christozentrismus des späten Zinzendorf* (Bern: Herbert Lang, 1973).

24. For some philosophical discussion of Eckhart's thought see Martin Heidegger, *Der Satz vom Grund* (Pfullingen: Neske, 1957), pp. 71–74; *Gelassenheit,* 2nd ed. (Pfullingen: Neske, 1970); and John D. Caputo, *The Mystical Element in Heidegger's Thought* (Columbus, OH: Ohio University Press, 1978).

25. Meister Eckhart, *Deutsche Predigten und Traktate,* ed. Josef Quint (Munich: Hanser, 1979), pp. 53–57, 303–306; and *Meister Eckhart: The Essential Sermons, Commentaries, Treatises and Defenses,* trans. Edmund College and Bernard McGinn (New York: Paulist Press, 1981), pp. 177–181 (Sermon 2). For a discussion of the sermon "*Beati pauperes spiritu*" see Otto Pöggeler, "Sein und Nichts: Mystische Elemente bei Heidegger und Celan," in Böhme, *Zu Dir Hin,* pp. 282–283. For a discussion of the sermon on Mary and Martha, see J. Matthew Ashley, "Contemplation in Prophetic Action," pp. 28–29. As

Ashley comments, in his sermon Eckhart showed himself as a proponent of medieval "contemplation in action" and as a forerunner of the "mysticism of everyday life" favored by later Protestant Pietists.

26. Jacques Derrida, *Sauf le Nom* (Paris: Editions Galileé, 1993), pp. 15–16, 31, 39, 76. See also Angelus Silesius, *Cherubinischer Wandersmann/Pélerin cherubinique* (Paris: Aubier, 1946).

27. For the above citations see Alois M. Haas, "Christförmig sein: Die Christusmystik des Angelus Silesius," in Böhme, *Zu Dir Hin*, pp. 181–183, 185, 188. Haas relies on H. L. Held, *Angelus Silesius: Sämtliche Poetische Werke in drei Bänden* (Munich: Hanser, 1949–53).

28. Although rarely the target of *agape*, the Prophet himself is sometimes endowed with qualities of gnostic spirituality. A prominent example is this statement attributed to him: "I am an 'Arab without the letter *ayn* [i.e., a *rabb* or Lord]; I am Ahmad without the *mim* [mortality]; he who has seen me has seen the Truth." See the entry *"al-Insan al-Kamil"* ("the perfect man") in Cyril Glassé, ed., *The Concise Encyclopedia of Islam* (San Francisco: Harper Press, 1989), p. 189.

29. Cited in Glassé, ed., *The Concise Encyclopedia of Islam*, p. 168. (*Tarjumán al-Ashwaq* means "The Interpreter of Longings.") Among Ibn Arabi's most celebrated writings are *al-Futúhát al-Makkiyyah* ("The Meccan Revelations") and *Fusus al-Hikam* ("Bezels of Wisdom").

30. There is a sprawling literature surrounding Ibn Arabi's work. Compare especially Rom Landau, *The Philosophy of Ibn Arabi* (London: Allen and Unwin, 1959); Ibn al-Arabi, *Sufis of Andalusia* (Berkeley: University of California Press, 1972); Claude Addas, *Ibn Arabi ou, La quête du soufre rouge* (Paris: Gallimard, 1989). In the Indian tradition, *"wahdat al-wujud"* can be broadly compared with a radical form of *Advaita Vedanta* according to which all finite beings are illusory and dissolved in the unity of *brahman*.

31. Ibn Arabi, "Whoso Knoweth Himself . . . ," trans. T. H. Weir (Glouces-teshire, UK: Beshara Press, 1976), pp. 4–5.

32. "Whoso Knoweth Himself . . . ," pp. 15, 20–23. A famous esoteric mystic who had claimed "I am God" long before Ibn Arabi was the Persian Husayn ibn Mansur, known as al-Hallaj (857–922). He was put to death by the Abbasid authorities in Baghdad.

33. See the entries on "Ismailis" and "Assassins" in Glassé, ed., *The Concise Encyclopedia of Islam*, pp. 53–55, 194–200. In accordance with their dualistic doctrine, some Ismailis ascribed to the Prophet Muhammad a merely

exoteric knowledge, while crediting Ali (the fourth caliph and first imam) with esoteric or "ineffable" knowledge. For a different and more favorable account see Farhad Daftarg, *A Short History of the Ismailis* (Edinburgh: Edinburgh University Press, 1998), pp. 15–16.

34. Frithjof Schuon, *Gnosis: Divine Wisdom,* trans. G. E. H. Palmer (London: John Murray, 1959), p. 80. Even more gnostic, in Ibn Arabi's vein, is this passage (p. 77): "There are various ways of expressing or defining the difference between gnosis and love—or between *jñana* and *bhakti*—but here we wish to consider one criterion only, and it is this: for the 'volitional' or 'affective' man (the *bhakta*) God is 'He' and the ego is 'I', whereas for the 'gnostic' or 'intellective' man (the *jñani*) God is 'I'—or 'Self'—and the ego is 'he' or 'other'. . . . Most men are individualists and consequently but little suited to make 'a concrete abstraction' of their empirical 'I', a process which is an intellectual and not a moral one: in other words, few have the gift of impersonal contemplation . . . such as will allow 'God to think in us'." Compare also his *Esoterism as Principle and as Way,* trans. William Stoddart (Bedfont, Middlesex, UK: Perennial Books, 1981). For arguments along lines similar to those of Schuon see Sayyed Hossein Nasr, *Knowledge and the Sacred* (Albany, NY: State University of New York Press, 1989).

35. *The Essential Rumi,* trans. Coleman Barks, with John Moyne et al. (Edison, NJ: Castle Books), pp. 21, 53, 131; also the entry "Jalal ad-Din ar-Rumi," in Glassé, ed., *The Concise Encyclopedia of Islam,* p. 205.

36. *The Essential Rumi,* p. 199; also William C. Chittick, *The Sufi Path of Love: The Spiritual Teachings of Rumi* (Albany, NY: State University of New York Press, 1983), p. 242.

37. See *The Essential Rumi,* p. 109; and Glassé, ed., *The Concise Encyclopedia of Islam,* p. 205.

38. Ashley, "Contemplation in Prophetic Action," p. 30. Regarding the danger of a global class division see, e.g., Richard Falk, *Predatory Globalization: A Critique* (Cambridge, UK: Polity Press, 1999). That altruism may occasionally lead to a meddlesome manipulation of other lives can readily be acknowledged. However, it is possible to distinguish between such an attitude and a caring orientation which precisely respects and nurtures the freedom and integrity of others. See in this respect Martin Heidegger's distinction between a "managerial" care and an "anticipating-emancipatory" solicitude; *Being and Time,* trans. Joan Stambaugh (Albany, NY: State University of New York Press, 1996), pp. 113–115 (Part One, par. 26).

39. Ashley, "Contemplation in Prophetic Action," p. 29.

40. See Wilder Foote, ed., *Servant of Peace: A Selection of the Speeches and Statements of Dag Hammarskjöld* (New York: Harper & Row, 1977), pp. 24, 58. In this connection, one may also recall an address given by Czech President Václav Havel at Harvard University in 1996 under the title "A Challenge to Nourish Spiritual Roots Buried Under Our Thin Global Skin." In that address, Havel spoke of an "archetypal spirituality" implanted in humankind, beyond the confines of organized faiths, and "lying dormant in the deepest roots of most, if not all, cultures." See *Just Commentary*, no. 28 (July 1996), p. 3.

CHAPTER FIVE. Cosmopolitanism: Religious, Moral, and Political

1. The idea of a "struggle for recognition" goes back to Hegel's *Phenomenology*, where the process is described, somewhat darkly or starkly, as a "struggle of life and death." See G. W. F. Hegel, *The Phenomenology of Mind*, trans. J. B. Baillie (New York: Harper & Row, 1967), pp. 229–240. In an attenuated form, the idea of mutual recognition has been taken up and developed by Charles Taylor, especially in "The Politics of Recognition," in Amy Gutmann, ed., *Multiculturalism and "The Politics of Recognition"* (Princeton: Princeton University Press, 1992), pp. 25–73.

2. Hans Küng, *Global Responsibility: In Search of a New World Ethic* (New York: Crossroad, 1991). For the text of the "Declaration Toward a Global Ethic" see Hans Küng and Karl-Josef Kuschel, eds., *A Global Ethic: The Declaration of the Parliament of the World's Religions* (New York: Continuum, 1995). In the latter text, Küng provides comments on the "history, significance and method" of the declaration (pp. 43–76), while Kuschel traces the historical development of the Parliament of the World's Religions from 1893 to 1993 (pp. 77–105). Compare also Marcus Braybrooke, *Pilgrimage of Hope: One Hundred Years of Global Interfaith Dialogue* (New York: Crossroad, 1992).

3. Küng, *Global Responsibility*, pp. xv–xvi, 9, 28, 35. Curiously, Küng adds (p. 35): "Postmodern men and women need common values, goals, ideals, visions." Despite the congruence of the idea of an "undivided" or universal ethics with central postulates of "modern" Western philosophy, the text repeatedly associates itself with a "postmodern" outlook—whose character, however, remains ambivalent and amorphous (being linked with such phenomena as feminism, postindustrialism, and postcolonialism, pp. 3–4, 17–20).

4. *Global Responsibility,* pp. 30, 32, 42. Specific references are made to Apel, *Diskurs und Verantwortung* (Frankfurt-Main: Suhrkamp, 1988); Habermas, *Moralbewusstsein und kommunikatives Handeln* (Frankfurt-Main: Suhrkamp, 1983); Weber, "Politik als Beruf," in *Gesammelte politische Schriften* (Tübingen: Mohr, 1958), pp. 505–560; and Jonas, *Das Prinzip Verantwortung: Versuch einer Ethik für die technologische Zivilisation* (Frankfurt-Main: Suhrkamp, 1984). Turning against the critics of a transcendental-universal approach, Küng observes (p. 43): "Those who want to dispense with a transcendent principle have to follow a long path of horizontal communication with the possibility that, in the end, they have just been going round in a circle."

5. Küng, *Global Responsibility,* pp. 51, 53. As he adds confidently (p. 87): "Religion can unambiguously demonstrate why morality, ethical values and norms must be unconditionally binding (and not just where it is convenient for me) and thus universal (for all strata, classes, and races). Precisely in this way the *humanum* is rescued by being seen to be grounded in the *divinum.*"

6. Küng and Kuschel, eds., *A Global Ethic,* pp. 14, 17, 19, 21–23, 36. Regarding the objections raised by Buddhist representatives see Küng's commentary, pp. 61–65.

7. John Rawls, *A Theory of Justice* (Cambridge, MA: Harvard University Press, 1971). In some subsequent writings Rawls has toned down or qualified the universalism of his early work. Regarding Apel and Habermas compare Seyla Benhabib and Fred Dallmayr, eds., *The Communicative Ethics Controversy* (Cambridge, MA: MIT Press, 1990).

8. For some of Martha Nussbaum's earlier writings see *The Fragility of Goodness: Luck and Ethics in Greek Tragedy and Philosophy* (Cambridge, UK: Cambridge University Press, 1986); *The Therapy of Desire: Theory and Practice in Hellenistic Ethics* (Cambridge, UK: Cambridge University Press, 1993).

9. Martha Nussbaum, "Kant and Stoic Cosmopolitanism," *Journal of Political Philosophy,* vol. 5 (1997), pp. 1–3.

10. "Kant and Stoic Cosmopolitanism," pp. 4–5, 7–8, 10, 12. For the reference to Marcus Aurelius see *The Meditations,* trans. G. M. Grube (Indianapolis, IN: Hacket, 1983), IV:4; for the Kant reference see *Kant: Political Writings,* ed. Hans Reiss, trans. H. B. Nisbet (2nd ed.; Cambridge, UK: Cambridge Univesity Press, 1991), pp. 93–130.

11. Martha Nussbaum, "Citizens of the World," in *Cultivating Humanity: A Classical Defense of Reform in Liberal Education* (Cambridge, MA: Harvard

University Press, 1997), pp. 52, 56–57, 59–61, 67. Nussbaum (p. 67) adds an attack on "difference politics" or "identity politics" (paralleling her cited attack on Nietzscheans): "Frequently, groups who press for the recognition of their group think of their struggle as connected with goals of human respect and social justice. And yet their way of focusing their demands, because it neglects commonalities and portrays people as above all members of identity groups, tends to subvert the demand for equal respect and love, and even the demand for attention to diversity itself." Compare also Nussbaum, *In Defense of Universal Values* (Notre Dame, IN: University of Notre Dame Press, 1999).

12. For these disagreements see Küng and Kuschel, eds., *A Global Ethic,* pp. 70, 94–96. In the words of Kuschel (p. 83): "The assessment that the 1893 Parliament was still shaped by 'a strong dose of Anglo-Saxon triumphalism' may also be true."

13. G. W. F. Hegel, "The Spirit of Christianity and Its Fate," in *Early Theological Writings,* trans. T. M. Knox (Philadelphia: University of Pennsylvania Press, 1971), pp. 212–215; *Hegel's Philosophy of Right,* trans. T. M. Knox (Oxford, UK: Oxford University Press, 1967), pp. 75–79. Nussbaum does refer to the role of inclinations (under the rubric of "passions"), but without drawing implications for the primacy of universalism.

14. Theodor W. Adorno, *Negative Dialektik* (Frankfurt-Main: Suhrkamp, 1966), pp. 226, 236–237. For a somewhat inadequate translation see *Negative Dialectics,* trans. E. B. Ashton (New York: Seabury Press, 1973), pp. 229, 240–241. Compare also my "The Politics of Nonidentity: Adorno, Postmodernism, and Edward Said," in *Alternative Visions: Paths in the Global Village* (Lanham, MD: Rowman & Littlefield, 1998), pp. 47–69.

15. Michel Foucault, *The History of Sexuality,* vol. 2: *The Use of Pleasure,* trans. Robert Hurley (New York: Vintage Books, 1986), pp. 26–28. Compare also his portrayal of moral practices or "arts of existence" as "those intentional and voluntary actions by which men not only set themselves rules of conduct, but also seek to transform themselves, to change themselves in their singular being, and to make their life into an *oeuvre* that carries certain aesthetic values and meets certain stylistic criteria."

16. *The History of Sexuality,* vol. 2: *The Use of Pleasure,* pp. 28, 54–55, 73; vol. 3: *The Care of the Self,* trans. Robert Hurley (New York: Pantheon Books, 1986). See also "The Ethic of Care for the Self as a Practice of Freedom: An Interview with Michel Foucault on January 29, 1984," trans. J. D. Gauthier,

in James Bernauer and David Rasmussen, eds., *The Final Foucault* (Cambridge, MA: MIT Press, 1988), pp. 4–7.

17. Zygmunt Bauman, *Postmodern Ethics* (Oxford, UK: Blackwell, 1993), pp. 13, 31, 34–36, 48, 54. On the relation between Foucault and Levinas see Barry Smart, "Foucault, Levinas, and the Subject of Responsibility," in Jeremy Moss, ed., *The Later Foucault* (London: SAGE Publications, 1998), pp. 78–92. On this issue, I am drawn to Paul Ricoeur's balanced position (inspired by Aristotle); see my "Oneself as Another: Paul Ricoeur's 'Little Ethics'," in *Achieving Our World* (Lanham, MD: Rowman & Littlefield, 2001), pp. 171–188.

18. Carol Gilligan, *In a Different Voice: Psychological Theory and Women's Development* (Cambridge, MA: Harvard University Press, 1982), pp. 2, 6, 16–17, 19. Among other feminist writers, the study refers especially to Nancy Chodorow, *The Reproduction of Mothering* (Berkeley: University of California Press, 1978). Regarding Kohlberg see his "Stage and Sequence," in David A. Goslin, ed., *Handbook of Socialization Theory and Research* (Chicago: University of Chicago Press, 1969), and "From Is to Ought," in Theodore Mischel, ed., *Cognitive Development and Epistemology* (New York: Academic Press, 1971), pp. 151–236; also Jürgen Habermas, "Moral Development and Ego Identity," in *Communication and the Evolution of Society,* trans. Thomas McCarthy (Boston: Beacon Press, 1979), pp. 69–94.

19. Luce Irigaray, *Between East and West: From Singularity to Community,* trans. Stephen Pluhacek (New York: Columbia University Press, 2002), pp. 136–137, 139–141. Irigaray's arguments had been prepared in some of her earlier studies, especially *Je, tu, nous: Toward a Culture of Difference,* trans. Alison Martin (New York: Routledge, 1993), and *I Love to You,* trans. Alison Martin (New York: Routledge, 1995).

20. Thus, she writes: "The Vedas, the Upanishads, and Yoga have for their principal function to assure the articulation between the instant and immorality or eternity. . . . The Vedic gods, the Brahmins, and the yogis care about the maintenance of the life of the universe and that of their body as cosmic nature. . . . What I wish to see become from these ancient texts, alas too neglected in our Western(ized) teaching, is that love come to pass between two freedoms." *Between East and West,* pp. 31, 63.

21. Tu Wei-ming, "Neo-Confucian Religiosity and Human Relatedness," in *Confucian Thought: Selfhood as Creative Transformation* (Albany, NY: State University of New York Press, 1985), pp. 138–139, 145–146. Compare also his

essay "The 'Moral Universal' from the Perspectives of East Asian Thought," in the same volume, pp. 19–34.

22. Nussbaum, "Kant and Stoic Cosmopolitanism," pp. 4, n. 11, 5, 8, 12, 14; and "Citizens of the World," in *Cultivating Humanity,* pp. 52, 57, 59–60. The sidelining of politics in favor of morality was also clearly evident in the deliberations of the Parliament of the World's Religions in 1993; see in this respect Küng and Kuschel, eds., *A Global Ethic,* pp. 54, 56.

23. Foucault, *The Care of the Self,* pp. 82, 86, 89, 94. As he adds, displaying admirable (nearly Aristotelian) good judgment (p. 93): "The basic attitude that one must have toward political activity was related to the general principle that whatever one is, it is not owing to the rank one holds, to the responsibility one exercises, to the position in which one finds oneself—above or beneath other people. What one is, and what one needs to devote one's attention to as to an ultimate purpose, is the expression of a principle that is singular in its manifestation within each person, but universal by the form it assumes in everyone, and collective by the community bond its establishes between individuals. Such is, at least for the Stoics, human reason as a divine principle present in all of us."

24. Peter Euben, "The Polis, Globalization, and the Politics of Place," in Aryeh Botwinick and William E. Connolly, eds., *Democracy and Vision: Sheldon Wolin and the Vicissitudes of the Political* (Princeton: Princeton University Press, 2001), pp. 266, 268–270. As he adds, highlighting the political effects of exclusiveness (p. 270): "Stoicism denied in practice the radical political possibilities of its philosophical commitments. Even when the Stoic ideal of virtuous and capable man was not primarily defined in political terms, it proved, nonetheless, especially congenial to monarchical and personal rule. Its leveling potential remained abstract, because (especially) early Stoics frequently refused to relate their thinking to the political and material conditions in which men lived their daily lives."

25. "The Polis, Globalization, and the Politics of Place," pp. 271–274. Soberly Euben continues (p. 274): "This is not to claim that cosmopolitanism is necessarily ethnocentric, but to caution against the unobstrusive ways in which dominant particulars represent themselves as the universal and actually become them in the sense of being the point of reference in relation to which others recognize themselves as particular."

26. In his words: "The challenge is to keep the critical moral edge of cosmopolitanism *and* the political focus of the polis in tension." "The Polis,

Globalization, and the Politics of Place," p. 270. Euben also adopts the notion of "parallel polis," articulated by Václav Havel and Adam Michnik, as "a way of naming the places within civil society where participatory opportunities existed that were otherwise denied by mendacious regimes" (p. 282).

27. Nussbaum, "Kant and Stoic Cosmopolitanism," p. 25. On bifocal justice see my "'Rights' versus 'Rites': Justice and Global Democracy," in *Alternative Visions: Paths in the Global Village* (Lanham, MD: Rowman & Littlefield, 1998), pp. 253–276.

CHAPTER SIX.   On Violence: Post-Arendtean Reflections

1. Hannah Arendt, "On Violence," in *Crises of the Republic* (New York: Harcourt Brace Jovanovich, 1972), p. 155. The essay was first published as *On Violence* (New York: Harcourt Brace Jovanovich, 1970). In the following the citations are from *Crises of the Republic*. On violence in general compare Martin Jay, *Refractions of Violence* (New York: Routledge, 2003), John Keane, *Reflections on Violence* (London: Verso, 1995), and Sheldon S. Wolin, "Violence and the Western Tradition," *American Journal of Orthopsychology*, vol. 33 (1962), pp. 15–28.

2. Arendt, "On Violence," pp. 115–116.

3. "On Violence," pp. 115, 117–119. As she adds (p. 120): "Violence has remained mostly a matter of theory and rhetoric where the clash between generations did not coincide with a clash of tangible group interests. . . . In America, the student movement has been seriously radicalized wherever police and police brutality intervened in essentially nonviolent demonstrations: occupations of administrative buildings, sit-ins, et cetera. Serious violence entered the scene only with the appearance of the Black Power movement on the campuses." She also draws attention to the report of the National Commission on the Causes and Prevention of Violence of June 1969.

4. Arendt, "On Violence," pp. 110, 113–114, 166–168, 170–171. For the citations from Sorel see *Reflections on Violence*, ed. Jeremy Jennings (Cambridge: Cambridge University Press, 1999), pp. 65, 77, 126, 130.

5. Arendt, "On Violence," pp. 114, 122, 164, 172. As one needs to add, however, Arendt is somewhat ambivalent in her treatment of Fanon. She cites with apparent approval (p. 168, note 96) an essay by Barbara Deming which says: "It is my conviction that he can be quoted as well to plead for nonviolence. . . .

Every time you find the word 'violence' in his pages, substitute for it the phrase 'radical and uncompromising action.'" See also Fanon, *The Wretched of the Earth*, trans. Constance Farrington (New York: Grove Press, 1968), pp. 85, 93, 95.

6. Arendt, "On Violence," pp. 156–158, 160. Her essay refers at this point chiefly to such sociobiologists as Adolf Portmann, Nikolas Tinbergen, and Konrad Lorenz.

7. Arendt, "On Violence," pp. 134–138. Compare John Stuart Mill, *Considerations on Representative Government* (1861; New York: Liberal Arts Press, 1958), pp. 59, 65; Max Weber, "Politics as a Vocation" (1921), in H. H. Gerth and C. Wright Mills, eds., *From Max Weber: Essays in Sociology* (New York: Oxford University Press, 1958), p. 78; C. Wright Mills, *The Power Elite* (New York: Oxford University Press, 1956), p. 171; Bertrand de Jouvenel, *Power: The Natural History of Its Growth* (New York: Hutchinson, 1948), p. 122. The passage quoted by Arendt in the above citation is taken from Alexander Passerin d'Entrèves, *The Notion of the State: An Introduction to Political Theory* (Oxford: Oxford University Press, 1967), p. 64. Going back in history, Arendt traces the "command" conception of power ultimately to "the Hebrew-Christian tradition and its 'imperative conception of law,'" saying ("On Violence," p. 138): "This concept was not invented by the 'political realists' but was, rather, the result of a much earlier, almost automatic generalization of God's 'commandments'."

8. Arendt, "On Violence," pp. 139–141.

9. "On Violence," pp. 142–145. Compare in this context also Arendt's "What Is Authority?" in her *Between Past and Future: Exercises in Political Thought* (New York: Meridian Books, 1963), pp. 91–141.

10. Arendt, "On Violence," pp. 145–148, 152, 161, 177. As she writes at one point, quoting Conor Cruise O'Brien (p. 176): "Sometimes 'violence is the only way of ensuring a hearing for moderation'. To ask the impossible in order to obtain the possible is not always counterproductive. And indeed, violence, contrary to what its prophets try to tell us, is more a weapon of reform than of revolution."

11. Sorel, *Reflections on Violence*, pp. 39, 105–106.

12. See Jean-Paul Sartre, *Being and Nothingness: An Essay on Phenomenological Ontology*, trans. Hazel E. Barnes (first French ed. 1943; New York: Philosophical Library, 1956), pp. 263, 265–267, 364; *Critique of Dialectical Reason*, vol. I: *Theory of Practical Ensembles*, trans. Alan Sheridan-Smith (first French

ed. 1960; London: NLB, 1976), pp. 108–115, 253–260; and his preface to Fanon's *The Wretched of the Earth,* p. 18. As one should note in fairness, some of Sartre's posthumously published writings on ethics complicate and mitigate the earlier emphasis on stark conflict; see in this respect especially Ronald E. Santoni, *Sartre on Violence: Curiously Ambivalent* (University Park, PA: Pennsylvania State University Press, 2003).

13. See Jacques Derrida, "The Ends of Man," in *Margins of Philosophy,* trans. Alan Bass (Chicago: University of Chicago Press, 1982), p. 135; also his "Violence and Metaphysics: An Essay on the Thought of Emmanuel Levinas," in *Writing and Difference,* trans. Alan Bass (Chicago: University of Chicago Press, 1978), pp. 116–117. At another point in the latter essay (p. 128), Derrida speaks of a "transcendental and pre-ethical violence," stating that this kind of violence "does not spring from an ethical resolution or freedom," but "originally institutes the relationship between two identities."

14. Derrida, "Force of Law: The 'Mystical Foundation of Authority'," in Drucilla Cornell, Michel Rosenfeld, and David G. Carlson, eds., *Deconstruction and the Possibility of Justice* (New York: Routledge, 1992), pp. 24–28 (translation slightly altered). Partly under the influence of Derrida and other "postmodern" writers, the language of rupture and irruptive violence has spread from philosophy into many other fields, including political theory, literary criticism, anthropology, and popular theology. In the latter two domains, one of the most influential figures is René Girard. Although trained as a literary critic, and without engaging in the kind of extensive fieldwork customary among anthropologists, Girard has developed a comprehensive, and ostensibly empirical, anthropological theory: a theory stipulating that violence is and has been endemic in human society from immemorial times and that traditional religion was basically designed to provide an answer to that problem—an answer, however, that by ritualizing killing, amounted itself to an act of violence. The "sacred" in this theory correlates closely with violence by representing both the terror of uncontrolled killing and the controlled rituals of religious sacrifice. See Girard, *Violence and the Sacred* (Baltimore: Johns Hopkins University Press, 1977), p. 300; also *The Scapegoat* (Baltimore: Johns Hopkins University Press, 1986) and *A Theater of Envy: William Shakespeare* (New York: Oxford University Press, 1991). The theologian Burton Mack seems correct in raising the question of criteria which could possibly disconfirm Girard's thesis, given his privileged access to the data (a

question parallel to the Marxist conundrum of "false consciousness"). See his "Introduction" to *Violent Origins: Walter Burkert, René Girard, and Jonathan Z. Smith on Ritual Killing and Cultural Formation,* ed. Robert G. Hamerton-Kelly (Stanford, CA: Stanford University Press, 1987), p. 11; compare also Andrew J. McKenna, *Violence and Difference: Girard, Derrida, and Deconstruction* (Urbana, IL: University of Illinois Press, 1992), and Wendy C. Hamblet, *The Sacred Monstrous: A Reflection on Violence in Human Communities* (Lanham, MD: Lexington Books, 2003).

15. See Bat-Ami Bar On, *The Subject of Violence: Arendtean Exercises in Understanding* (Lanham, MD: Rowman & Littlefield, 2002), pp. xi, xiii, 7–8. Compare also Julia Kristeva, *Hannah Arendt: Life Is a Narrative* (Toronto: University of Toronto Press, 2001).

16. Arendt, "We Refugees," *Menorah Journal,* vol. 31 (1943), pp. 71, 76–77. Compare also Arendt, "The Jew as Pariah: A Hidden Tradition," *Jewish Social Studies,* vol. 6 (1944), pp. 99–122; and Judith Shklar, "Hannah Arendt as Pariah," *Partisan Review,* vol. 50 (1983), pp. 64–77.

17. Bar On, *The Subject of Violence,* pp. 31–32. See also Arendt, "The Concentration Camps," *Partisan Review,* vol. 15 (1948), pp. 743–763.

18. Bar On, *The Subject of Violence,* pp. 32–33, 36. As she adds (p. 37): "The kind of understanding whose possibility [Arendt] is interested in and is trying to describe in 'Understanding and Politics' is specifically an ethico-political understanding of the violent world that comes to be with the rise of totalitarianism." See also Arendt, "Understanding and Politics," *Partisan Review,* vol. 20 (1953), pp. 377–392, and her "On the Nature of Totalitarianism: An Essay in Understanding" (1953), in Jerome Kohn, ed., *Essays in Understanding* (New York: Harcourt Brace, 1994), pp. 328–360; also Theodor W. Adorno, "What Does Coming to Terms with the Past Mean?" (1959), in Geoffrey H. Hartman, ed., *Bitburg in Moral and Political Perspective* (Bloomington, IN: Indiana University Press, 1986), pp. 114–129 (at p. 115).

19. Among many others, one might point here to Chantal Mouffe, a political thinker otherwise scrupulous in matters of terminology. Arguing against a rational-consensual model of politics, as articulated in John Rawls's *Political Liberalism,* she states that this perspective "offers us a picture of the well-ordered society as one from which—through rational agreement on justice—antagonism, violence, power and repression have disappeared." See Mouffe, *The Democratic Paradox* (London: Verso, 2000), p. 31; also Rawls, *Political Liberalism* (New York: Columbia University Press, 1993).

20. Arendt, "On Violence," pp. 109, 178, 180. As she adds, in a nearly prophetic vein (p. 119): "The seemingly irresistible proliferation of techniques and machines, far from only threatening certain classes with unemployment, menaces the existence of whole nations and conceivably of all mankind."

21. In Merleau-Ponty's words: "Empiricism cannot see that we need to know what we are looking for, otherwise we would not be looking for it; and intellectualism fails to see that we need to be ignorant of what we are looking for, or equally again we should not be searching." See *Phenomenology of Perception*, trans. Colin Smith (New York: Humanities Press, 1962), p. 28.

22. Merleau-Ponty, *Humanism and Terror: An Essay on the Communist Problem*, trans. John O'Neill (Boston: Beacon Press, 1969), pp. xiv–xv. These statements are accompanied by this famous and memorable passge (p. xiv): "Whatever one's philosophical or even theological position, a society is not the temple of value-idols that figure on the front of its monuments or in its constitutional scrolls; the value of a society is the value it places upon man's relation to man. . . . To understand and judge a society, one has to penetrate its basic structure to the human bond upon which it is built; this undoubtedly depends upon legal relations, but also upon forms of labor, ways of loving, living, and dying."

23. Merleau-Ponty, *Humanism and Terror*, pp. xviii–xxiv, xxxv. In some of his later writings, Merleau-Ponty sided in favor of a reformist politics over revolutionary rupture. As he observed at one point: "The question arises whether there is not more of a future in a regime that does not intend to remake history from the ground up but only to change it, and whether it is not the regime that one must look for, instead of once again entering the circle of revolution." See *Adventures of the Dialectic,* trans. Joseph Bien (Evanston, IL: Northwestern University Press, 1973), p. 207.

24. See Mahatma Gandhi, *Satyagraha* (Ahmedabad: Navajivan, 1958), p. 6; *India's Case for Swaraj* (Ahmedabad: Yeshanand, 1932), p. 369. The passages are cited in Thomas Pantham, "Beyond Liberal Democracy: Thinking with Mahatma Gandhi," in Pantham and Kenneth L. Deutsch, eds., *Political Thought in Modern India* (New Delhi: SAGE Publications, 1986), pp. 340–341. Compare also Indira Rothermund, "Gandhi's *Satyagraha* and Hindu Thought," in the same volume, pp. 297–306; and my "*Satyagraha*: Gandhi's Truth Revisited," in *Alternative Visions: Paths in the Global Village* (Lanham, MD: Rowman and Littlefield, 1998), pp. 105–121.

25. Arendt, "On Violence," pp. 152, 177.

CHAPTER SEVEN.   Gandhi and Islam: A Heart-and-Mind Unity?

1. Rajmohan Gandhi, "Understanding Gujarat," *Just Commentary,* vol. 2, no. 5 (May 2002), p. 7. (Reprinted from *The Hindu,* March 12, 2002.) The reference to Rama was prompted by the fact that the attacked train near Godhra was returning from Ayodhya, the supposed hometown of Lord Rama and the site of a planned temple in his honor (involving the destruction of a Muslim mosque on the same site). The last phrase is itself a "healing" phrase since the name of Rama is used in conjunction with "almighty" and "compassionate," which are epithets of Allah.

2. Margaret Chatterjee, *Gandhi's Religious Thought* (Notre Dame, IN: University of Notre Dame Press, 1983), p. 120. Chatterjee (p. 1) quotes C. F. Andrews's opinion that Gandhi was "a saint of action rather than of contemplation"—a view which probably underestimates the reflective quality of Gandhi's writings and utterances.

3. Muhammad Mujeeb, *The Indian Muslims* (London: Allen & Unwin, 1967), p. 167.

4. Mohandas K. Gandhi, *An Autobiography, or The Story of My Experiments with Truth,* trans. Mahadev Desai (Ahmedabad: Navajivan Publ. House, 1927), p. 28. See also Sheila McDonough, *Gandhi's Responses to Islam* (New Delhi: Printworld, 1994), pp. 5, 7, 12.

5. *The Collected Works of Mahatma Gandhi,* vol. 2 (Delhi: Government of India, 1967), p. 72.

6. McDonough, *Gandhi's Responses to Islam,* p. 21. As she adds (p. 27): "Gandhi often used Muslim and Hindu imagery in this way because his fundamental assertion was that the symbols from the two religious traditions both made sense in the immediate context of the suffering of the Indians in South Africa. . . . Gandhi believed that the essential struggle of Muhammad's lifetime, the struggle to create a new form of civilization, could be equated with the mystical struggle of [Lord] Rama against Ravana as portrayed in the epic, the *Ramayana.* . . . In this respect, Gandhi was a follower of the *bhakti* and *Sufi* traditions in which the importance of religious symbols lies in the illumination the symbols may awaken in the hearts of believers." See also S. Abid Husain, *Gandhiji and Communal Unity* (Bombay: Orient Longmans, 1969), p. 57.

7. As McDonough writes: "Gandhi hoped to win the support of these Muslims by himself joining the *Khilafat* movement, and becoming one of its

organizers. He did not get much strong support from the other Hindu leaders in India for this activity." See *Gandhi's Responses to Islam,* p. 42. As she also mentions (pp. 46–48), he used again vocabulary from both religions to promote his efforts. Thus he invoked the martyrdom of Hasan and Husain, the grandsons of the Prophet, as equivalents to the Hindu notion of "*tapascharya,*" meaning the power of self-suffering and self-purification. On another occasion, he compared the Indian struggle for independence from England with the Prophet's exodus (*hijra*) from Mecca to Medina.

8. McDonough, *Gandhi's Responses to Islam,* pp. 49–55. See also *The Collected Works of Mahatma Gandhi,* vol. 19, p. 153.

9. Assessing the long-range significance of the Khilafat movement, Gail Minault remarks: "The national alliance disintegrated, but Muslim community self-consciousness, with or without the *Khilafat* to symbolize it, had become a factor in Indian politics. . . . The alternative structures which developed as the vehicles for Muslim consciousness during the *Khilafat* movement provided the techniques, and much of the personnel, for the development of a specifically Muslim nationalism in the subcontinent later." See *The Khilafat Movement: Religious Symbolism and Political Mobilization in India* (New York: Columbia University Press, 1982), p. 212.

10. B. R. Nanda, *Mahatma Gandhi: A Biography* (New York: Barrons Educational Series, 1965), p. 238.

11. McDonough, *Gandhi's Responses to Islam,* pp. 83, 86, 94–95. See also Abdul Wahid Khan, *India Wins Freedom: The Other Side* (Karachi: Pakistan Education Publishers, 1961), p. 253.

12. Mushirul Hasan, *A Nationalist Conscience* (New Delhi: Manohar, 1987), p. 93.

13. S. Abid Husain, *The Destiny of Indian Muslims* (Bombay: Asia Publishing House, 1965), p. 118; P. C. Chaudhury, *Gandhi and His Contemporaries* (New Delhi: Sterling Publishers, 1972), p. 136. Summarizing the motives of affection, Roland E. Miller writes: "We can suggest that Muslim trust of Gandhi was based on four things: his respect for religion and religious commitment; his regard for Muslims as full members of what he once called India's 'joint family'; his peace-loving nature; and his honest friendship." See "Indian Muslim Critiques of Gandhi," in Harold Coward, ed., *Indian Critiques of Gandhi* (Albany, NY: State University of New York Press, 2003), p. 194.

14. Exemplifying Muslim suspicions, Muhammad Ali (his onetime friend) in 1930 charged Gandhi's program with being "not a covenant for complete

independence of India but of making seventy million Indian Muslims dependent on the Hindu Mahasabha." On his part, the president of the Hindu Mahasabha, V. D. Savarkar, declared in 1938 that the Gandhi-inspired National Congress "has been, since its inception down to this day, a Hindu body." See Hasan, *A Nationalist Conscience*, p. 173; Mushir U. Haq, *Muslim Politics in India* (Meerut: Meenakshi Prakashan, 1976), p. 135.

15. Muhammad Mujeeb, *Dr. Zakir Husain: A Biography* (New Delhi: National Book Trust, 1972), p. 236; quoted in McDonough, *Gandhi's Responses to Islam*, p. 69.

16. As Gandhi stated at one point: "The Moplahs have sinned against God and have suffered grievously for it. Let the Hindus also remember that they have not allowed the opportunity for revenge to pass by." *The Collected Works of Mahatma Gandhi*, vol. 23, p. 514. See also Roland E. Miller, *The Mappila Muslims of Kerala* (Madras: Orient Longman, rev. ed., 1992); and his "Indian Muslim Critiques of Gandhi," in Coward, ed., *Indian Critiques of Gandhi*, pp. 202–205.

17. Quoted in Miller, *The Mappila Muslims of Kerala*, p. 130.

18. See Judith Brown, *Gandhi's Rise to Power: Indian Politics, 1915–1922* (Cambridge: Cambridge University Press, 1972), p. 331; M. Zaidi, ed., *Congress Presidential Addresses* (New Delhi: Indian Institute of Applied Political Research, 1989), vol. 4, p. 137. The final qualification can be gathered from his additional comment (p. 138): "In spite of my utter abhorrence of violence I will say with all deliberation that on the Day of Judgment I would rather stand before God's White Throne guilty of all this violence than to have to answer for the unspeakable sin of so cowardly a surrender."

19. See Bhikhu Parekh, *Gandhi's Political Philosophy: A Critical Examination* (Notre Dame, IN: University of Notre Dame Press, 1989), pp. 140, 147; and Raghavan Iyer, *The Moral and Political Writings of Mahatma Gandhi* (Oxford: Clarendon Press, 1987), vol. 2, part 4.

20. Zaidi, ed., *Congress Presidential Addresses*, vol. 4, p. 136.

21. In McDonough's words: "Jinnah was negotiating as a lawyer representing his clients, most of the Muslims, who did not trust the majority community to treat them justly and fairly once the British were gone. . . . Jinnah saw Gandhi as a fellow lawyer who was trying to fog up the issues of drawing up a mutually satisfactory contract. A lawyer trying to draw up a contract is not interested in 'heart-unity' with the lawyer from the other side." See

Gandhi's Responses to Islam, p. 88. Compare also Stanley Wolpert, *Jinnah of Pakistan* (New York: Oxford University Press, 1984), especially pp. 230–236; S. K. Majumdar, *Jinnah and Gandhi: Their Role in India's Quest for Freedom* (Calcutta: Mukhopadhyay, 1966).

22. McDonugh oversimplifies matters considerably when she presents Jinnah simply as a liberal modernist, stating: "He was not interested in keeping alive and recreating some model society from the remote past, but of moving into the future to create new forms of life." She even compares Jinnah's vision of Pakistan with the Prophet's exodus (*hijra*) from Mecca to Medina, "from the known into the unknown." See *Gandhi's Responses to Islam,* p. 91.

23. Parekh, *Gandhi's Political Philosophy,* p. 173. As he adds: "The British brought liberal political culture to India but, thanks to the inherent logic of colonialism, corrupted it by embodying it in non-liberal representative institutions."

24. Parekh's account of these developments is instructive. As he writes: "Jinnah's great contribution lay in defining the Muslims as a nation, articulating Muslim nationalism in easily intelligible idioms and mobilizing the masses behind it. . . . [By 1946, however] he radically changed his tune and began to speak the secular language of the modern state. . . . He evidently used the ideological language of nationalism to legitimize and realize his political objectives. Once they were secured and the arduous task of running the state began, the ideological baggage became a grave liability and had to be abandoned at the first opportunity." See *Gandhi's Political Philosophy,* pp. 175, 182; also M. A. Karandikar, *Islam: India's Transition to Modernity* (Delhi: Eastern Publishers, 1961), pp. 281–282.

25. Parekh, *Gandhi's Political Philosophy,* p. 121.

26. B. R. Nanda, *Gandhi and His Critics* (Delhi: Oxford University Press, 1985), p. 103.

27. Foreword to Sir Abdullah Suhrawardy, *The Sayings of Muhammad* (New York: Carol Publishing Group, 1990), p. 7; quoted in McDonough, *Gandhi's Responses to Islam,* p. 1.

28. Chatterjee, *Gandhi's Religious Thought,* pp. 154, 181.

29. McDonough, *Gandhi's Responses to Islam,* pp. 27–29, 71, 84.

30. See *The Collected Works of Mahatma Gandhi,* vol. 24, p. 153; Abdul Wahid Khan, *India Wins Freedom: The Other Side,* p. 269. Quoted in McDonough, *Gandhi's Responses to Islam,* pp. 53, 95–96.

31. Parekh, *Gandhi's Political Philosophy,* p. 123. In a similar vein, McDonough remarks: "As the government of the new secular India swung into action, he [Gandhi] would most probably have become both a loyal citizen and a hard-working critic. . . . He would have been an unceasing voice of protest within the structures of a democratic state." See *Gandhi's Responses to Islam,* p. 93. Gandhi's views on this matter were echoed by Michel Foucault when he stated: "Nothing is more inconsistent than a political regime that is indifferent to truth; but nothing is more dangerous than a political system that claims to lay down the truth. The function of 'telling the truth' must not take the form of law." See *Politics, Philosophy, Culture,* ed. L. Kritzman (New York: Routledge, 1990), p. 43.

32. *Young India,* November 5, 1931; quoted in Parekh, *Gandhi's Political Philosophy,* p. 146. The notion of "heart-and-mind" is familiar from the Confucian tradition (*hsin*); it also resonates distantly with Erasmus's motto of "*eruditio et pietas*" (learning and piety).

33. See Rajmohan Gandhi, "Understanding Gujarat," p. 8; also his *Eight Lives: A Study of the Hindu-Muslim Encounter* (Albany, NY: State University of New York Press, 1986), p. ix. For some empirical evidence that interreligious or intercommunal engagement can curb social violence compare Ashutosh Varshney, *Ethnic Conflict and Civic Life: Hindus and Muslims in India* (New York: Oxford University Press, 2002).

CHAPTER EIGHT.   Confucianism and the Public Sphere:
Five Relationships Plus One?

1. For an eloquent tribute to this tendency compare Husserl's statement: "To bring latent reason to the understanding of its own possibilities and thus to bring to insight the possibility of metaphysics as a true possibility— this is the only way to put metaphysics or universal philosophy on the strenuous road to realization. It is the only way to decide whether the *telos* which was inborn in European humanity at the birth of Greek philosophy . . . whether this *telos* is merely a factual, historical delusion . . . or whether Greek humanity was not rather the first breakthrough to what is essential to humanity as such, its *entelechy*." See Edmund Husserl, *The Crisis of European Sciences and Transcendental Phenomenology: An Introduction to Phenomeno-*

logical Philosophy, trans. David Carr (Evanston, IL: Northwestern University Press, 1970), p. 15.

2. Aristotle, *Politics,* 1252a1, 1253a15–16; quoted from *The Politics of Aristotle,* trans. Ernest Barker (Oxford: Clarendon Press, 1946), pp. 1, 7. As Barker elaborates in his "Introduction" (pp. xlix–xlx): If Aristotle "speaks of the growth of the household into the village and of villages into the state [*polis*], he does not rest his belief in the natural character of political society on the simple fact of such growth. . . . Indeed, it would seem that Aristotle, true to the general Greek conception of politics as a sphere of conscious creation in which legislators had always been active, believed in the conscious construction of the *polis.* . . . There is no contradiction in such a sentence; for there is no contradiction between the immanent impulses of human nature and the conscious art which is equally, or even more, a part of the same human nature."

3. Aristotle, *Politics,* 1252a2, 1279a9–11; in *The Politics of Aristotle,* pp. 1–2, 112. That even in Aristotle's time this maxim carried a critical edge is revealed by his comment (p. 112): "Today the case is different: moved by the profits to be derived from office and the handling of public property, men want to hold office continuously." In our own time, the critical edge emerges even more sharply.

4. Aristotle, *Politics,* 1252b6, 1253b1, 1254b6–7, 1255b12, 1259b2–3; in *The Politics of Aristotle,* pp. 4, 8, 13, 17, 33.

5. Aristotle, *Politics,* 1252b4, 1275a6, 1275b12, 1295b7; see *The Politics of Aristotle,* pp. 3, 93, 95, 181. As Aristotle adds at another point (p. 16): "The same line of thought is followed in regard to nobility as well as slavery. Greeks regard themselves as noble not only in their own country, but absolutely and in all places; but they regard barbarians as noble only [or at best] in their own country—thus assessing that there is one sort of nobility and freedom which is absolute or universal, and another which is only relative."

6. For the above account see Barker, "Introduction," in *The Politics of Aristotle,* pp. lix–lxi.

7. See Thomas Hobbes, *Leviathan* (New York: Dutton & Co., 1953), Introduction and Chapter 1; also *De Cive or The Citizen,* ed. Sterling P. Lamprecht (New York: Appleton-Century-Crofts, 1949), pp. 21–22 (Chapter 1, section 2).

8. John Locke, *Two Treatises of Civil Government* (New York: Dutton & Co., 1953), p. 5 (Book I, Chapter 2).

9. Locke, *Two Treatises,* pp. 159, 164–165, 206 (Book II, Chapter 7, section 87; Chapter 8, sections 95–97; Chapter 15, Section 173).

10. Hannah Arendt, *The Human Condition: A Study of the Central Dilemmas Facing Modern Man* (Chicago: University of Chicago, 1958), pp. 29–30, 268, 292–297.

11. As Hall and Ames observe correctly: "What gives the discussion of Confucius' 'sociopolitical theory' such an unfamiliar ring is the absence in his thinking of certain distinctions that Western social and political thinkers have deemed fundamental. The most important of these distinctions is that of the 'private' and 'public' realms. Allied with this distinction is the equally important division between the 'social' and 'political' modes of organization." See David L. Hall and Roger T. Ames, *Thinking Through Confucius* (Albany, NY: State University of New York Press, 1987), p. 146.

12. Herbert Fingarette, *Confucius—The Secular as Sacred* (New York: Harper Torchbooks, 1972), pp. 37, 41, 45, 75–76. The lines are from *Analects* 6:28. For a slightly different rendering of these lines see *The Analects of Confucius,* trans. Arthur Waley (New York: Vintage Books, 1989), p. 122.

13. Wing-tsit Chan, "Chinese and Western Interpretations of *Jen* (Humanity)," *Journal of Chinese Philosophy,* vol. 2 (1975), p. 109.

14. Tu Wei-ming, "*Jen* as a Living Metaphor," in his *Confucian Thought: Selfhood as Creative Transformation* (Albany, NY: State University of New York Press, 1985), pp. 81, 88. As he remarks in another context, *jen* not only transgresses the inner/outer, private/public bifurcation, but also mediates between humanity and nature as well as between humanity and "Heaven" (or celestial immortals). The person striving for *jen,* he writes, "must also be able to realize the nature of the 'myriad things' and assist Heaven and Earth in their transforming and nourishing functions. . . . Unless one can realize the nature of all things to form a trinity with Heaven and Earth, one's self-realization cannot be complete." See Tu Wei-ming, *Humanity and Self-Cultivation: Essays in Confucian Thought* (Berkeley: Asian Humanities Press, 1979), p. 97.

15. Tu Wei-ming, "Neo-Confucian Religiosity and Human Relatedness," in *Confucian Thought,* pp. 133, 137. The "Western Inscription" reads (p. 137): "Heaven is my father and Earth is my mother, and even such a small creature as I finds an intimate place in their midst. Therefore that which fills the universe I regard as my body and that which directs the universe I consider as my nature. All people are my brothers and sisters, and all things are my companions."

16. Robert N. Bellah, *Beyond Belief: Essays on Religion in a Post-Traditional World* (New York: Harper & Row, 1976), pp. 94–95.

17. Tu Wei-ming, "Selfhood and Otherness: The Father-Son Relationship in Confucian Thought" and "Neo-Confucian Religiosity and Human Relatedness," in *Confucian Thought*, pp. 121–124, 138.

18. *Analects* 1:1; *The Analects of Confucius*, p. 83. See also Tu Wei-ming, *Confucian Thought*, p. 139.

19. David L. Hall and Roger T. Ames, *The Democracy of the Dead: Dewey, Confucius, and the Hope for Democracy in China* (Chicago: Open Court, 1999), pp. 11, 204. As they candidly add (p. 12): "We do not ignore the serious defects to traditional Confucianism illustrated by the isolation of minorities, gender inequities, and an overall disinterest in the rule of law. In spite of these past failings, we argue that, on balance, there are resources within the Confucian tradition for constructing a coherent model of a viable and humane democracy that remains true to the communitarian sensibilities of traditional China while avoiding many of the defects of rights-based liberalism." Compare also their *Thinking Through Confucius* (Albany, NY: State University of New York Press, 1987); *Anticipating China: Thinking Through the Narratives of Chinese and Western Culture* (Albany, NY: State University of New York Press, 1995); *Thinking From the Han: Self, Truth, and Transcendence in Chinese and Western Culture* (Albany, NY: State University of New York Press, 1998); and for some critical comments my "Humanity and Humanization: Comments on Confucianism," in *Alternative Visions: Paths in the Global Village* (Albany, NY: State University of New York Press, 1998), p. 123–144.

20. Tu Wei-ming, *Confucian Thought*, pp. 144–146.

21. Masao Abe, *Zen and Western Thought,* ed. William R. LaFleur (Honolulu: University of Hawaii Press, 1985), pp. 160, 255.

22. Apart from the writings of Hannah Arendt, the above considerations are indebted to the work of Jürgen Habermas, especially his *The Structural Transformation of the Public Sphere,* trans. Thomas Burger and Frederick Lawrence (Cambridge, MA: MIT Press, 1989), and *The Inclusion of the Other: Studies in Political Theory,* ed. Ciaran Cronin and Pablo De Greiff (Cambridge, MA: MIT Press, 1998). Compare also Craig Calhoun, ed., *Habermas and the Public Sphere* (Cambridge, MA: MIT Press, 1992). For a discussion of the possible role of the public sphere (*kung*) in Asian societies see, e.g., Wm. Theodore de Bary, *The Trouble with Confucianism* (Cambridge, MA: Harvard

University Press, 1991), pp. 100–101; also William T. Rowe, "The Public Sphere in Modern China," *Modern China,* vol. 16 (1990), pp. 303–329, and David Strand, *"Civil Society" and "Public Sphere" in Modern China: A Perspective of Popular Movements in Beijing, 1919–1989* (Durham, NC: Asian-Pacific Studies Institute, Duke University, 1990).

23. John G. A. Pocock, "The Ideal of Citizenship Since Classical Times," in Ronald Beiner, ed., *Theorizing Citizenship* (Albany, NY: State University of New York Press, 1995), pp. 30–31. Compare also the comment of Gershon Shafir: "Citizenship is the legal foundation and social glue of the new communality [of the *polis*]. It is founded on the definition of the human being as 'a creature formed by nature to live a political life' and, in Pocock's words, this is 'one of the great Western definitions of what it is to be human'." See Shafir, ed., *The Citizenship Debates* (Minneapolis, MN: University of Minnesota Press, 1998), p. 3.

24. Norberto Bobbio, "Racism Today," in his *In Praise of Meekness: Essays on Ethics and Politics* (Cambridge, UK: Polity Press, 2000), p. 112.

25. Shafir, "Introduction: The Evolving Tradition of Citizenship," in *The Citizenship Debates,* pp. 23–24. For an argument in favor of differentiated citizenship see especially Iris Marion Young, "Polity and Group Difference: A Critique of the Ideal of Universal Citizenship," in the same volume, pp. 263–290. In Bobbio's view, the solution resides in "the reconciliation of the two opposing trends" (of equality and difference); see *In Praise of Meekness,* p. 8.

CHAPTER NINE. Religion, Ethics, and Liberal Democracy:
A Possible Symbiosis

1. See Maulana Wahiduddin Khan, ed., *Words of the Prophet Muhammad: Selections from the Hadith* (New Delhi: Al-Risala Books, 1996), p. 3.

2. See Matthew 5:5, 5:7, and 2 Timothy 1:7. For the Buddhist notions of non-ego and compassion see, e.g., Masao Abe, *Zen and Western Thought,* ed. William R. LaFleur (Honolulu: University of Hawaii Press, 1985), pp. 176–178, 222–223.

3. See Samuel P. Huntington, "Culture, Power, and Democracy," in Marc F. Plattner and Aleksander Smolar, eds., *Globalization, Power, and Democracy* (Baltimore: Johns Hopkins University Press, 2000), p. 5. The definition of politics in terms of a "friend-enemy" confrontation was introduced

by Carl Schmitt, *The Concept of the Political,* trans. George Schab (New Brunswick, NJ: Rutgers University Press, 1976).

4. P. S. Allen, *Opus epistularum Desiderii Erasmi* (Oxford: Clarendon Press, 1906), Ep. 179; cited from Lester K. Born, ed. and trans., *The Education of a Christian Prince, by Desiderius Erasmus* (New York: Columbia University Press, 1936), p. 6. As Born states, in view of the many traditional sources of Erasmus's treatise, "we can readily state that great originality in political thinking was not his contribution. . . . [However,] the mere fact that Erasmus did not originate—in fact could not have originated—most of the doctrines he expounded in no way militates against his importance in the world of political theory" (pp. 24–25). In his "Introduction," Born provides an overview of the "mirror of princes" literature from antiquity to the Renaissance (pp. 94–124). On this score, Erasmus's text clearly differs markedly from Nietzsche's goal of a radical "transvaluation of all values." In the political domain, Nietzsche's approach appears both too difficult (being accessible only to a select few intellectuals) and too easy—since many politicians naturally believe themselves to be "beyond good and evil" (without having made even the first step toward self-overcoming or "overman").

5. Allen, *Opus epistularum,* Ep. 423; cited from Born, *The Education of a Christian Prince,* p. 27. Thomas More's *Utopia* was published in the same year (1516).

6. *The Education of a Christian Prince,* pp. 133–134, 150–151.

7. *The Education of a Christian Prince,* pp. 140, 151, 154, 157, 162–163.

8. *The Education of a Christian Prince,* pp. 161, 177, 183, 209, 233.

9. *The Education of a Christian Prince,* pp. 150, 153, 220.

10. Al-Farabi, *Fusul al-Madani (Aphorisms of the Statesman),* ed. D. M. Dunlap (Cambridge: Cambridge University Press, 1961), pp. 40, 53, 57. As al-Farabi adds: "Similarly, if people have enraged him [the ruler] by some injustice, but what they deserve for that injustice falls short of war or killing, war and killing are undoubtedly unjust" (p. 57). On broadly Aristotelian grounds, the text distinguishes between virtue and "self-restraint" (p. 33)—which seems to suggest that virtue can become so habitual as to no longer need fostering (which does not concur with ordinary experience). For a somewhat different rendering of the text see *Alfarabi, The Political Writings,* trans. Charles E. Butterworth (Ithaca, NY: Cornell University Press, 2001), pp. 11–67.

11. See Wm. Theodore de Bary, *Neo-Confucian Orthodoxy and the Learning of the Mind-and-Heart* (New York: Columbia University Press, 1981),

pp. 69, 85. For the sayings of Confucius see *Analects*, 12:7 and 12:22. Compare in this context also Roger T. Ames, *The Art of Rulership: A Study of Ancient Chinese Political Thought* (Albany, NY: State University of New York Press, 1994). Concentrating on the ninetieth book of the classical text *Huai Nan Tzu* (140 B.C.), Ames demonstrates the importance in classical rulership of the notion of "benefiting the people" (*li min*).

12. Norberto Bobbio is emeritus professor of legal and political philosophy at the University of Turin and senator-for-life in the Italian Senate. Among his many publications, the following seem most pertinent here: *The Future of Democracy* (Cambridge, UK: Polity Press, 1987); *Democracy and Dictatorship* (Cambridge, UK: Polity Press, 1989); *Liberalism and Democracy* (London: Verso, 1990); *The Age of Rights* (Cambridge, UK: Polity Press, 1996).

13. Bobbio, *In Praise of Meekness: Essays on Ethics and Politics,* trans. Teresa Chataway (Cambridge, UK: Polity Press, 2000), pp. 68–70.

14. *In Praise of Meekness,* pp. 47–48, 79–80. The reference is to Gerhard Ritter, *The Corrupting Influence of Power* (Tower Bridge, UK: Hadleigh, 1952).

15. Bobbio, *In Praise of Meekness,* p. 67.

16. *In Praise of Meekness,* pp. 23, 25, 27. Although Bobbio states (p. 27) that he "could not locate meekness" in Erasmus's text, this seems to be more a terminological than a substantive issue.

17. *In Praise of Meekness,* pp. 24–25. Bobbio's text does not give a citation for Mazzantini. For the distinction between power and violence see also Hannah Arendt, "On Violence," in *Crises of the Republic* (New York: Harcourt Brace Jovanovich, 1972), pp. 105–184. For Martin Heidegger's treatment of power, see my "Heidegger on *Macht* and *Machenschaft*," *Continental Philosophy Review,* vol. 34 (2001), pp. 247–267.

18. Bobbio, *In Praise of Meekness,* pp. 27–33. For Bobbio, meekness exceeds or transcends toleration or recognition because of their reliance on mutuality. As he states, in a passage evoking Derrida's and Levinas's praise of unreciprocated gift-giving (p. 32): "A meek person does not ask for or expect any reciprocity. Meekness is an attitude toward others that does not need to be reciprocated for it to be fully actualized. This is also the case with altruism, kindness, generosity, and mercy, all of which are social as well as unilateral values.... Meekness, instead, is a gift and has no predetermined or prescribed limits." See in this context Jacques Derrida, *The Gift of Death,* trans. David Wills (Chicago: University of Chicago Press, 1995); Emmanuel Levinas, *To-*

tality and Infinity, trans. Alphonso Lingis (Pittsburgh, PA: Duquesne University Press, 1961).

19. Bobbio, *In Praise of Meekness*, pp. 25–26, 28. The text repeatedly criticizes Carl Schmitt's "friend-enemy" concept; see especially pp. 73–74.

20. *In Praise of Meekness*, p. 35, note 4.

21. Speech in Malikanda, February 21, 1940; in Raghavan Iyer, ed., *The Moral and Political Writings of Mahatma Gandhi*, vol. I: *Civilization, Politics, and Religion* (Oxford: Clarendon Press, 1986), p. 416.

22. Iyer, ed., *The Moral and Political Writings of Mahatma Gandhi*, vol. I, p. 395. The verses are from *Bhagavad Gita*, Book 2, lines 47–48, and Book 3, line 30. See *The Bhagavad Gita*, trans. Juan Mascaró (New York: Penguin Books, 1962), pp. 52, 58–59.

23. While the maintenance of lawfulness and order is a regular task of government—a part of its "police function"—the label "war on terrorism" unduly militarizes this function with detrimental effects on politics and the rule of law. See in this regard Richard Falk, *The Great Terror War* (New York: Olive Branch Press, 2003).

24. Bobbio, In *Praise of Meekness*, pp. 34–35.

25. In *Praise of Meekness*, p. 33. Somewhat provocatively (but entirely correctly) Bobbio ascribes to this city a "feminine virtue," adding (p. 34): "I am aware that, by saying that meekness has always seemed desirable to me precisely because of its femininity, I am disappointing all those women who stood up against centuries-old male domination. [But] I believe the practice of kindness is bound to prevail when the city of women is realized." In this connection, one may recall not only the ending of Goethe's *Faust*, but also the assignment of certain feminine qualities to Gandhi by Ashis Nandy, who writes that "Gandhi's androgyny sought to give back to femininity a part of the traditional sacredness and magic associated with it." See "From Outside the Imperium," in Nandy, *Traditions, Tyranny, and Utopias: Essays in the Politics of Awareness* (Delhi: Oxford University Press, 1987), p. 144.

CHAPTER TEN.   Homelessness and Pilgrimage: Heidegger on the Road

1. Martin Heidegger, "Letter on Humanism," in David F. Krell, ed., *Martin Heidegger: Basic Writings* (New York: Harper & Row, 1977), p. 219.

Regarding refugees and displaced persons in our time compare, e.g., Mary Bray Pipher, *The Middle of Everywhere: The World's Refugees Come to Our Town* (New York: Harcourt, 2002); Michael A. Dummett, *On Immigration and Refugees* (New York: Routledge, 2001); Jeremy Harding, *The Uninvited: Refugees at Rich Man's Gate* (London: Profile, 2000); Alastair Ager, *Perspectives on the Experience of Forced Migration* (New York: Cassell, 1999).

2. Heidegger, *An Introduction to Metaphysics,* trans. Ralph Manheim (Garden City, NY: Anchor Books, 1961), pp. 123–124. For the German text see Heidegger, *Einführung in die Metaphysik,* ed. Petra Jaeger (*Gesamtausgabe,* vol. 40; Frankfurt-Main: Klostermann, 1983), pp. 155–156.

3. *An Introduction to Metaphysics,* pp. 127–128 (translation slightly altered); *Einführung,* pp. 160–161.

4. Heidegger, *Being and Time,* trans. Joan Stambaugh (Albany, NY: State University of New York Press, 1996), pp. 13 (Introduction, II, 5), 103 (Part One, Division One, III, 24; translation slightly altered). See also *An Introduction to Metaphysics,* p. 137; *Einführung,* p. 172. Compare Gilbert Ryle, *The Concept of Mind* (New York: Barnes & Noble, 1949), pp. 11–12.

5. Heidegger, *Die Kunst und der Raum* (St. Gallen: Erker-Verlag, 1969), p. 11; "Letter on Humanism," in Krell, ed., *Martin Heidegger: Basic Writings,* pp. 228–229.

6. This reading of the "*Kehre*" concurs with the interpretation offered by William J. Richardson in his justly celebrated book *Heidegger: Through Phenomenology to Thought* (4th ed.; New York: Fordham University Press, 2003).

7. Heidegger, *Hölderlins Hymne "Der Ister,"* ed. Walter Biemel (*Gesamtausgabe,* vol. 53; Frankfurt-Main: Klostermann, 1984), p. 59. For an English translation (not followed here) see Heidegger, *Hölderlin's Hymn "The Ister,"* trans. William McNeill and Julia Davis (Bloomington, IN: Indiana University Press, 1996).

8. *Hölderlins Hymne "Der Ister,"* pp. 87, 127–129. For a more detailed discussion of the lecture course on Hölderlin's "Der Ister" and also of the slightly earlier (1941/42) lecture course on Hölderlin's hymn "Andenken" see the chapter "Homecoming Through Otherness" in my *The Other Heidegger* (Ithaca, NY: Cornell University Press, 1993), pp. 149–180.

9. Heidegger, *Hölderlins Hymne "Der Ister,"* pp. 89, 91–93. In large measure, Heidegger's comments on adventurism were meant as a critical response to Ernst Jünger's (quasi-Nietzschean) book *Das abenteuerliche Herz* (1929; 2nd ed., Hamburg: Hanseatische Verlagsanstalt, 1938).

10. Heidegger, *Hölderlins Hymne "Der Ister,"* p. 60. The above lines indicate that, at the latest by this time, Heidegger had renounced any sympathy for a chauvinistic nationalism. Compare also Walter Biemel, "Zu Heideggers Deutung der Ister-Hymne," *Heidegger Studies,* vol. 3/4 (1987–88), pp. 41–60.

11. For some discussions of the deeper sense of pilgrimage, compare Ali Shari'ati, *Hajj: Reflections on Its Rituals,* trans. Laleh Bakhtia (Tehran: Kazi Publications, 1996); Dorothy M. Richardson, *Pilgrimage* (New York: Knopf, 1938); Stringfellow Barr, *The Pilgrimage of Western Man* (New York: Harcourt Brace, 1949); Douglas C. Macintosh, *The Pilgrimage of Faith in the World of Modern Thought* (Calcutta: University of Calcutta, 1931).

12. See Philip C. Engblom, "Introduction," in D. B. Mokashi, *Palkhi: An Indian Pilgrimage,* trans. P. C. Engblom (Albany, NY: State University of New York Press, 1987), pp. 23, 27; also Gabriel Marcel, *Homo Viator,* trans. Emma Craufurd (New York: Harper Torchbooks, 1962).

13. Eleanor Zelliot, "A Historical Introduction to the *Warkari* Movement," in Mokashi, *Palkhi,* pp. 39–40, 42–43. See also James F. Edwards, *Dynaneshwar: The Out-Caste Brahmin* (Poona: Aryabhushan Press, 1941). Compare B. P. Bahirat, *The Philosophy of Jnanadeva* (Delhi: Motilal Banarsidass, 1984).

14. Regarding the "call of conscience" see *Being and Time,* pp. 251–258 (Part I, Division Two, II, 56–57). See also Heidegger, *Holzwege* (Frankfurt-Main: Klostermann, 1950); *Der Feldweg* (3rd ed.; Frankfurt-Main: Klostermann, 1962); *Wegmarken* (Frankfurt-Main: Klostermann, 1967). Shortly before his death Heidegger stipulated that his writings should be seen as "ways not works."

15. Heidegger, ". . . Poetically Man Dwells . . . ," in *Poetry, Language, Thought,* trans. Albert Hofstadter (New York: Harper & Row, 1971), pp. 213, 220–222 (translation slightly altered). For the German original of the essay see ". . . *Dichterisch wohnet der Mensch . . .* ," in *Vorträge und Aufsätze,* Part II (3rd ed.; Pfullingen: Neske, 1967), pp. 61–78.

16. *Poetry, Language, Thought,* pp. 222–223 (translation slightly altered). Heidegger (p. 225) also cites some other verses of Hölderlin, composed roughly at the same time, which read: "What is God? Unknown, yet / full of His qualities is the / face of the sky. For the lightnings / are the wrath of God. The more something / is invisible, the more it yields to what's alien (*Fremdes*)."

17. *Poetry, Language, Thought,* pp. 228–229 (translation slightly altered).

18. Raimon Panikkar, *A Dwelling Place for Wisdom,* trans. Annemarie S. Kidder (Louisville, KY: Westminster/John Knox Press, 1993), pp. 17–18. The

passage is from *Brihadaranyaka Upanishad,* IV, 1, 7. Panikkar also cites the verse from Proverbs 9:1, "Wisdom has prepared a dwelling place for itself," and comments (pp. 13–14): "A dwelling place is not a garment. It is not an individual affair, nor a kind of private salvation. . . . I cannot simply occupy, manipulate, and enjoy wisdom. I cannot simply use it, not even for some beneficial cause; nor can I use it up or abuse it. . . . It exists only where there is abundance, only where wisdom is allowed to overflow out of its plenitude."

APPENDIX.   Lessons of September 11

1. Samuel P. Huntington, "The Clash of Civilizations?" *Foreign Affairs,* vol. 72 (Summer 1993), pp. 22–49.

2. World Bank, *World Development Report 2000* (Oxford: Oxford University Press, 2000), cited from *World Faiths Development Dialogue,* Occasional Paper no. 4 (Oxford, 2000), p. 3. A year earlier, a United Nations report had noted that global inequalities in income and living standards have now reached "grotesque proportions," manifest (for example) in the fact that the combined wealth of the world's three richest families (about $135 billion) is greater than the annual income of 600 million people in the economically least developed countries. See UN Development Program (UNDP), *Human Development Report 1999* (Oxford: Oxford University Press, 1999). For the comments of Shirley Williams see *The Observer* (University of Notre Dame), September 14, 2001, p. 4.

3. Hannah Arendt, *The Human Condition: A Study of the Central Dilemmas Facing Modern Man* (Chicago: University of Chicago Press, 1958), p. 231. As one might add, some forms of recent "postmodernism" in America simply tend to exacerbate this penchant for "world-alienation."

4. Rear Admiral Eugene J. Carroll, Jr. (USN, Ret.), "Unilateralism Amok," in *Inforum* (Fourth Freedom Forum), no. 29 (Fall 2001), p. 3.

5. "Final Statement" of the Organization of Islamic States (OIC), *London Quds Press,* October 10, 2001.

6. For reflections on this point see Ziauddin Sardar, "Muslims in Denial," *The Observer* (London), October 21, 2001, pp. 4–5.

7. Bernard Lewis, *What Went Wrong? Western Impact and Middle Eastern Response* (Oxford: Oxford University Press, 2001), p. 116.

8. In this connection, the OIC Final Statement deserves attention when it rejects "any link between terrorism and the right of the Muslim and Arab people, including the Palestinian and Lebanese people, to self-determination, self-defense, sovereignty, and resistance against foreign occupation and aggression. These are legitimate rights guaranteed by the UN Charter and international law."

9. Compare in this respect, e.g., Pheng Cheah and Bruce Robbins, eds., *Cosmopolitics: Thinking and Feeling Beyond the Nation* (Minneapolis, MN: University of Minnesota Press, 1998); Martin J. Matustick, *Postnational Identity* (New York: Guilford Press, 1993); Fred Dallmayr and José M. Rosales, eds., *Beyond Nationalism? Sovereignty and Citizenship* (Lanham, MD: Lexington Books, 2001).

10. Compare on this point especially Richard Falk, *The Great Terror War* (New York: Olive Branch Press, 2003); James P. Sterba, ed., *Terrorism and International Justice* (New York: Oxford University Press, 2003); Teresa Brennan, *Globalization and Its Terrors* (London: Routledge, 2003).

11. One may note here the comments by Jürgen Habermas and Jacques Derrida: "At the international level and in the framework of the United Nations, Europe has to throw its weight on the scale to counterbalance the hegemonic unilateralism of the United States. . . . If Europe has solved [its earlier problems], why should it not issue a further challenge: to defend and promote a cosmopolitan order on the basis of international law against competing visions?" See "For a European Foreign Policy," *Constellations*, vol. 10 (2003), pp. 293–294. Compare also Giovanna Borradori, *Philosophy in a Time of Terror: Dialogues with Jürgen Habermas and Jacques Derrida* (Chicago: University of Chicago Press, 2003).

12. See Immanuel Kant, "Perpetual Peace: A Philosophical Sketch," in Hans Reiss, ed., *Kant's Political Writings*, trans. H. B. Nisbet (Cambridge, UK: Cambridge University Press, 1970), pp. 93–130; also my "Global Governance and Cultural Diversity," in *Achieving Our World: Toward a Global and Plural Democracy* (Lanham, MD: Rowman & Littlefield, 2001), pp. 35–50.

Abe, Masao, 168
Achilles, 3
Adorno, Theodor W., 15, 99, 125
agency, 34, 47
—political, 34
ahimsa, 17, 142–143
Ajmal Khan, Hakim, 139–140
Alexander the Great, 153, 157, 179
al-Farabi, 180–181
al-Ghazali, 83, 148
Ali, Muhammad, 139, 143
alienation, 192, 201, 204
Allende, Salvador, 61
Ambrose, Saint, 26
Ames, Roger, 167
Angelus Silesius, 77, 86
Ansari, Mukhtar, 140
anthropocentrism, 164
anthropology, philosophical, 32, 221n14
Antigone, 193–194, 196–197
antiquity, 43
anti-Semitism, 113
anti-universalism, 102
Apel, Karl-Otto, 93–94
Aquinas, Thomas, 47, 158
Arbenz, Jacobo, 61

Arendt, Hannah, 11, 16, 111–127, 129–131, 160–161
Aristotle, 3, 18, 30–33, 54, 98, 105, 108, 153–158, 162, 166, 180, 251n5
Ashley, Matthew, 65–66, 87
authority, 118
autonomy, 99, 101, 121
Azad, Abul Kalam, 137, 140

barbarism, 26
Barker, Ernest, 157–158
Bar On, Bat-Ami, 16, 112, 123–125
Basilides, 72
Bauman, Zygmunt, 15, 101
behaviorism, 127
Bellah, Robert, 165
Benjamin, Walter, 11, 122
Bergson, Henri, 114–115
Bernard of Clairvaux, 69, 76
Berrigan, Daniel, 9
Bhagavad Gita, 134–135, 189, 200
bhakti, 148, 200
Bobbio, Norberto, 19, 170, 174, 181–191, 220n21, 256n12
Bonaventure, Saint, 69, 78
Brierly, James, 53
Brunner, Emil, 72

FRED DALLMAYR is Packey J. Dee Professor of Political Theory at the University of Notre Dame.